LONDON

2 0 0 3

■ *Selection of hotels and restaurants*

Sélection d'hôtels et de restaurants ■

■ *Selezione di alberghi e ristoranti*

LONDON

This new edition of the Red Guide London
offers you a comprehensively revised selection
of hotels, restaurants and pubs.
Every year our dedicated team
of professional inspectors seeks out
and tests the full range of establishments,
visiting anonymously
and making their own impartial decisions.

For the first time we have included
a short descriptive text for each establishment,
complementing the familiar Michelin symbols
and offering an insight into the character
and surroundings so that our readers can be sure
of making the right choice.
Also new this year is the ♀ symbol
which highlights establishments offering
a good selection of quality wines by the glass.

Additionally, don't forget
to follow the **"Bib Gourmand"** 🍴 :
it will lead you to restaurants
offering good food at moderate prices.

The Red Guide is written for you
and influenced by you.
Please send us your comments
and recommendations by post or by e-mail to
theredguide-gbirl@uk.michelin.com .
You can consult the complete listings
of The Red Guide London at
www.ViaMichelin.co.uk

Contents

How to use
this guide

Choosing a hotel or restaurant

This guide offers a selection of hotels and restaurants to help motorists on their travels. In each category establishments are listed in order of preference according to the degree of comfort they offer.

Categories

🏨	XXXXX	*Luxury in the traditional style*
🏨	XXXX	*Top class comfort*
🏨	XXX	*Very comfortable*
🏨	XX	*Comfortable*
🏨	X	*Quite comfortable*
	🍺	*Traditional pubs serving food*
🏠		*Other recommended accommodation (Guesthouses and private homes)*
without rest.		*The hotel has no restaurant*
	with rm	*The restaurant also offers accommodation*

Peaceful atmosphere and setting

Certain establishments are distinguished in the guide by the red symbols shown below.

Your stay in such hotels will be particularly pleasant or restful, owing to the character of the building, its decor, the setting, the welcome and services offered, or simply the peace and quiet to be enjoyed there.

 to 🏠, 🏠	*Pleasant hotels*
to X	*Pleasant restaurants*
	Very quiet or quiet, secluded hotel
🏠	*Quiet hotel*
≤ London	*Exceptional view*
≤	*Interesting or extensive view*

Hotel facilities

In general the hotels we recommend have full bathroom and toilet facilities in each room.
This may not be the case, however for certain rooms in categories 🛏 and ⭡.

30 rm	*Number of rooms*
🛗	*Lift (elevator)*
▤	*Air conditioning*
TV	*Television in room*
⇝	*Establishment either partly or wholly reserved for non-smokers*
✆	*Modem point in the bedrooms*
⅋	*Rooms accessible to disabled people*
⌂	*Meals served in garden or on terrace*
⚊ ⚊	*Outdoor or indoor swimming pool*
⽊ ⊆s	*Exercise room – Sauna*
⌺	*Garden*
⚲	*Park*
⚲ ⏸8	*Hotel tennis court – Golf course and number of holes*
⌂ 150	*Equipped conference hall; maximum capacity*
⇔	*Hotel garage (additional charge in most cases)*
⊡	*Car park for customers only*
⚞	*Dogs are excluded from all or part of the hotel*
Fax	*Telephone document transmission*
closed Saturday and August	*Dates when closed as indicated by the restaurateur*
season	*Probably open for the season – precise dates not available.* *Where no date or season is shown, establishments are open all year round.*
LL35 0SB	*Postal code*

Cuisine

Stars

*Certain establishments deserve to be brought to your attention for the particularly fine quality of their cooking. **Michelin stars** are awarded for the standard of meals served. For such restaurants we list three culinary specialities typical of their style of cooking to assist you in your choice.*

✿✿✿ Exceptional cuisine, worth a special journey

One always eats here extremely well, sometimes superbly. Fine wines, faultless service, elegant surroundings. One will pay accordingly!

✿✿ Excellent cooking, worth a detour

Specialities and wines of first class quality. This will be reflected in the price.

✿ A very good restaurant in its category

The star indicates a good place to stop on your journey. But beware of comparing the star given to an expensive «de luxe» establishment to that of a simple restaurant where you can appreciate fine cuisine at a reasonable price.

🍜 The "Bib Gourmand"

Good food at moderate prices

*You may also like to know of other restaurants with less elaborate, moderately priced menus that offer good value for money and serve carefully prepared meals. We bring them to your attention by marking them with the **"Bib Gourmand"** 🍜 and Meals in the text of the Guide, e.g. Meals 19.00/25.00.*

Prices

Prices quoted are valid for autumn 2002. Changes may arise if goods and service costs are revised.

Hotels and restaurants in bold type
have supplied details of all their rates
and have assumed responsibility for maintaining
them for all travellers in possession of this guide.

Prices are given in £ sterling.
All accommodation prices include both service and V.A.T. All restaurant prices include V.A.T. Service is also included when an s. appears after the prices. Where no s. is shown, prices may be subject to the addition of a variable service charge that is usually between 10% - 15%.

*Your recommendation is self-evident
if you always walk into a hotel guide in hand.*

Meals

Meals 13.00/28.00 · **Set meals**
Lowest 13.00, and highest 28.00 – prices for set meals including cover charge, where applicable

Meals 19.00/25.00 · *See page 8*

s. · *Service included*

♀ · *Wine served by the glass*

Meals a la carte · **A la carte meals**
20.00/35.00 · The prices represent the range of charges from a simple to an elaborate 3 course meal and include a cover charge where applicable

↑: *Dinner in this category of establishment will generally be offered from a fixed price menu of limited choice, served at a set time to residents only. Lunch is rarely offered. Many will not be licensed to sell alcohol.*

Rooms

rm 120.00/250.00   *Lowest price* 120.00, *per room for a comfortable single and highest price* 250.00 *per room for the best double or twin*

suites   *Check with the hotelier for prices*

rm 125.00/255.00   *Full cooked breakfast (whether taken or not) is included in the price of the room*

9.50   *Price of breakfast*

Short breaks

Many hotels offer a special rate for a stay of two or more nights which comprises dinner, room and breakfast usually for a minimum of two people. Please enquire at hotel for rates.

Alcoholic beverages-conditions of sale

The sale of alcoholic drinks is governed in Great Britain and Ireland by licensing laws which vary greatly from country to country.

Allowing for local variations, restaurants may stay open and serve alcohol with a bona fide meal during the afternoon. Hotel bars and public houses are generally open between 11am and 11pm at the discretion of the licensee. Hotel residents, however, may buy drinks outside the permitted hours at the discretion of the hotelier.

Children under the age of 14 are not allowed in bars.

Deposits

Some hotels will require a deposit, which confirms the commitment of customer and hotelier alike. Make sure the terms of the agreement are clear.

Credit cards

Credits cards accepted by the establishment: MasterCard (Eurocard) – American Express – Diners Club – Visa – Japan Credit Bureau

London

✉ SW7	*Postal address*
London G.	*See the Michelin Green Guide*
BX A	*Letters giving the location of a place on the town plan*
🏌18	*Golf course and number of holes (handicap sometimes required, telephone reservation strongly advised)*
⁂, ≼	*Panoramic view, viewpoint*
✈	*Airport*
🛈	*Tourist Information Centre*

Standard Time

In winter standard time throughout the British Isles is Greenwich Mean Time (G.M.T.). In summer British clocks are advanced by one hour to give British Summer Time (B.S.T.). The actual dates are announced annually but always occur over weekends in March and October.

Sights

Star-rating

★★★	*Highly recommended*
★★	*Recommended*
★	*Interesting*

Car, tyres

*The wearing of seat belts in Great Britain
is obligatory for drivers, front seat passengers
and rear seat passengers where seat belts are fitted.
It is illegal for front seat passengers
to carry children on their lap.*

Michelin tyre suppliers
ATS Euromaster tyre dealers

*The address of the nearest ATS Euromaster tyre dealer
can be obtained by contacting the address below
between 9am and 5pm.*

> *ATS Euromaster*
> *Jill Lane*
> *Sambourne*
> *Redditch*
> *Worcs. B96 6ES*
> *☎ 0800 750 850*

Motoring organisations

*The major motoring organisations in Great Britain
are the Automobile Association and the Royal
Automobile Club. Each provides services in varying
degrees for non-resident members
of affiliated clubs.*

AUTOMOBILE ASSOCIATION
Fanum House
Basingstoke, Hants
RG21 2EA
☎ (08705) 448866

ROYAL AUTOMOBILE CLUB
RAC House, Boston Drive
Bourne End Bucks SL8 5YS
☎ (01628) 843888

Town plans

ⓐ ● a   *Hotels – Restaurants*

Sights

Place of interest
Interesting place of worship

Roads

M 1   *Motorway*
❹ ❹   *Junctions: complete, limited*
Dual carriageway with motorway characteristics
Main traffic artery
A 2   *Primary route (GB)*
and National route (IRL)
◄   *One-way street – Unsuitable for traffic, street subject*
to restrictions
Pedestrian street – Tramway
Piccadilly   *Shopping street – Car park – Park and Ride*
Gateway – Street passing under arch – Tunnel
Low headroom (16'6" max.) on major through routes
Station and railway
Funicular – Cable-car
△ B   *Lever bridge – Car ferry*

Various signs

Tourist Information Centre
Church/Place of worship – Mosque – Synagogue
Communications tower or mast – Ruins
Garden, park, wood – Cemetery
Stadium – Racecourse – Golf course
Golf course (with restrictions for visitors) – Skating rink
Outdoor or indoor swimming pool
View – Panorama
Monument – Fountain – Hospital – Covered market
Pleasure boat harbour – Lighthouse
Airport – Underground station – Coach station
Ferry services:
- passengers and cars
Main post office
Public buildings located by letter:
C H J   *County Council Offices – Town Hall – Law Courts*
M T U   *Museum – Theatre – University, College*
POL.   *Police (in large towns police headquarters)*

London

BRENT WEMBLEY   *Borough – Area*
Borough boundary – Area boundary

13

Cette nouvelle édition du Guide Rouge Londres
propose une sélection actualisée d'hôtels,
maisons d'hôtes, restaurants et pubs.
Elle a été réalisée en toute indépendance
par les Inspecteurs Michelin,
des professionnels passionnés qui visitent
et testent dans un total anonymat.

Cette année, l'introduction d'un texte descriptif,
clair et concis, complète nos informations
sur chaque établissement et permet au lecteur
de le situer dans son cadre,
d'en sentir l'ambiance
et de le choisir en toute confiance.
Nous avons également introduit le symbole ♀
qui vous indique des adresses
où sont servis des vins de qualité au verre.

De plus, n'oubliez pas de suivre
le **"Bib Gourmand"** 😊 :
il vous conduira à des restaurants
proposant des repas soignés à prix modérés.

Le Guide Rouge Michelin vit et progresse
grâce à ses lecteurs. N'hésitez pas à nous écrire.
Vous pouvez également consulter
la sélection du Guide Rouge Londres sur
www.ViaMichelin.co.uk
et nous envoyer vos commentaires à
theredguide-gbirl@uk.michelin.com

Sommaire

Comprendre

17

Le choix d'un hôtel, d'un restaurant

*Ce guide vous propose une sélection d'hôtels
et restaurants établie à l'usage de l'automobiliste
de passage. Les établissements, classés
selon leur confort, sont cités par ordre
de préférence dans chaque catégorie.*

Catégories

🏨	XXXXX	*Grand luxe et tradition*
🏨	XXXX	*Grand confort*
🏨	XXX	*Très confortable*
🏨	XX	*De bon confort*
🏠	X	*Assez confortable*
	🍴	*Traditionnel pub anglais servant des repas*
⌂		*Autres formes hébergement conseillé (maison d'hôtes et cottages)*
without rest.		*L'hôtel n'a pas de restaurant*
	with rm	*Le restaurant possède des chambres*

Agrément et tranquillité

*Certains établissements se distinguent dans le guide
par les symboles rouges indiqués ci-après.
Le séjour dans ces hôtels se révèle particulièrement
agréable ou reposant.
Cela peut tenir d'une part au caractère de l'édifice,
au décor original, au site, à l'accueil
et aux services qui sont proposés,
d'autre part à la tranquillité des lieux.*

🏨 à 🏠, ⌂		*Hôtels agréables*
XXXXX à X		*Restaurants agréables*
🦢		*Hôtel très tranquille ou isolé et tranquille*
🦢		*Hôtel tranquille*
⪦ London		*Vue exceptionnelle*
⪦		*Vue intéressante ou étendue*

L'installation

Les chambres des hôtels que nous recommandons possèdent, en général, des installations sanitaires complètes. Il est toutefois possible que dans les catégories 🏠 et ⌂, certaines chambres en soient dépourvues.

30 ch	Nombre de chambres
⬚	Ascenseur
▤	Air conditionné
TV	Télévision dans la chambre
⇥✖	Établissement entièrement ou en partie réservé aux non-fumeurs
☎	Prise modem dans la chambre
⅋	Chambres accessibles aux handicapés physiques
⌂	Repas servis au jardin ou en terrasse
⌆ ⌇	Piscine : de plein air ou couverte
⅃♨	Salle de remise en forme – Sauna
☂	Jardin de repos
⚘	Parc
✗ ⌸18	Tennis à l'hôtel – Golf et nombre de trous
⌲ 150	Salles de conférences : capacité maximum
⇔	Garage dans l'hôtel (généralement payant)
▣	Parking réservé à la clientèle
⌀	Accès interdit aux chiens (dans tout ou partie de l'établissement)
Fax	Transmission de documents par télécopie
closed Saturday and August	Fermeture communiquée par le restaurateur
LL35 OSB	Code postal de l'établissement

La table

Les étoiles

*Certains établissements méritent d'être signalés
à votre attention pour la qualité de leur cuisine.
Nous les distinguons par les étoiles de bonne table.
Nous indiquons, pour ces établissements,
trois spécialités culinaires qui pourront orienter
votre choix.*

❀❀❀ **Une des meilleures tables, vaut le voyage**

*On y mange toujours très bien, parfois
merveilleusement, grands vins, service impeccable,
cadre élégant... Prix en conséquence.*

❀❀ **Table excellente, mérite un détour**

*Spécialités et vins de choix...
Attendez-vous à une dépense en rapport.*

❀ **Une très bonne table dans sa catégorie**

*L'étoile marque une bonne étape
sur votre itinéraire.
Mais ne comparez pas l'étoile d'un établissement
de luxe à prix élevés avec celle d'une petite maison
où à prix raisonnables, on sert également
une cuisine de qualité.*

Le "Bib Gourmand"

Repas soignés à prix modérés

*Vous souhaitez parfois trouver des tables plus
simples, à prix modérés; c'est pourquoi nous avons
sélectionné des restaurants proposant, pour un
rapport qualité-prix particulièrement favorable,
un repas soigné.*
Ces restaurants sont signalés par le **"Bib Gourmand"**
et Meals.
Ex. Meals 19.00/25.00.

Les prix

Les prix que nous indiquons dans ce guide
ont été établis en automne 2002. Ils sont susceptibles
de modifications, notamment en cas de variations
des prix des biens et services.

Les hôtels et restaurants figurent en gros caractères
lorsque les hôteliers nous ont donné tous leurs prix
et se sont engagés, sous leur propre responsabilité,
à les appliquer aux touristes de passage
porteurs de notre guide.

Les prix sont indiqués en livres sterling
(1 L = 100 pence). Les tarifs de l'hébergement
comprennent le service et la T.V.A.
La T.V.A. est également incluse dans les prix des
repas. Toutefois, le service est uniquement compris
dans les repas si la mention « s » apparaît après
le prix. Dans le cas contraire, une charge
supplémentaire variant de 10 à 15 % du montant de
l'addition est demandée.

*Entrez à l'hôtel le guide à la main, vous montrerez
ainsi qu'il vous conduit là en confiance.*

Repas

Repas à prix fixe

Meals 13.00/28.00	Minimum 13.00, Maximum 28.00. Ces prix s'entendent couvert compris
Meals 19.00/25.00	Voir page 20
s.	Service compris
♀	Vin servi au verre

Repas à la carte

Meals à la carte
20.00/35.00

Le 1er prix correspond à un repas simple mais soigné,
comprenant : petite entrée, plat du jour garni, dessert.
Le 2e prix concerne un repas plus complet,
comprenant : hors-d'œuvre, plat principal, fromage
ou dessert. Ces prix s'entendent couvert compris

⌂ : Dans les établissements de cette catégorie, le dîner
est servi à heure fixe exclusivement aux personnes ayant
une chambre. Le menu, à prix unique, offre un choix
limité de plats. Le déjeuner est rarement proposé.
Beaucoup de ces établissements ne sont pas autorisés
à vendre des boissons alcoolisées.

Chambres

rm 120.00/250.00	*Prix minimum* 120.00 *d'une chambre pour une personne et prix maximum* 250.00 *de la plus belle chambre occupée par deux personnes*
suites	*Se renseigner auprès de l'hôtelier*
rm ☕ 125.00/255.00	*Le prix du petit déjeuner à l'anglaise est inclus dans le prix de la chambre, même s'il n'est pas consommé*
☕ 9.50	*Prix du petit déjeuner*

Short breaks

Certains hôtels proposent des conditions avantageuses ou «Short Break» pour un séjour minimum de 2 nuits. Ce forfait, calculé par personne pour 2 personnes au minimum, comprend la chambre, le dîner et le petit déjeuner. Se renseigner auprès de l'hôtelier.

La vente de boissons alcoolisées

En Grande-Bretagne, la vente de boissons alcoolisées est soumise à des lois pouvant varier d'une région à l'autre.

D'une façon générale, les restaurants peuvent demeurer ouverts l'après-midi et servir des boissons alcoolisées dans la mesure où elles accompagnent un repas suffisamment consistant. Les bars d'hôtel et les pubs sont habituellement ouverts de 11 heures à 23 heures. Néanmoins, l'hôtelier a toujours la possibilité de servir, à sa clientèle, des boissons alcoolisées en dehors des heures légales.

Les enfants au-dessous de 14 ans n'ont pas accès aux bars.

Les arrhes

Certains hôteliers demandent le versement d'arrhes. Il s'agit d'un dépôt-garantie qui engage l'hôtelier comme le client. Bien faire préciser les dispositions de cette garantie.

Cartes de crédit

🔵 AE 🔵 VISA JCB *Cartes de crédit acceptées par l'établissement : MasterCard (Eurocard) – American Express – Diners Club – Visa – Japan Credit Bureau*

Londres

✉ *SW7*	*Bureau de poste desservant la localité*
London G.	*Voir le guide vert Michelin*
BX A	*Lettres repérant un emplacement sur le plan*
🏌18	*Golf et nombre de trous (Handicap parfois demandé, réservation par téléphone vivement recommandée)*
☀, ≤	*Panorama, point de vue*
✈	*Aéroport*
🛈	*Information touristique*

Heure légale

Les visiteurs devront tenir compte de l'heure officielle en Grande-Bretagne : une heure de retard sur l'heure française.

Les curiosités

Intérêts

★★★	*Vaut le voyage*
★★	*Mérite un détour*
★	*Intéressant*

La voiture, les pneus

En Grande-Bretagne, le port de la ceinture
de sécurité est obligatoire pour le conducteur
et le passager avant ainsi qu'à l'arrière, si le
véhicule en est équipé. La loi interdit au passager
avant de prendre un enfant sur ses genoux.

Fournisseurs de pneus michelin
ATS Euromaster Spécialistes du pneu

Des renseignements sur le plus proche point
de vente de pneus ATS Euromaster pourront être
obtenus en s'informant entre 9 h et 17 h
à l'adresse indiquée ci-dessous.

ATS Euromaster
Jill Lane
Sambourne
Redditch
Worcs. B96 6ES
℡ 0800 750 850

Automobile clubs

Les principales organisations de secours automobile
dans le pays sont l'Automobile Association
et le Royal Automobile Club,
toutes deux offrant certains de leurs services
aux membres de clubs affiliés.

AUTOMOBILE ASSOCIATION
Fanum House
Basingstoke, Hants
RG21 2EA
℡ (08705) 448866

ROYAL AUTOMOBILE CLUB
RAC House, Boston Drive
Bourne End Bucks SL8 5YS
℡ (01628) 843888

Les plans

◉ ● a   *Hôtels – Restaurants*

Curiosités

Bâtiment intéressant
Édifice religieux intéressant

Voirie

Autoroute
- échangeurs : complet, partiel
Route à chaussées séparées de type autoroutier
Grand axe de circulation
Itinéraire principal (Primary route : GB)
(National route : IRL)
Sens unique – Rue impraticable, réglementée
Rue piétonne – Tramway
Rue commerçante – Parking – Parking Relais
Porte – Passage sous voûte – Tunnel
Passage bas (inférieur à 16'6") sur les grandes voies
de circulation
Gare et voie ferrée
Funiculaire – Téléphérique, télécabine
Pont mobile – Bac pour autos

Signes divers

Information touristique
Église/édifice religieux – Mosquée – Synagogue
Tour ou pylône de télécommunication – Ruines
Jardin, parc, bois – Cimetière
Stade – Hippodrome – Golf
Golf (réservé) – Patinoire
Piscine de plein air, couverte
Vue – Panorama
Monument   Fontaine – Hôpital – Marché couvert
Port de plaisance – Phare
Aéroport – Station de métro – Gare routière
Transport par bateau :
- passagers et voitures
Bureau principal
Bâtiment public repéré par une lettre :
- Bureau de l'Administration du Comté – Hôtel de ville
- Musée – Théâtre – Université, grande école
- Police (commissariat central) – Palais de Justice

C H
M T U
POL. J

Londres

BRENT WEMBLEY   *Nom d'arrondissement (borough) – de quartier (area)*
Limite de « borough » – d'« area »

*Questa nuova edizione della Guida Rossa Londra
propone una selezione aggiornata di alberghi,
B&B, ristoranti e pubs.
E' realizzata in assoluta autonomia di giudizio
dagli ispettori Michelin, persone competenti
che visitano e provano gli esercizi
in totale anonimato.*

*Una grande novità accompagna
questa edizione 2003 :
l'introduzione di un breve testo descrittivo
per ogni esercizio segnalato. In questo modo,
il lettore potrà identificare un locale anche
in base all'ambiente, alla posizione,
alle caratteristiche della struttura...
e scegliere così con maggiore sicurezza.*

*Per di più, abbiamo introdotto il nuovo simbolo ♀
che vi indica gli indirizzi per trovare vini di qualità
serviti al bicchiere.
Un ultimo consiglio :
Seguite il* **"Bib Gourmand"** *:
vi indica numerosi ristoranti
dove troverete pasti accurati a prezzi contenuti.*

*La Guida Rossa vive e evolve grazie ai suoi Lettori.
Non esitate a scriverci,
anche via internet presso l'indirizzo*
theredguide-gbirl@uk.michelin.com
*o a consultare l'intera selezione
della Guida Rossa Londra sul sito*
www.ViaMichelin.co.uk _____

Sommario

Come servisi della guida

29

La scelta di un albergo, di un ristorante

*Questa guida propone una selezione
di alberghi e ristoranti stabilita ad uso
dell'automobilista di passaggio. Gli esercizi,
classificati in base al confort che offrono,
vengono citati in ordine di preferenza
per ogni categoria.*

Categorie

🏨🏨🏨	🍽🍽🍽🍽🍽	*Gran lusso e tradizione*
🏨🏨🏨	🍽🍽🍽🍽	*Gran confort*
🏨🏨	🍽🍽🍽	*Molto confortevole*
🏨	🍽🍽	*Di buon confort*
🏨	🍽	*Abbastanza confortevole*
	🍲	*Pub tradizionali con cucina*
⌂		*Altra forme di alloggio consigliate (Pensioni e Case private)*
without rest.		*L'albergo non ha ristorante*
	with rm	*Il ristorante dispone di camere*

Amenità e tranquillità

*Alcuni esercizi sono evidenziati nella guida dai
simboli rossi indicati qui di seguito. Il soggiorno
in questi alberghi dovrebbe rivelarsi particolarmente
ameno o riposante.*

*Ciò può dipendere sia dalle caratteristiche
dell'edifico, dalle decorazioni non comuni,
dalla sua posizione e dal servizio offerto,
sia dalla tranquillità dei luoghi.*

🏨🏨🏨 a 🏨, ⌂		*Alberghi ameni*
🍽🍽🍽🍽🍽 a 🍽		*Ristoranti ameni*
	🦢	*Albergo molto tranquillo o isolato e tranquillo*
	🦢	*Albergo tranquillo*
⬐ London		*Vista eccezionale*
	⬐	*Vista interessante o estesa*

Installazioni

Le camere degli alberghi che raccomandiamo possiedono, generalmente, delle installazioni sanitarie complete. È possibile tuttavia che nelle categorie 🏠 e 🏠 alcune camere ne siano sprovviste.

30 rm	*Numero di camere*
🛗	*Ascensore*
🗐	*Aria condizionata*
📺	*Televisione in camera*
🚭	*Esercizio riservato completamente o in parte ai non fumatori*
📞	*Presa modem in camera*
🚹	*Camere di agevole accesso per portatori di handicap*
🏡	*Pasti serviti in giardino o in terrazza*
🏊 🏊	*Piscina: all'aperto, coperta*
🏋 🜚s	*Palestra – Sauna*
🌳	*Giardino*
🛝	*Parco*
🎾 🏌️18	*Tennis appatenente all'albergo – Golf e numero di buche*
🏛 150	*Sale per conferenze: capienza massima*
🚗	*Garage nell'albergo (generalmente a pagamento)*
🅿	*Parcheggio riservato alla clientela*
🐕	*Accesso vietato ai cani (in tutto o in parte dell'esercizio)*
Fax	*Trasmissione telefonica di documenti*
closed Saturday and August	*Periodo di apertura, comunicato dall'albergatore*
LL35 OSB	*Codice postale dell'esercizio*

31

La tavola

Le stelle

*Alcuni esercizi meritano di essere segnalati alla Vostra attenzione per la qualità tutta particolare della loro cucina. Noi li evidenziamo con le «stelle di ottima tavola».
Per questi ristoranti indichiamo tre specialità culinarie e alcuni vini locali che potranno aiutarVi nella scelta.*

✿✿✿ Una delle migliori tavole, vale il viaggio

Vi si mangia sempre molto bene, a volte meravigliosamente, grandi vini, servizio impeccabile, ambientazione accurata... Prezzi conformi.

✿✿ Tavola eccellente, merita una deviazione

*Specialità e vini scelti...
AspettateVi una spesa in proporzione.*

✿ Un'ottima tavola nella sua categoria

*La stella indica una tappa gastronomica sul Vostro itinerario.
Non mettete però a confronto la stella di un esercizio di lusso, dai prezzi elevati, con quella di un piccolo esercizio dove, a prezzi ragionevoli, viene offerta una cucina di qualità.*

🍽 Il "Bib Gourmand"

Pasti accurati a prezzi contenuti

*Per quando desiderate trovare delle tavole più semplici a prezzi contenuti abbiamo selezionato dei ristoranti che, per un rapporto qualità-prezzo particolarmente favorevole, offrono un pasto accurato.
Questi ristoranti sono evidenziati nel testo con il "Bib Gourmand"* 🍽 *e* Meals *evidenziata in rosso, davanti ai prezzi.
Ex.* 🍽 Meals 19.00/25.00.

I prezzi

I prezzi che indichiamo in questa guida sono stati stabiliti nel l'autunno 2002. Potranno pertanto subire delle variazioni in relazione ai cambiamenti dei prezzi di beni e servizi.

Gli alberghi e i ristoranti vengono menzionati in carattere grassetto quando gli albergatori ci hanno comunicato tutti i loro prezzi e si sono impegnati, sotto la propria responsabilità, ad applicarli ai turisti di passaggio, in possesso della nostra guida.

I prezzi sono indicati in lire sterline (1 £ = 100 pence).

Tutte le tariffe per il soggiorno includono sia servizio che I.V.A. Tutti i prezzi dei ristoranti includono l'I.V.A., il servizio è incluso quando dopo il prezzo appare s. Quando non compare s., il prezzo può essere soggetto ad un aumento per il servizio solitamente compreso tra il 10% e il 15%.

Entrate nell'albergo o nel ristorante con la guida in mano, dimostrando in tal modo la fiducia in chi vi ha indirizzato.

Pasti

Meals 13.00/28.00	**Prezzo fisso** *Prezzo minimo* 13.00, *massimo* 28.00.
Meals 19.00/25.00	*Vedere p. 32*
s.	*Servizio compreso*
♀	*Vino servito a bicchiere*
Meals a la carte 20.00/35.00	**Alla carta** *Il 1º prezzo corrisponde ad un pasto semplice comprendente : primo piatto, piatto del giorno con contorno, dessert. Il 2º prezzo corrisponde ad un pasto più completo comprendente : antipasto, piatto principale, formaggio e dessert*

↑ : Negli alberghi di questa categoria, la cena viene servita, ad un'ora stabilita, esclusivamente a chi vi alloggia. Il menu, a prezzo fisso, offre una scelta limitata di piatti. Raramente viene servito anche il pranzo. Molti di questi esercizi non hanno l'autorizzazione a vendere alcolici.

Camere

rm 120.00/250.00	*Prezzo minimo* 120.00, *per una camera singola e prezzo massimo* 250.00 *per la camera più bella per due persone*
suites	*Informarsi presso l'albergatore*
rm ☐ 125.00/255.00	*Il prezzo della prima colazione inglese è compreso nel prezzo della camera anche se non viene consumata*
☐ 9.50	*Prezzo della prima colazione*

«Short Breaks»

Alcuni alberghi propongono delle condizioni particolarmente vantaggiose o short break per un soggiorno minimo di due notti.
Questo prezzo, calcolato per persona e per un minimo di due persone, comprende; camera, cena e prima colazione. Informarsi presso l'albergatore.

La vendita di bevande alcoliche

La vendita di bevande alcoliche in Gran Bretagna è regolata da leggi che variano considerevolmente da regione a regione.

Eccezion fatta per varianti locali, i ristoranti possono rimanere aperti o servire bevande alcoliche con i pasti il pomeriggio. I bar degli hotel e i pub sono generalmente aperti dalle 11 alle 23, a discrezione del gestore. I clienti dell'hotel, comunque, possono acquistare bevande al di fuori delle ore stabilite se il direttore lo permette.

Il bambini al di sotto del 14 anni non possono entrare nei bar.

La caparra

Alcuni albergatori chiedono il versamento di una caparra. Si tratta di un deposito-garanzia che impegna tanto l'albergatore che il cliente. Vi raccomandiamo di farVi precisare le norme riguardanti la reciproca garanzia.

Carte di credito

Carte di credito accettate dall'esercizio :
MasterCard (Eurocard) – American Express – Diners Club – Visa – Japan Credit Bureau

Londra

✉ SW7	*Sede dell'ufficio postale*
London G.	*Vedere la Guida Verde Michelin*
BX A	*Lettere indicanti l'ubicazione sulla pianta*
⌐₁₈	*Golf e numero di buche (handicap generalmente richiesto, prenotazione telefonica vivamente consigliata)*
☀, ≤	*Panorama, punto di vista*
✈	*Aeroporto*
🛈	*Ufficio informazioni turistiche*

Ora legale

I visitatori dovranno tenere in considerazione l'ora ufficiale in Gran Bretagna : un'ora di ritardo sull'ora italiana.

Luoghi d'interesse

Grado di interesse

★★★	*Vale il viaggio*
★★	*Merita una deviazione*
★	*Interessante*

L'automobile, I pneumatici

*In Gran Bretagna, l'uso delle cinture di sicurezza
è obbligatorio per il conducente e il passeggero
del sedile anteriore, nonchè per i sedili posteriori,
se ne sono equipaggiati. La legge non consente
al passaggero seduto davanti di tenere un bambino
sulle ginocchia.*

Pneumatici Michelin

*Potrete avere delle informazioni sul più vicino
punto vendita di pneumatici ATS Euromaster,
rivolgendovi, tra le 9 e le 17, all'indirizzo indicato
qui di seguito :*

> *ATS Euromaster*
> *Jill Lane*
> *Sambourne*
> *Redditch*
> *Worcs. B96 6ES*
> ✆ *0800 750 850*

*Le nostre Succursali sono in grado di dare ai
nostri clienti tutti i consigli relativi alla migliore
utilizzazione dei pneumatici.*

Automobile clubs

*Le principali organizzazioni di soccorso
automobilistico sono l'Automobile Association
ed il Royal Automobile Club :
entrambe offrono alcuni loro servizi
ai membri dei club affiliati.*

AUTOMOBILE ASSOCIATION
Fanum House
Basingstoke, Hants
RG21 2EA
✆ *(08705) 448866*

ROYAL AUTOMOBILE CLUB
RAC House, Boston Drive
Bourne End Bucks SL8 5YS
✆ *(01628) 843888*

Le piante

ⓐ ● a *Alberghi – Ristoranti*

Curiosità

Edificio interessante
Costruzione religiosa interessante

Viabilità

Autostrada
- svincoli: completo, parziale
Strada a carreggiate separate di tipo autostradale
Asse principale di circolazione
Itinerario principale (Primary route : GB)
(National Route : IRL)
Senso unico – Via impraticable, a circolazione regolamentata
Via pedonale – Tranvia
.Piccadilly *Via commerciale – Parcheggio – Parcheggio Ristoro*
Porta – Sottopassaggio – Galleria
Sottopassaggio (altezza inferiore a 16'6") sulle grandi
vie di circolazione
Stazione e ferrovia
Funicolare – Funivia, Cabinovia
Ponte mobile – Traghetto per auto

Simboli vari

Ufficio informazioni turistiche
Chiesa/edificio religioso – Moschea – Sinagoga
Torre o pilone per telecomunicazioni – Ruderi
Giardino, parco, bosco – Cimitero
Stadio – Ippodromo – Golf
Golf riservato – Pattinaggio
Piscina all'aperto, coperta
Vista – Panorama
Monumento – Fontana – Ospedale – Mercato coperto
Porto per imbarcazioni da diporto – Faro
Aeroporto – Stazione della Metropolitana – Autostazione
Trasporto con traghetto:
- passeggeri ed autovetture
Ufficio centrale
Edificio pubblico indicato con lettera:
C H *- Sede dell'Amministrazione di Contea – Municipio*
M T U *- Museo – Teatro – Università, grande scuola*
POL. J *- Polizia (Questura, nelle grandi città) – Palazzo di Giustizia*

Londra

BRENT WEMBLEY *Nome del distretto amministrativo (borough) –*
del quartiere (area)
Limite del « borough » – di « area »

37

London

🏛 *Victoria Station Forecourt – City of London Information Centre, St. Paul's Church-yard, EC4* ☎ *(020) 7332 1456 – Selfridges, Basement Services Arcade, Oxford Street, WI – Britain Visitor Centre, I Regent Street, WI.*

✈ *Heathrow,* ☎ *08700 000123, p. 10* AX *–* **Terminal** : *Airbus (A1) from Victoria, Airbus (A2) from Paddington – Underground (Piccadilly line) frequent service daily.*

✈ *Gatwick,* ☎ *08700 002468 p. 11 : by A 23* EZ *and M 23 –* **Terminal** : *Coach service from Victoria Coach Station (Flightline 777, hourly service) – Railink (Gatwick Express) from Victoria (24 h service).*

✈ *London City Airport* ☎ *(020) 7646 0000, p. 9* HV.

✈ *Stansted, at Bishop's Stortford,* ☎ *08700 000303, NE : 34 m. p. 9 : by M 11* JT *and A 120.*

British Airways : *Ticket sales and reservations Paddington Station, London W2,* ☎ *0845 7799977.*

Major hotel groups
Central reservation telephone numbers

Principales chaînes hôtelières
Centraux téléphoniques de réservation

Principali catene alberghiere
Centrali telefoniche di prenotazione

ACCOR HOTELS (IBIS, MERCURE & NOVOTEL)	*0208 2834500*
CHOICE HOTELS	*0800 444444 (Freephone)*
CORUS & REGAL HOTELS	*08457 334400*
DE VERE HOTELS PLC	*0870 6063606*
HILTON HOTELS	*08705 515151*
HOLIDAY INN WORLDWIDE	*0800 897121 (Freephone)*
HYATT HOTELS WORLDWIDE	*0845 8881234*
INTERCONTINENTAL HOTELS LTD	*0800 0289387 (Freephone)*
JURYS/DOYLE HOTELS	*0870 9072222*
MACDONALD HOTELS PLC	*08457 585593*
MARRIOTT HOTELS	*0800 221222 (Freephone)*
MILLENNIUM & COPTHORNE HOTELS PLC	*0845 3020001*
PREMIER LODGES	*08702 010203*
QUEENS MOAT HOUSES PLC	*0500 213214 (Freephone)*
RADISSON EDWARDIAN HOTELS	*0800 374411 (Freephone)*
RAMADA JARVIS HOTELS	*08457 581811*
SHERATON HOTELS	*0800 353535 (Freephone)*
THISTLE HOTELS	*0800 181716 (Freephone)*
TRAVEL INNS	*0870 2428000*
TRAVELODGES	*08700 850950*

PRACTICAL INFORMATION

Banks

Open, generally 9.30 am to 4.30 pm weekdays (except public holidays). Most have cash dispensers. You need ID (passport) for cashing cheques. Banks levy smaller commissions than hotels.
Many 'Bureaux de Change' around Piccadilly open 7 days.

Congestion Charging

From 17 February 2003 it is proposed to levy a £5 charge per day on all vehicles (except motor cycles and exempt vehicles) entering the central zone between 7.00 am and 6.30 pm - Monday to Friday except on Bank Holidays.
Payment can be made in advance, on the day, by post, on the Internet, by telephone or at retail outlets.
A charge of up to £80 will be made for non-payment.
Further information is available on the Transport for London website - www.tfl.gov.uk.

Getting around

As driving and parking in London are difficult, it is advisable to take the Underground, a bus or taxi and full details of these services can be obtained from London Transport Travel Enquiries ℘ (020) 7222 1234.

Underground – an extensive network covers the whole capital and a map can be found at the back of this guide. Single or return tickets may be purchased from tube stations only. To calculate an estimated journey time, count three minutes between stations and an average of fifteen minutes to change lines. Last trains run from Central London until 0.50am Mondays to Fridays and until 12 midnight on Sundays.

Buses – Bus-routes are displayed in bus shelters as well as inside the buses themselves. White signs with the red logo indicate bus stops at which all listed buses must stop – red signs with the white logo are request stops at which passengers must wave to the bus to stop and make a pick up.

Taxis – The traditional London cab is available at railway termini, Heathrow airport taxi ranks and cruising the streets. An orange roof light displays whether or not they are available for pick-up and when iluminated they can be hailed in the street.

Travelcards – Multi-journey zoned passes are more economical for a stay in the capital and these Travelcards are available for one day, a weekend, a week or longer.

Medical Emergencies

To contact a doctor for first aid, emergency medical advice and chemists night service: 07000 372255.
Accident & Emergency: dial 999 for Ambulance, Police or Fire Services.

Post Offices

Open Monday to Friday 9 am to 5.30 pm. Late collections made from Leicester Square.

Shopping

Most stores are found in Oxford Street (Selfridges, M & S), Regent Street (Hamleys, Libertys) and Knightsbridge (Harrods, Harvey Nichols). Open usually Monday to Saturday 9 am to 6 pm. Some open later (8 pm) once a week; Knightsbridge Wednesday, Oxford Street and Regent Street Thursday. Other areas worth visiting include Jermyn Street and Savile Row (mens outfitters), Bond Street (jewellers and haute couture).

Theatres

The "West End" has many major theatre performances and can generally be found around Shaftesbury Avenue. Most daily newspapers give details of performances. A half-price ticket booth is located in Leicester Square and is open Monday-Saturday 1 - 6.30 pm, Sunday and matinée days 12 noon - 6.30 pm. Restrictions apply.

Tipping

When a service charge is included in a bill it is not necessary to tip extra. If service is not included a discretionary 10% is normal.

Sights

Curiosités

Le curiosità

HISTORIC BUILDINGS AND MONUMENTS

Palace of Westminster★★★ : *House of Lords*★★, *Westminster Hall*★★ *(hammerbeam roof*★★★*)*, *Robing Room*★, *Central Lobby*★, *House of Commons*★, *Big Ben*★, *Victoria Tower*★ p. 30 LY – *Tower of London*★★★ *(Crown Jewels*★★★, *White Tower or Keep*★★★, *St. John's Chapel*★★, *Beauchamp Tower*★ *Tower Hill Pageant*★*)* p. 31 PVX, *British Airways London Eye (view*★★★*)*.

Banqueting House★★ p. 30 LX – *Buckingham Palace*★★ *(Changing of the Guard*★★, *Royal Mews*★★*)* p. 36 BVX – *Kensington Palace*★★ p. 28 FX – *Lincoln's Inn*★★ p. 37 EV – *London Bridge*★ p. 31 PVX – *Royal Hospital Chelsea*★★ p. 35 FU – *St. James's Palace*★★ p. 33 EP – *Somerset House*★★ p. 37 EXY – *South Bank Arts Centre*★★ *(Royal Festival Hall*★, *National Theatre*★, *County Hall*★*)* p. 30 MX – *The Temple*★★ *(Middle Temple Hall*★*)* p. 26 MV – *Tower Bridge*★★ p. 31 PX.

Albert Memorial★ p. 34 CQ – *Apsley House*★ p. 32 BP – *Burlington House*★ p. 33 EM – *Charterhouse*★ p. 27 NOU – *George Inn*★, *Southwark* p. 31 PX – *Gray's Inn*★ p. 26 MU – *Guildhall*★ *(Lord Mayor's Show*★★*)* p. 27 OU – *International Shakespeare Globe Centre*★ p. 31 OX T – *Dr Johnson's House*★ p. 27 NUV A – *Lancaster House*★ p. 33 EP – *Leighton House*★ p. 28 EY – *Linley Sambourne House*★ p. 28 EY – *Lloyds Building*★★ p. 27 PV – *Mansion House*★ *(plate and insignia*★★*)* p. 27 PV P – *The Monument*★ *(*★*)* p. 27 PV G – *Old Admiralty*★ p. 30 KLX – *Royal Albert Hall*★ p. 34 CQ – *Royal Exchange*★ p. 27 PV V – *Royal Opera Arcade*★ *(New Zealand House)* p. 33 FGN – *Royal Opera House*★ *(Covent Garden)* p. 37 DX – *Spencer House*★★ p. 33 DP – *Staple Inn*★ p. 26 MU Y – *Theatre Royal*★ *(Haymarket)* p. 33 GM – *Westminster Bridge*★ p. 30 LY.

CHURCHES

The City Churches

St. Paul's Cathedral★★★ *(Dome* ⩽★★★*)* p. 27 NOV.

St. Bartholomew the Great★★ *(choir*★*)* p. 27 OU K – *St. Dunstan-in-the-East*★★ p. 27 PV F – *St. Mary-at-Hill*★★ *(woodwork*★★, *plan*★*)* p. 27 PV B – *Temple Church*★★ p. 26 MV.

All Hallows-by-the-Tower (font cover★★ *brasses*★*)* p. 27 PV Y – *Christ Church*★ p. 25 OU N – *St. Andrew Undershaft (monuments*★*)* p. 27 PV A – *St. Bride*★ *(steeple*★★*)* p. 27 NV Y – *St. Clement Eastcheap (panelled interior*★★*)* p. 27 PV E – *St. Edmund the King and Martyr (tower and spire*★*)* p. 27 PV D – *St-Giles Cripplegate*★ p. 27 OU N – *St. Helen Bishopsgate*★ *(monuments*★★*)* p. 27 PUV R – *St. James Garlickhythe (tower and spire*★, *sword rests*★*)* p. 27 OV R – *St. Magnus the Martyr (tower*★, *sword rest*★*)* p. 27 PV K – *St. Margaret Lothbury*★ *(tower and spire*★, *woodwork*★, *screen*★, *font*★*)* p. 27 PU S – *St. Margaret Pattens (spire*★, *woodwork*★*)* p. 27 PV N – *St. Martin-within-Ludgate (tower and spire*★, *door cases*★*)* p. 27 NOV B – *St. Mary Abchurch*★ *(reredos*★★, *tower and spire*★, *dome*★*)* p. 27 PV X – *St. Mary-le-Bow (tower and steeple*★★*)* p. 27 OV G – *St. Michael Paternoster Royal (tower and spire*★*)* p. 27 OV D – *St. Nicholas Cole Abbey (tower and spire*★*)* p. 27 OV F – *St. Olave*★ p. 27 PV S – *St. Peter upon Cornhill (screen*★*)* p. 27 PV L – *St. Stephen Walbrook*★ *(tower and steeple*★, *dome*★*)*, p. 27 PV Z – *St. Vedast (tower and spire*★, *ceiling*★*)*, p. 27 OU E.

Other Churches

Westminster Abbey★★★ *(Henry VII Chapel*★★★, *Chapel of Edward the Confessor*★★, *Chapter House*★★, *Poets' Corner*★*)* p. 30 LY.

Southwark Cathedral★★ p. 31 PX.

Queen's Chapel★ p. 33 EP – *St. Clement Danes*★ p. 37 EX – *St. James's*★ p. 33 EM – *St. Margaret's*★ p. 30 LY A – *St. Martin-in-the-Fields*★ p. 37 DY – *St. Paul's*★ *(Covent Garden)* p. 37 DX – *Westminster Roman Catholic Cathedral*★ p. 30 KY B.

PARKS

Regent's Park★★★ p. 25 HI *(terraces*★★*)*, *Zoo*★★.

Hyde Park – Kensington Gardens★★ *(Orangery*★*)* pp. 28 and 29 – *St. James's Park*★★ p. 30 KXY.

STREETS AND SQUARES

The City★★★ *p. 27* NV.

Bedford Square★★ *p. 26* KLU – *Belgrave Square*★★ *p. 36* AVX – *Burlington Arcade*★★ *p. 33* DM – *Covent Garden*★★ *(The Piazza*★★ *) p. 37* DX – *The Mall*★★ *p. 33* FP – *Piccadilly*★ *p. 33* EM – *The Thames*★★ *pp. 29-31* – *Trafalgar Square*★★ *p. 37* DY – *Whitehall*★★ *(Horse Guards*★ *) p. 30* LX.

Barbican★ *p. 27* OU – *Bond Street*★ *pp. 32-33* CK-DM – *Canonbury Square*★ *p. 27* NS – *Carlton House Terrace*★ *p. 33* GN – *Cheyne Walk*★ *p. 29* GHZ – *Fitzroy Square*★ *p. 26* KU – *Jermyn Street*★ *p. 33* EN – *Leicester Square*★ *p. 33* GM – *Merrick Square*★ *p. 31* OY – *Montpelier Square*★ *p. 35* EQ – *Neal's Yard*★ *p. 37* DV – *Piccadilly Arcade*★ *p. 33* DEN – *Portman Square*★ *p. 32* AJ – *Queen Anne's Gate*★ *p. 30* KY – *Regent Street*★ *p. 33* EM – *Piccadilly Circus*★ *p. 33* FM – *St. James's Square*★ *p. 33* FN – *St. James's Street*★ *p. 33* EN – *Shepherd Market*★ *p. 32* CN – *Soho*★ *p. 33* – *Trinity Church Square*★ *p. 31* OY – *Victoria Embankment gardens*★ *p. 37* DEXY – *Waterloo Place*★ *p. 33* FN.

MUSEUMS

British Museum★★★ *p. 26* LU – *National Gallery*★★★ *p. 33* GM – *Science Museum*★★★ *p. 34* CR – *Tate Britain*★★★ *p. 30* LZ – *Victoria and Albert Museum*★★★ *p. 35* DR – *Wallace Collection*★★★ *p. 32* AH.

Courtauld Institute Galleries★★ *(Somerset House) p. 37* EXY – *Gilbert Collection*★★ *(Somerset House) p. 37* EX Y – *Museum of London*★★ *p. 27* OU **M** – *National Portrait Gallery*★★ *p. 33* GM – *Natural History Museum*★★ *p. 34* CS – *Sir John Soane's Museum*★★ *p. 26* MU **M** – *Tate Modern*★★ *(views*★★★ *from top floors) p. 31* OX **M**.

Clock Museum★ *(Guildhall) p. 26* OU – *Imperial War Museum*★ *p. 31* NY – *London's Transport Museum*★ *p. 37* DX – *Madame Tussaud's*★ *p. 25* IU **M** – *Museum of Mankind*★ *p. 33* DM – *National Army Museum*★ *p. 35* FU – *Percival David Foundation of Chinese Art*★ *p. 26* KLT **M** – *Planetarium*★ *p. 25* IU **M** – *Wellington Museum*★ *(Apsley House) p. 32* BP.

OUTER LONDON

Blackheath *p. 15* HX *terraces and houses*★, *Eltham Palace*★ **A**
Brentford *p. 12* BX *Syon Park*★★, *gardens*★
Bromley *p. 14* GY *The Crystal Palace Park*★
Chiswick *p. 13* CV *Chiswick Mall*★★, *Chiswick House*★ **D**, *Hogarth's House*★ **E**
Dulwich *p. 14* *Picture Gallery*★ FX **X**
Greenwich *pp. 14 and 15 : Cutty Sark*★★ GV **F**, *Footway Tunnel(*≤ ★★ *) – Fan Museum*★ *p. 10* GV **A**, – *National Maritime Museum*★★ *(Queen's House*★★ *) GV* **M**, *Royal Naval College*★★ *(Painted Hall*★, *the Chapel*★ *) GV* **G**, *The Park and Old Royal Observatory*★ *(Meridian Building : collection*★★ *) HV* **K**, *Ranger's House*★ GX **N**
Hampstead *Kenwood House*★★ *(Adam Library*★★, *paintings*★★ *) p. 9* EU **P**, *Fenton House*★★, *p. 24* ES
Hampton Court *p. 12* BY *(The Palace*★★★, *gardens*★★★, *Fountain Court*★, *The Great Vine*★ *)*
Kew *p. 13* CX *Royal Botanic Gardens*★★★ : *Palm House*★★, *Temperate House*★, *Kew Palace or Dutch House*★★, *Orangery*★, *Pagoda*★, *Japanese Gateway*★
Hendon★ *p. 9, Royal Air Force Museum*★★ CT **M**
Hounslow *p. 12* BV *Osterley Park*★★
Lewisham *p. 14* GX *Horniman Museum*★ **M**
Richmond *pp. 12 and 13 : Richmond Park*★★, ⚘★★★ CX, *Richmond Hill*⚘★★ CX, *Richmond Bridge*★★ BX **R**, *Richmond Green*★★ BX **S** *(Maids of Honour Row*★★, *Trumpeter's House*★ *)*, *Asgill House*★ BX **B**, *Ham House*★★ BX **V**
Shoreditch *p. 10* FU *Geffrye Museum*★ **M**
Tower Hamlets *p. 10* GV *Canary Wharf*★★ **B**, *Isle of Dogs*★ *St. Katharine Dock*★ **Y**
Twickenham *p. 12* BX *Marble Hill House*★ **Z**, *Strawberry Hill*★ **A** .

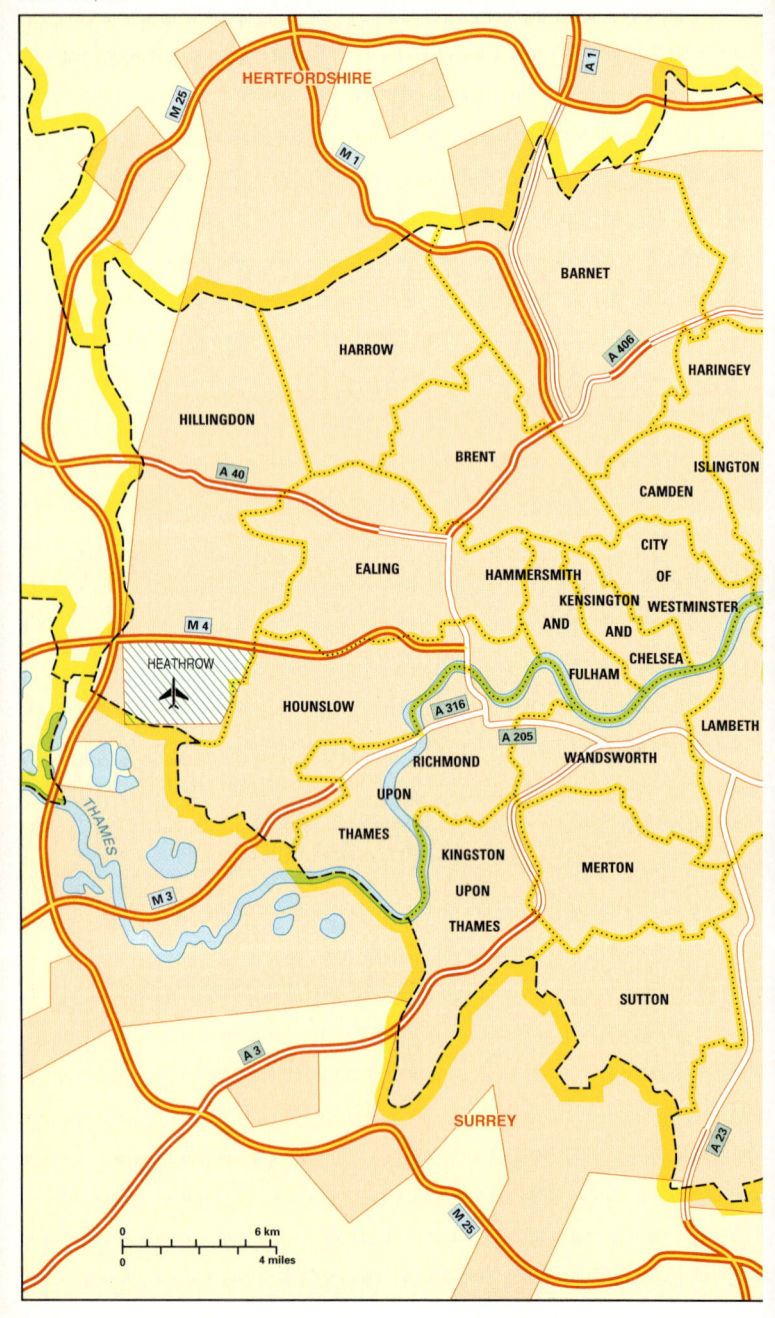

HERTFORDSHIRE

M 25

M 1

A 1

BARNET

HARROW

A 406

HARINGEY

HILLINGDON

BRENT

ISLINGTON

A 40

CAMDEN

EALING

CITY

HAMMERSMITH

OF

KENSINGTON

WESTMINSTER

M 4

AND

AND

HEATHROW

CHELSEA

FULHAM

HOUNSLOW

A 316

LAMBETH

A 205

RICHMOND

WANDSWORTH

THAMES

UPON

THAMES

KINGSTON

MERTON

M 3

UPON

THAMES

SUTTON

A 3

SURREY

A 23

0   6 km

0   4 miles

M 25

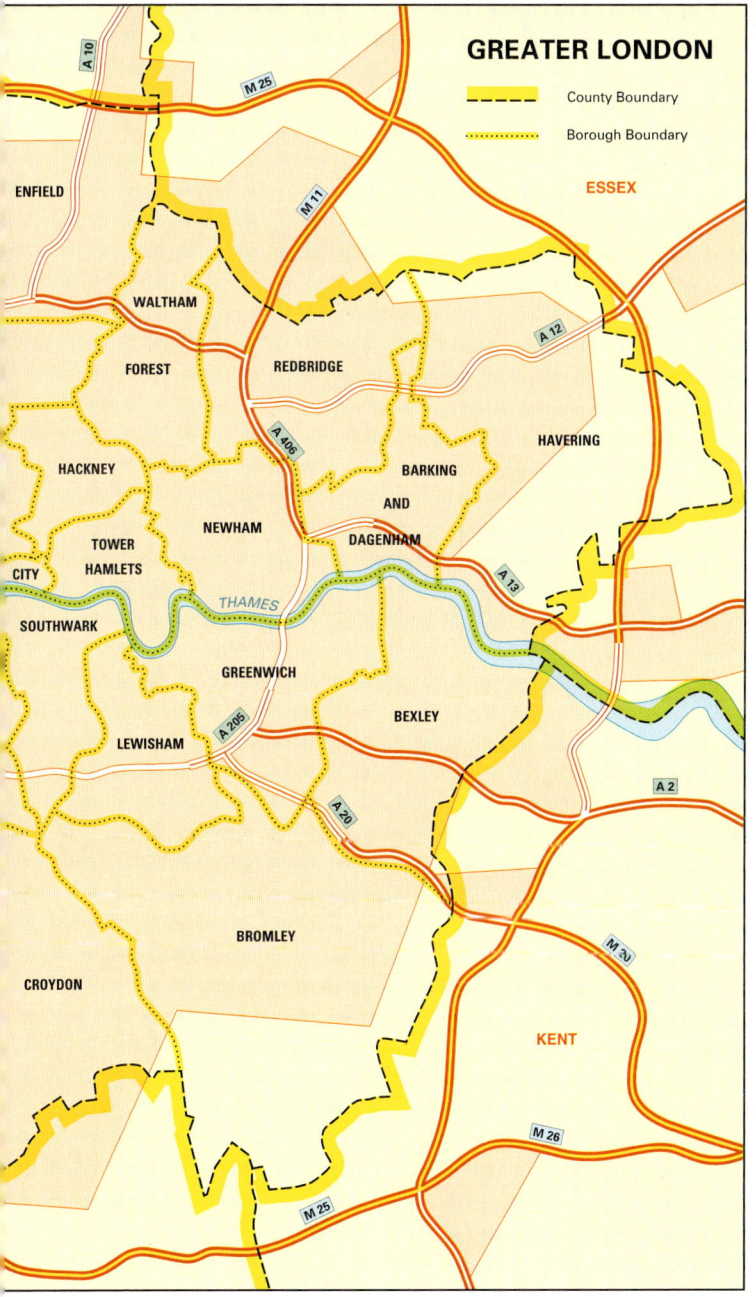

GREATER LONDON

County Boundary

Borough Boundary

ESSEX

ENFIELD

WALTHAM

FOREST

REDBRIDGE

HAVERING

HACKNEY

BARKING

AND

NEWHAM

DAGENHAM

TOWER

HAMLETS

CITY

THAMES

SOUTHWARK

GREENWICH

BEXLEY

LEWISHAM

A 2

BROMLEY

CROYDON

KENT

M 26

M 25

GREATER LONDON
NORTH-WEST

0 — 3 km
0 — 2 miles

Greater London Boundary
Through route
16.2 Low headroom : See map 404

pp 8-9	pp 10-11
pp 12-13	pp 14-15

AYLESBURY A 41 M 1 BIRMINGHAM

RADLETT

WATFORD JUNCTION

ELSTREE

MICHELIN

WATFORD
WATFORD HIGH STREET

BUSHEY

BUSHEY

CARPENDERS PARK

STANMORE

STANMORE

HATCH END

HEADSTONE LANE

HARROW

NORTHWOOD

HARROW AND WEALDSTONE

KENTON

NORTHWOOD HILLS

PINNER

KENTON

EASTCOTE

NORTH HARROW

WEST HARROW

HARROW ON-THE-HILL

NORTHWICK PARK

EASTCOTE

RAYNERS LANE

SOUTH KENTON

RUISLIP MANOR

WEST RUISLIP

RUISLIP

SOUTH HARROW

NORTH WEMBLEY

ICKENHAM

RUISLIP GARDENS

SOUTH RUISLIP

SUDBURY HILL

ICKENHAM

NORTHOLT AERODROME

SUDBURY TOWN

HILLINGDON

NORTHOLT

A 4090

UXBRIDGE

GREENFORD

ALPERTON

PERIVALE

HILLINGDON

YIEWSLEY

EALING

EALING BROADWAY

HAYES

A 4020

SOUTHALL

HANWELL

SOUTH EALING

NORTHFIELDS

BOSTON MANOR

OSTERLEY PARK

OSTERLEY

M 4

READING, WINDSOR

A 40 (M 40) OXFORD

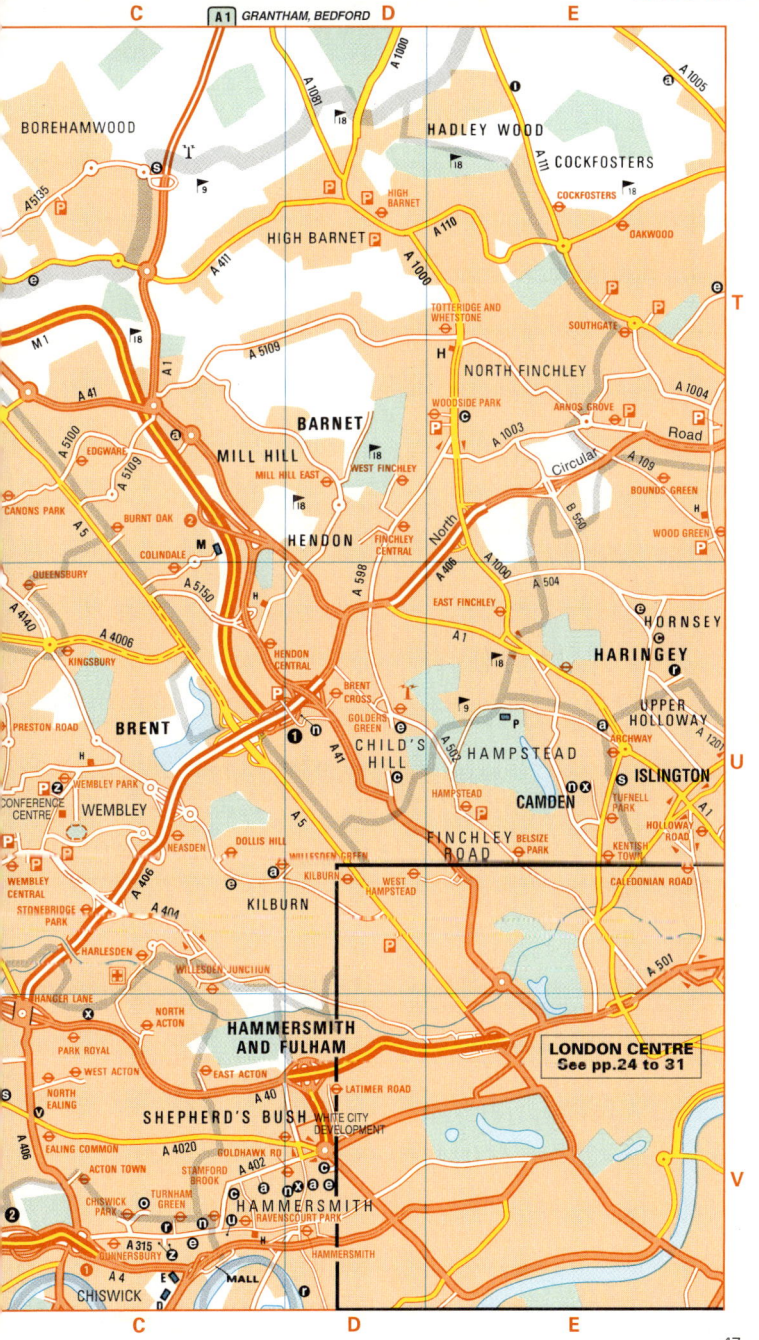

A1 GRANTHAM, BEDFORD

BOREHAMWOOD

HADLEY WOOD
COCKFOSTERS

COCKFOSTERS
OAKWOOD

HIGH BARNET
HIGH BARNET
A 110

TOTTERIDGE AND WHETSTONE

SOUTHGATE

NORTH FINCHLEY
WOODSIDE PARK
ARNOS GROVE
BOUNDS GREEN
WOOD GREEN
Road
North Circular

BARNET
MILL HILL
WEST FINCHLEY
MILL HILL EAST
HENDON
FINCHLEY CENTRAL

EDGWARE
BURNT OAK
COLINDALE

EAST FINCHLEY
HORNSEY
HARINGEY

QUEENSBURY
CANONS PARK
KINGSBURY
PRESTON ROAD

HENDON CENTRAL
BRENT CROSS
GOLDERS GREEN
CHILD'S HILL
HAMPSTEAD
UPPER HOLLOWAY
ARCHWAY

BRENT
WEMBLEY PARK
WEMBLEY
NEASDEN
DOLLIS HILL
KILBURN
CAMDEN
ISLINGTON
TUFNELL PARK
HOLLOWAY ROAD
KENTISH TOWN

CONFERENCE CENTRE
WEMBLEY CENTRAL
STONEBRIDGE PARK
HARLESDEN

FINCHLEY ROAD
BELSIZE PARK
WEST HAMPSTEAD
KILBURN
WILLESDEN GREEN
HAMPSTEAD

CALEDONIAN ROAD

HANGER LANE
NORTH ACTON
PARK ROYAL
WEST ACTON
NORTH EALING

WILLESDEN JUNCTION

HAMMERSMITH AND FULHAM

LONDON CENTRE
See pp.24 to 31

EAST ACTON
LATIMER ROAD

SHEPHERD'S BUSH
WHITE CITY DEVELOPMENT

EALING COMMON
ACTON TOWN
GOLDHAWK RD
STAMFORD BROOK
CHISWICK PARK
TURNHAM GREEN
HAMMERSMITH
RAVENSCOURT PARK

GUNNERSBURY
HAMMERSMITH
MALL

CHISWICK

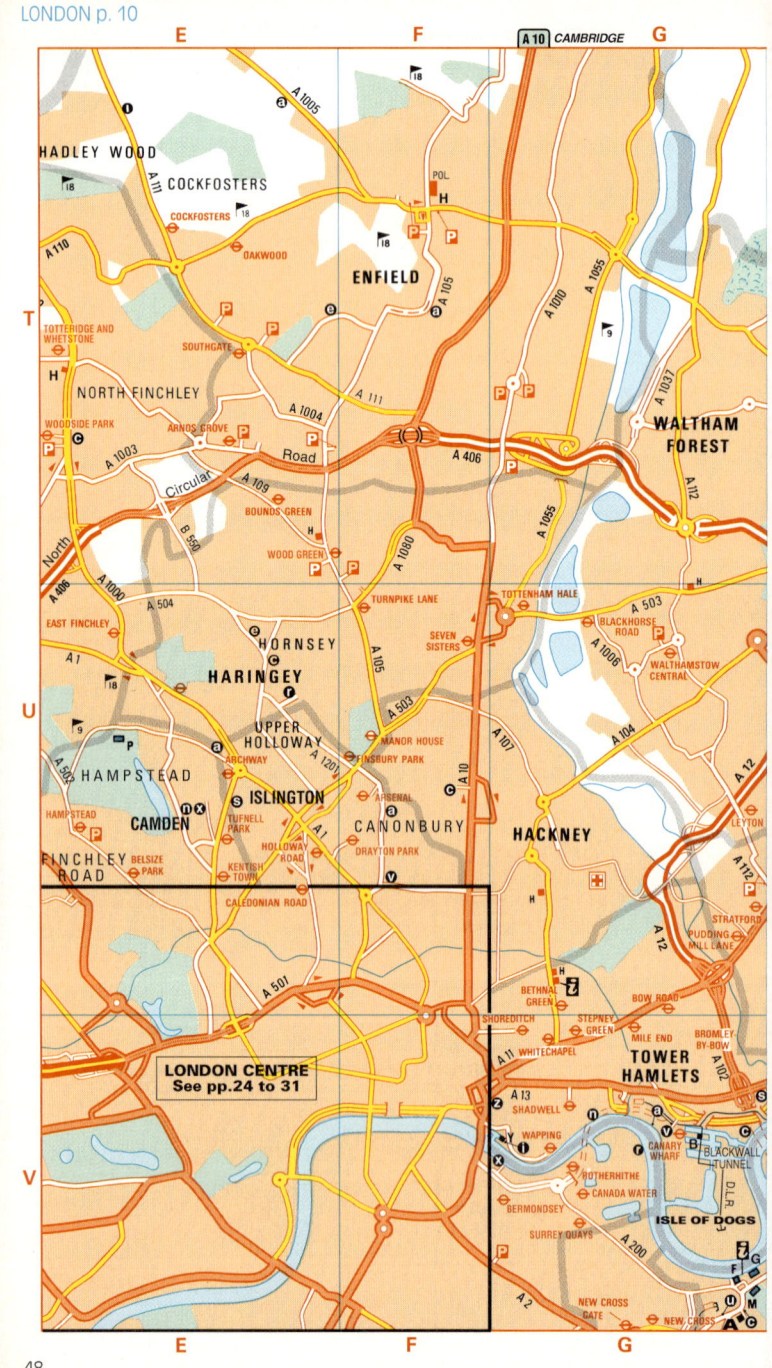

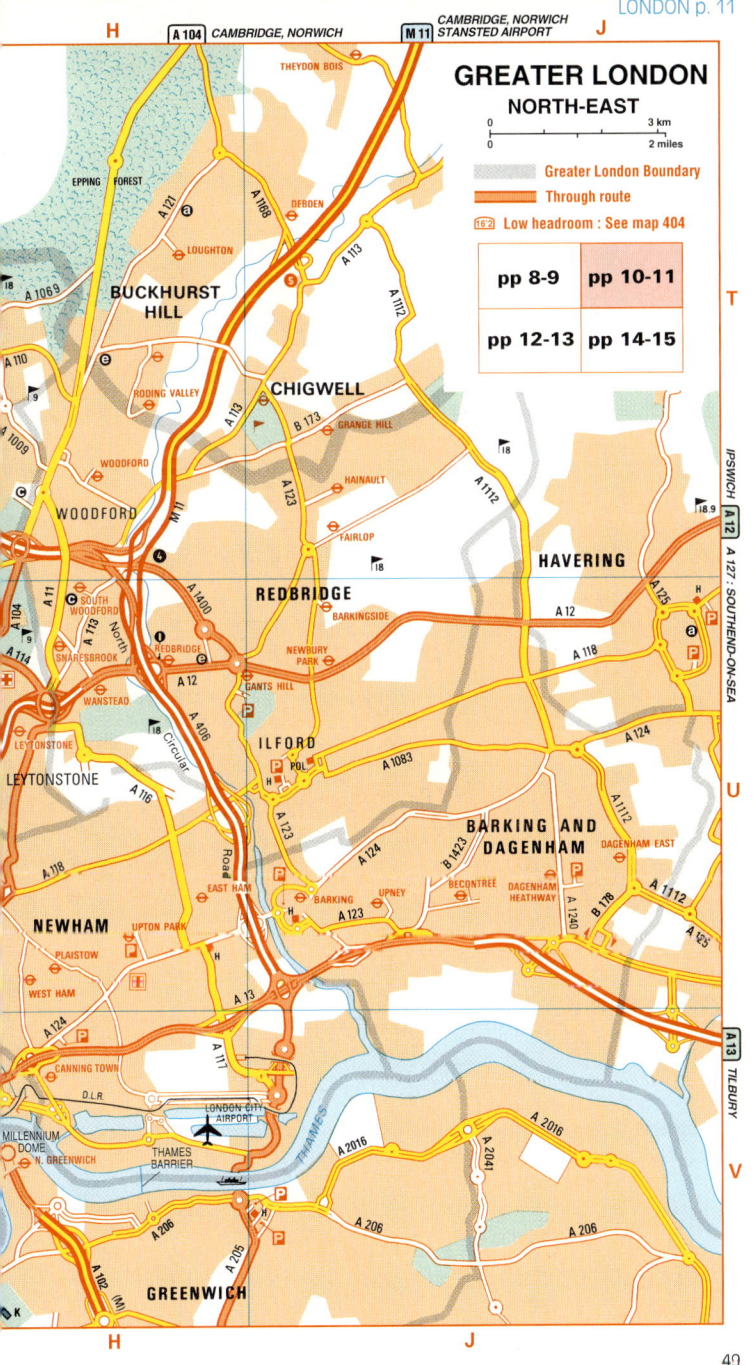

GREATER LONDON
NORTH-EAST

Greater London Boundary
Through route
Low headroom : See map 404

| pp 8-9 | pp 10-11 |
| pp 12-13 | pp 14-15 |

GREATER LONDON
SOUTH-WEST

| 0 | | 3 km |
| 0 | | 2 miles |

Greater London Boundary
Through route
Low headroom : See map 404

pp 8-9	pp 10-11
pp 12-13	pp 14-15

YIEWSLEY
HILLINGDON
EALING
EALING BROADWAY
HAYES
SOUTHALL
HANWELL
SOUTH EALING
NORTHFIELDS
BOSTON MANOR
OSTERLEY PARK
OSTERLEY
SYON PARK
HEATHROW
CRANFORD
HATTON CROSS
HOUNSLOW WEST
HOUNSLOW EAST
HOUNSLOW CENTRAL
HOUNSLOW
TERMINAL 1
TERMINAL 3
HEATHROW AIRPORT
TERMINAL 2
TERMINAL 4
HEATHROW 4
TWICKENHAM
RICHMOND
UPON THAMES
BUSHY PARK
SUNBURY
SHEPPERTON
HAMPTON COURT
Thames
WALTON-ON-THAMES
WEYBRIDGE
ESHER
CLAYGATE
CLAREMONT PARK
COBHAM
Mole

READING WINDSOR A4
SOUTHAMPTON BASINGSTOKE A30
SOUTHAMPTON BASINGSTOKE M3

PORTSMOUTH A3
WORTHING A243

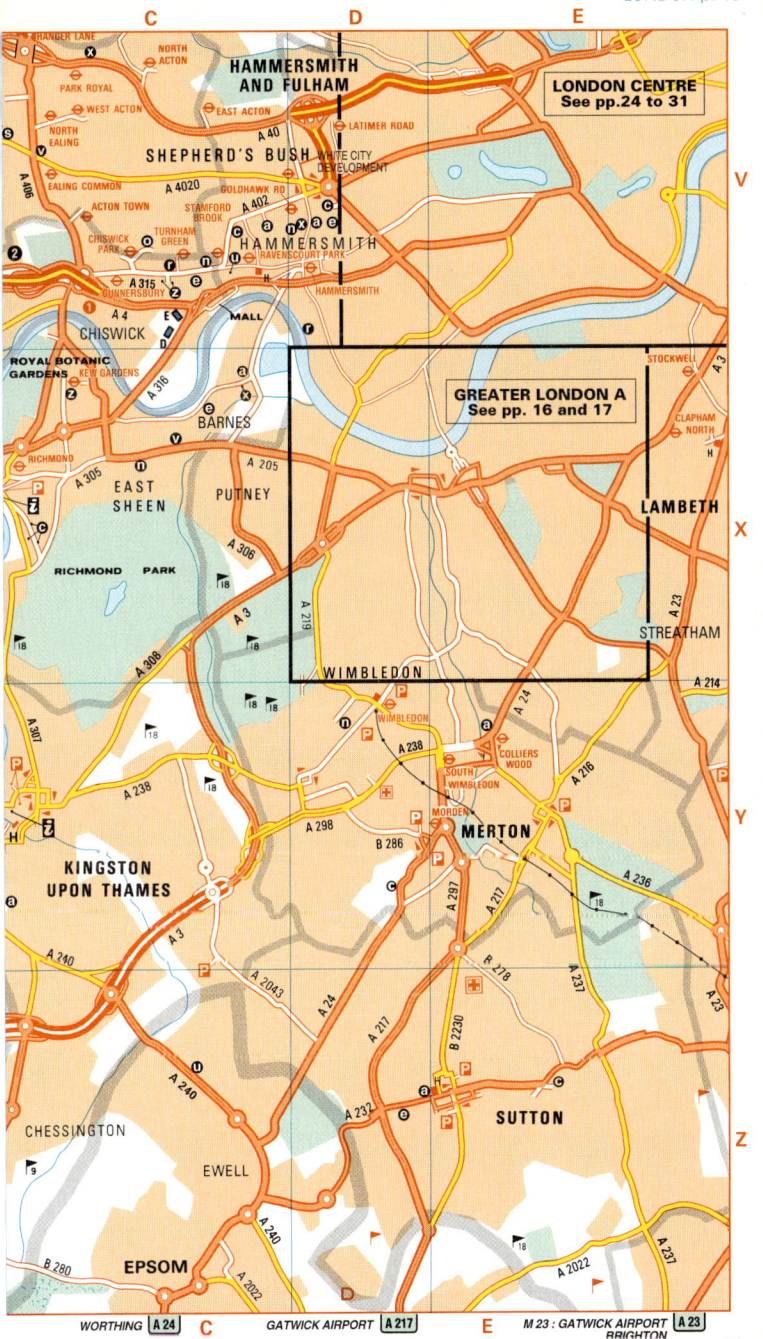

LONDON CENTRE
See pp.24 to 31

GREATER LONDON A
See pp. 16 and 17

SHOREDITCH
STEPNEY GREEN
MILE END
BROMLEY BY-BOW
A 11
WHITECHAPEL
TOWER HAMLETS
A 102
A 13
SHADWELL
WAPPING
CANARY WHARF
BLACKWALL TUNNEL
ROTHERHITHE
CANADA WATER
BERMONDSEY
ISLE OF DOGS
SURREY QUAYS
A 200
NEW CROSS GATE
NEW CROSS
A 2
STOCKWELL
A 3
A 2
A 202
A 20
D.L.R.
CLAPHAM NORTH
BRIXTON
A 2218
SOUTHWARK
LAMBETH
HERNE HILL
Circular
Road
LEWISHAM
A 205
South
DULWICH
A 23
STREATHAM
A 21
A 212
A 2218
A 214
A 2015
A 24
COLLIERS WOOD
A 216
A 212
A 234
A 222
SOUTH WIMBLEDON
MORDEN
A 215
A 213
MERTON
A 297
A 217
A 236
A 214
B 278
A 237
CROYDON
A 222
A 232
B 2230
A 23
A 212
SUTTON
SOUTH CROYDON
ADDINGTON
A 235
A 2022
18-9
A 2022
A 237
SANDERSTEAD
A 22

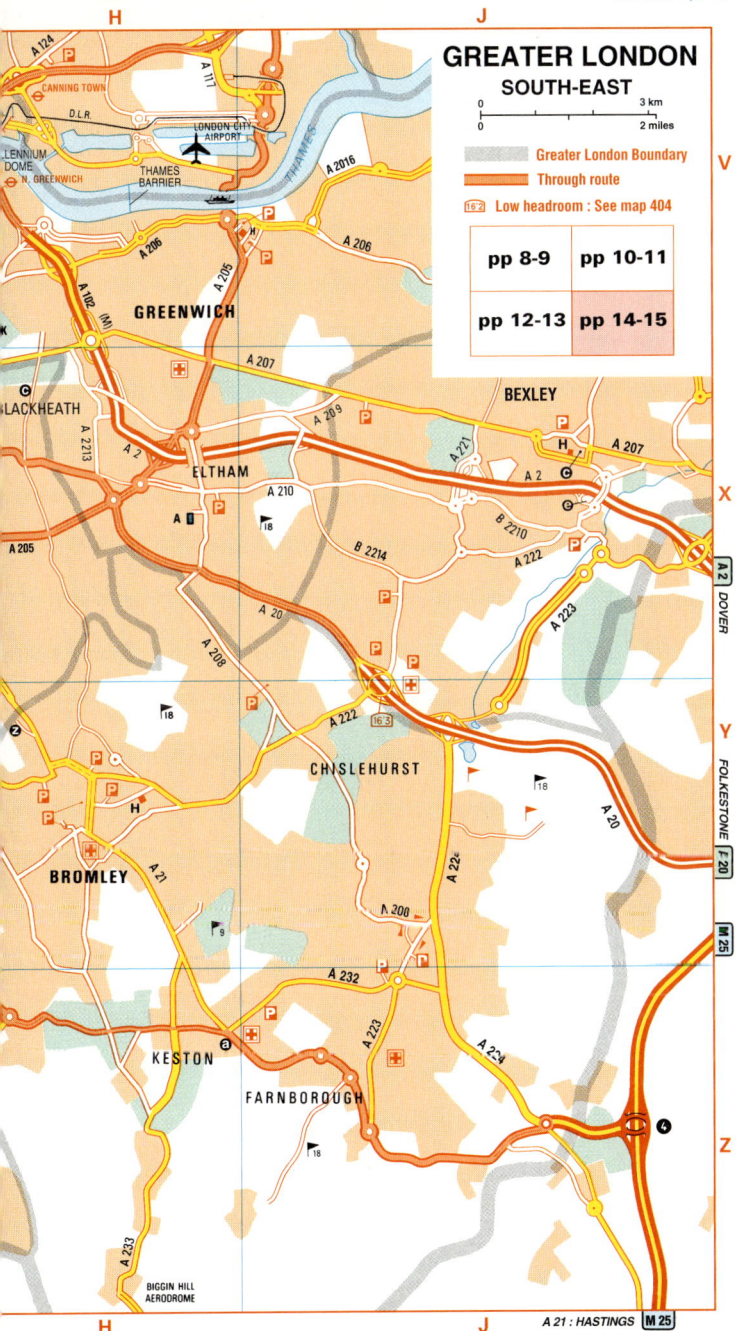

GREATER LONDON
SOUTH-EAST

| 0 | 3 km |
| 0 | 2 miles |

Greater London Boundary
Through route
Low headroom : See map 404

| pp 8-9 | pp 10-11 |
| pp 12-13 | pp 14-15 |

A 124
CANNING TOWN
A 111
D.L.R.
LONDON CITY AIRPORT
MILLENNIUM DOME
N. GREENWICH
THAMES BARRIER
THAMES
A 2016
A 206
A 206
A 102 (M)
A 205
GREENWICH
A 207
A 2213
BLACKHEATH
A 2
A 209
A 210
ELTHAM
A 2
BEXLEY
A 207
A 221
B 2210
A 222
A 223
DOVER A 2
A 18
B 2214
A 205
A 20
A 208
A 18
A 222
16.3
CHISLEHURST
A 18
A 20
FOLKESTONE A 20
P
P
H
P
BROMLEY
A 21
A 22
A 200
M 25
A 232
KESTON
a
A 223
FARNBOROUGH
A 224
A 18
Z
A 233
BIGGIN HILL AERODROME

53

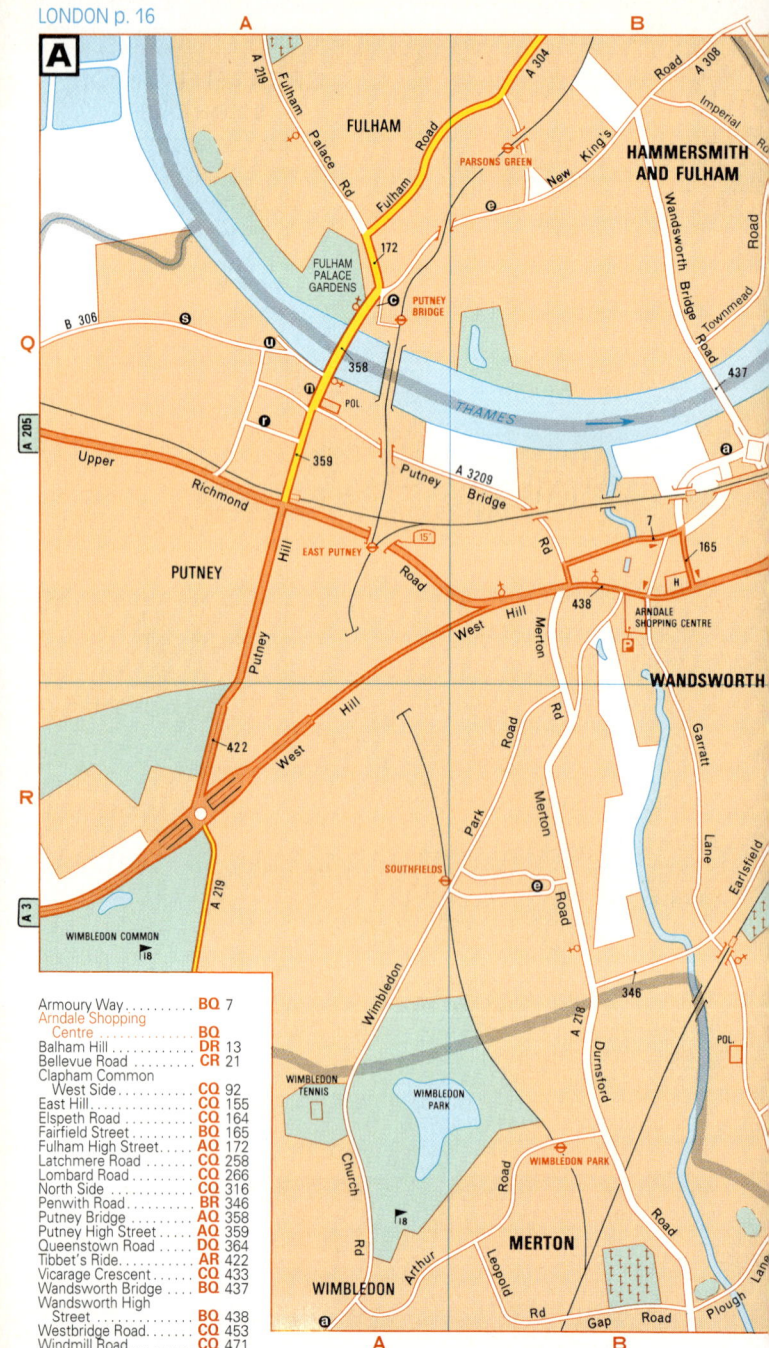

LONDON CENTRE

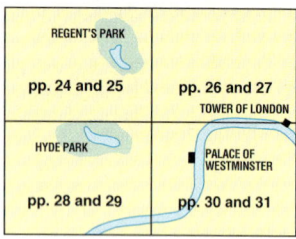

REGENT'S PARK	
pp. 24 and 25	pp. 26 and 27 TOWER OF LONDON
HYDE PARK	PALACE OF WESTMINSTER
pp. 28 and 29	pp. 30 and 31

STREET INDEX TO LONDON CENTRE TOWN PLANS

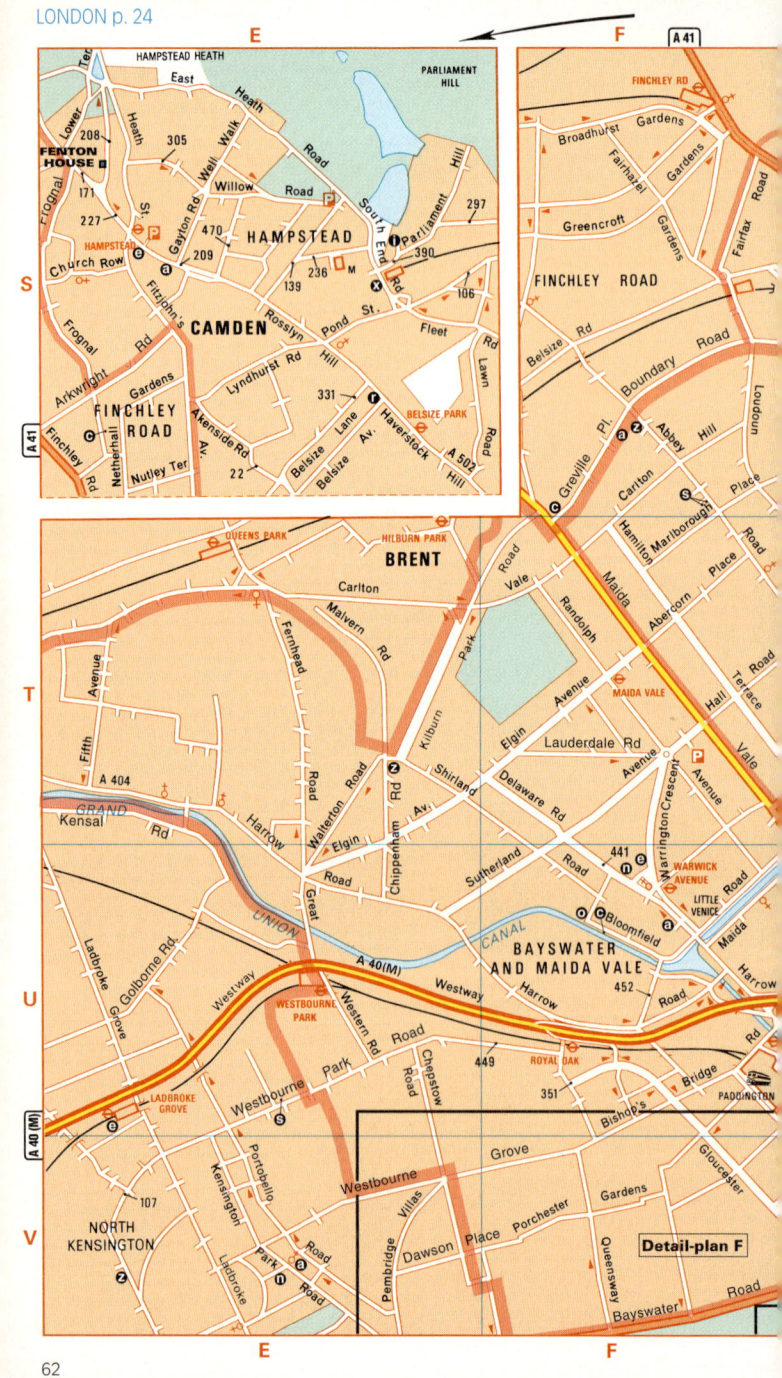

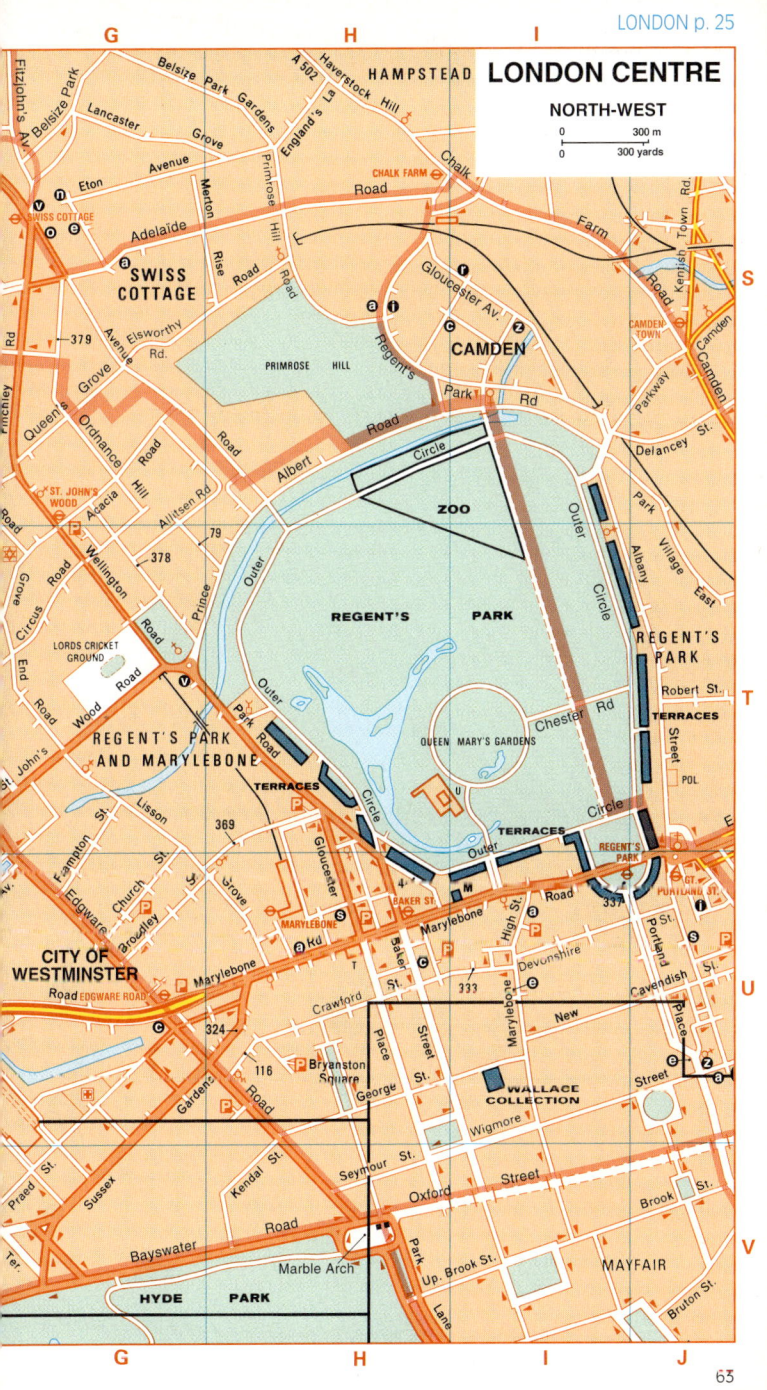

LONDON CENTRE
NORTH-WEST

0 — 300 m
0 — 300 yards

HAMPSTEAD

CHALK FARM
Chalk Farm Road

SWISS COTTAGE
SWISS COTTAGE

ST. JOHN'S WOOD

PRIMROSE HILL

CAMDEN
CAMDEN TOWN

ZOO

REGENT'S PARK

REGENT'S PARK

LORDS CRICKET GROUND

REGENT'S PARK AND MARYLEBONE

TERRACES

QUEEN MARY'S GARDENS

TERRACES

TERRACES

REGENT'S PARK
GT. PORTLAND ST.

MARYLEBONE

CITY OF WESTMINSTER
EDGWARE ROAD

Bryanston Square

George St.

WALLACE COLLECTION

Crawford

Wigmore

Oxford Street

Seymour St.

Bayswater Road

HYDE PARK

Marble Arch

MAYFAIR

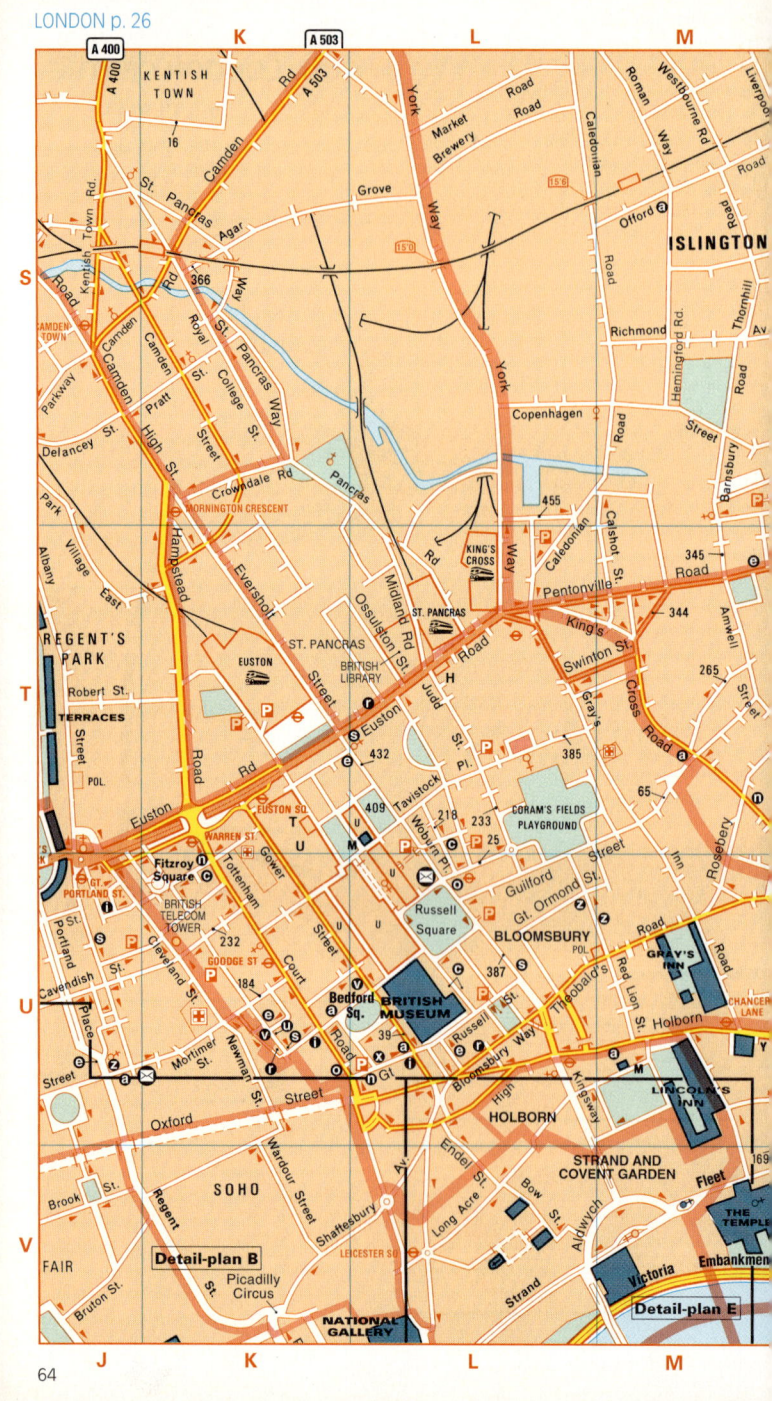

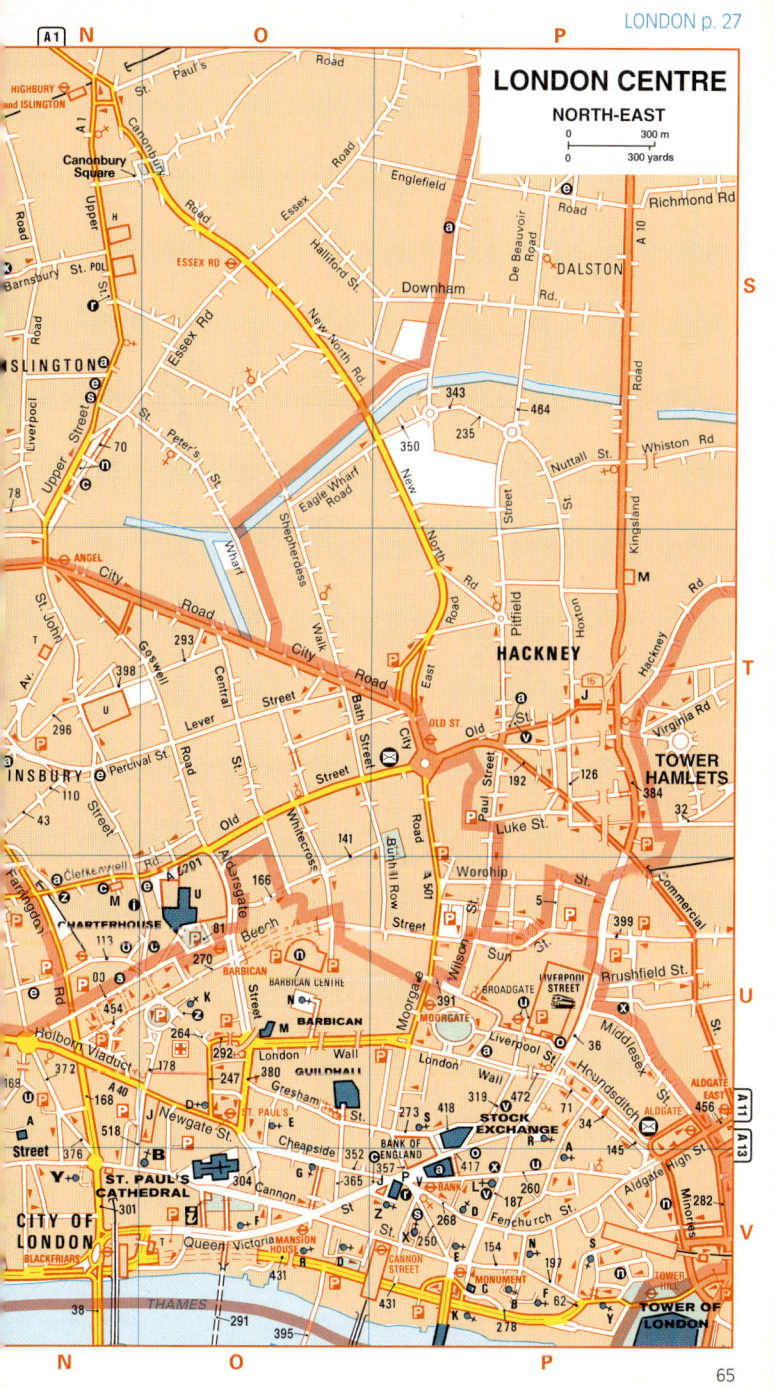

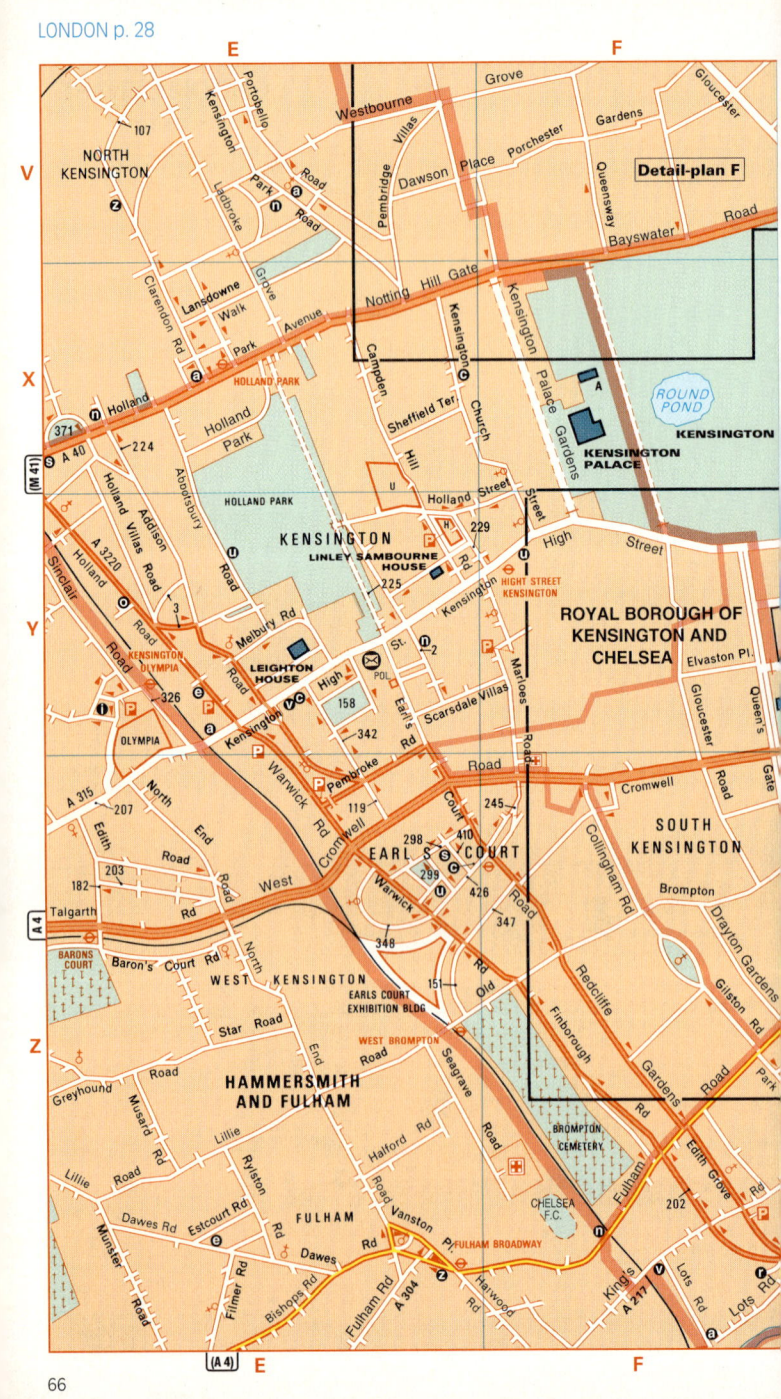

LONDON CENTRE

SOUTH-WEST

0   300 m
0   300 yards

G   H   I   J

Praed St.
Sussex
Kendal St.
Seymour St.
Oxford
Bayswater Road
Marble Arch
HYDE PARK
Up. Brook St
Park Lane
Bruton St.
South Audley St.
Berkeley St.
Piccadilly

CITY OF WESTMINSTER

The Long Water
Serpentine
The Serpentine
Park Lane
Curzon
GREEN PARK

GARDENS
HYDE PARK AND KNIGHTSBRIDGE
Road
HYDE PARK CORNER
Constitution Hill
Constitution Hill

Kensington
Road
Knightsbridge
a
Grosvenor Pl

Exhibition Road
Sloane Street
Belgrave Square
Chapel St.
Detail-plan D

VICTORIA AND ALBERT MUSEUM
Brompton Road
Pont Street
BELGRAVIA
Lyall St.
VICTORIA

SCIENCE MUSEUM
U
Walton Street
Cadogan Sq.
Street
King's Road
Ebury Street
Buckingham Palace Road
Belgr

Road
Pelham Street
Sloane Avenue
Cadogan Gdns
Saint
Belgr

Detail-plan C
Onslow Gdns
Sydney
Cale Street
Pimlico
Ebury Bridge Rd
Warwick Way
Sutherland St.
Gloucester

Old
Rd
Street
Rd
156
c
Lupus

CHELSEA
Smith Street
Chelsea Bridge Rd
Grosvenor

Fulham
Church
King's
Flood Street
Royal Hospital
Road
THE ROYAL HOSPITAL
14 9

Beaufort
Oakley Street
Chelsea
Embankment
Chelsea Bridge
Queenstown Road

Walk
Cheyne
a
Cheyne Walk
Albert Bridge
Battersea Bridge
The Parade
Carriage Drive East
75

Cheyne Walk
Battersea Bridge
Battersea Bridge Rd
Albert Bridge Rd
Parkgate Rd
75
BATTERSEA PARK
Road
361
19

WANDSWORTH

G   H   I   J

V
X
Y
Z

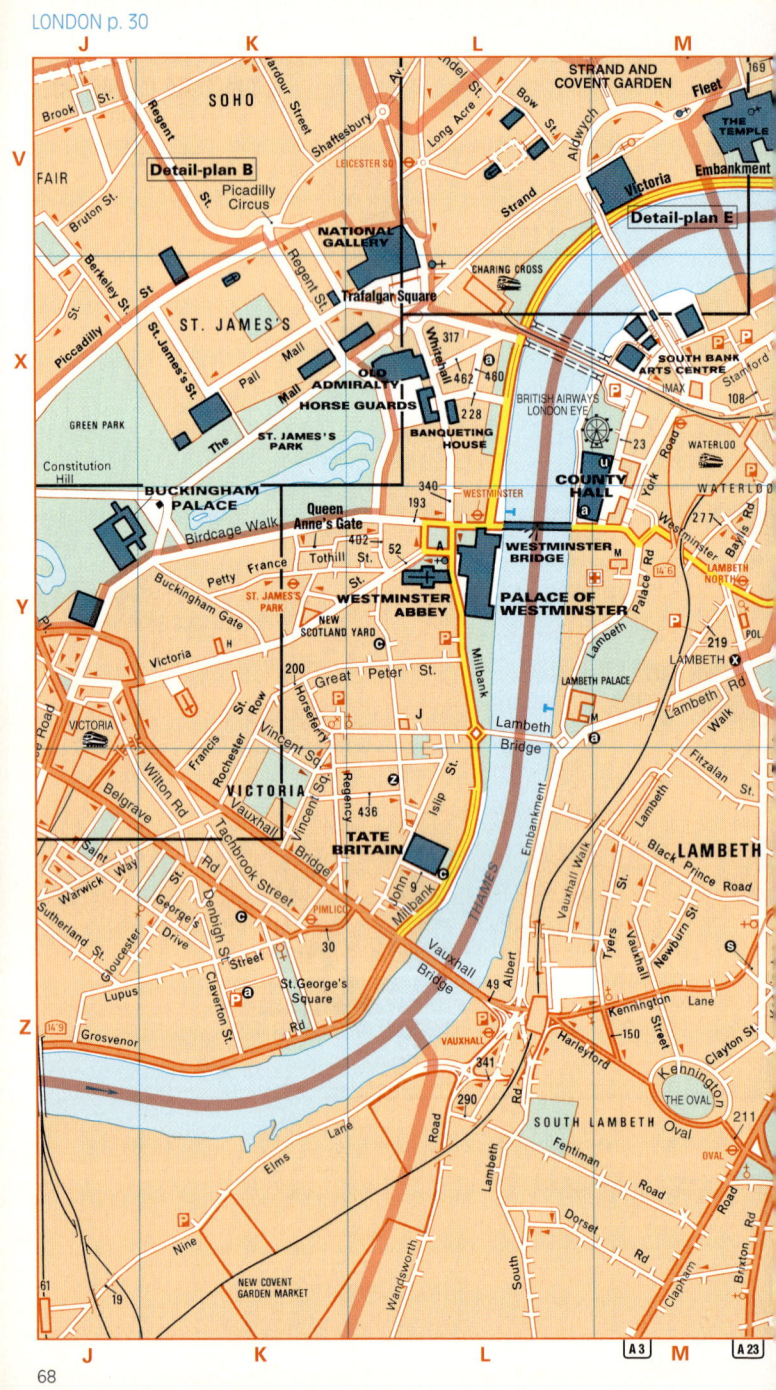

LONDON CENTRE
SOUTH-EAST

0   300 m
0   300 yards

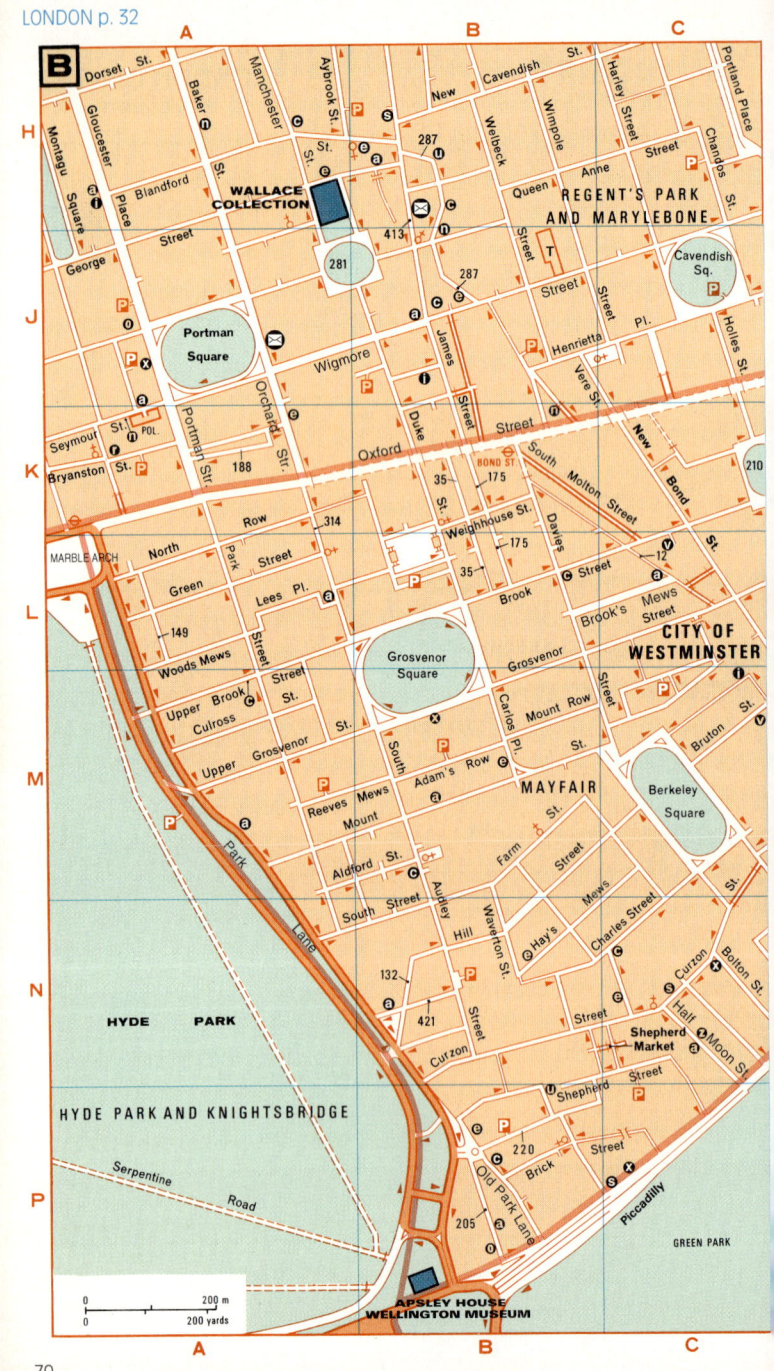

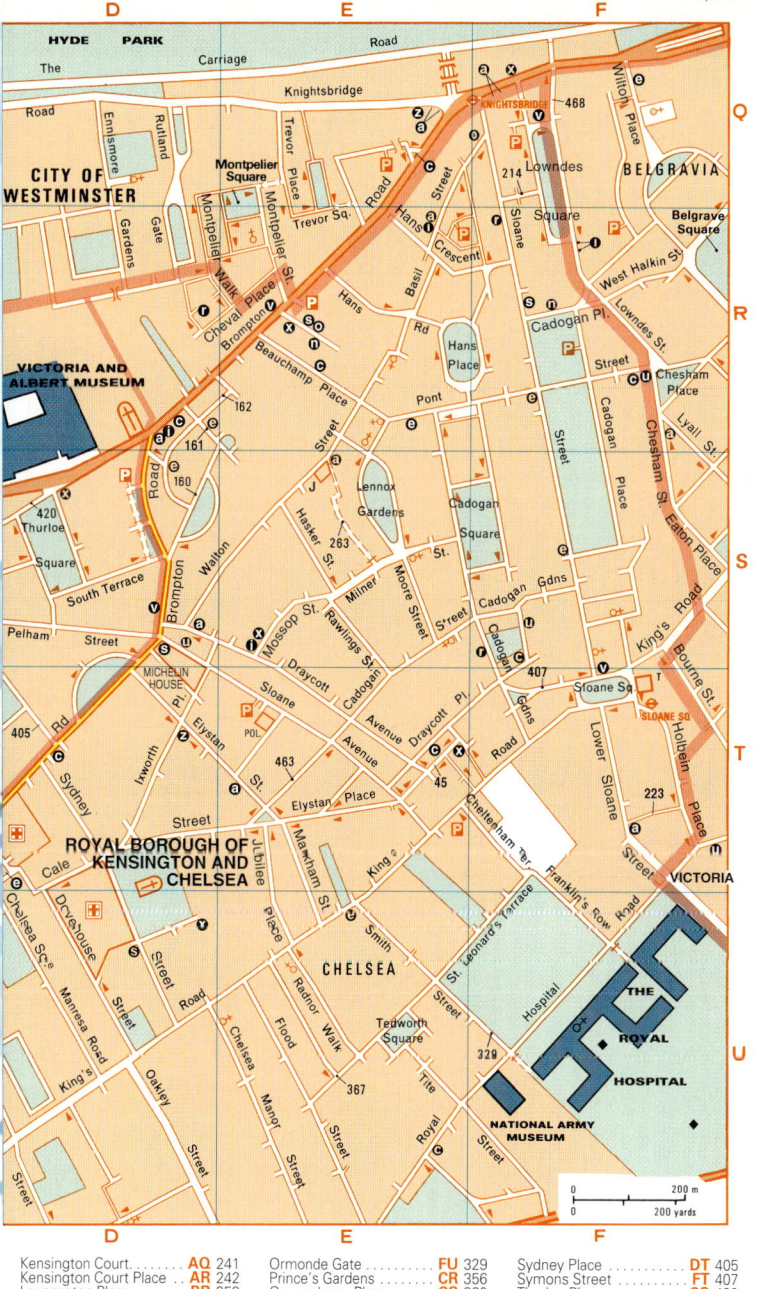

73

D
A
B
C
V
X
Y
WELLINGTON ARCH
142
GREEN PARK
Constitution Hill
QUEEN VICTORIA MEMORIAL
The Mall
St. James's Park Lake
ST. JAMES'S
ST. JAMES'S PARK
BUCKINGHAM PALACE GARDENS
BUCKINGHAM PALACE
Birdcage Walk
M
Grosvenor Cres.
Halkin St.
Chapel St.
Grosvenor Place
Belgrave Square
Chester St.
56
56 CITY OF WESTMINSTER
Petty France
Palmer St.
Wilton St.
Upper Belgrave St.
ROYAL MEWS
T
Palace St.
Castle La.
56
BELGRAVIA
Pl.
274
48
St.
Belgrave Place
Square
Hobart Pl.
Grosvenor Gdns
Rd
Victoria St.
H
Lower Belgrave St.
Victoria
T
St.
Street
Howick Pl.
8
Eaton Place
Eaton
Road
Square
88
412
Ashley Pl.
416
Street
Row
King's
Eccleston
Street
Carlisle Place
WESTMINSTER CATHEDRAL
Elizabeth
Eaton
88
Palace
VICTORIA
Vauxhall
Francis
Wilton
VICTORIA
Rochester
Vincent Square
St.
Hudson's Pl.
PASSPORT OFFICE
St.
389
Chester Row
Ebury
Buckingham
157
Gillingham St.
Bridge
Tachbrook
389
Street
201
Road
Street
Hugh Street
Belgrave
Warwick Way
St.
Road
0
200 m
0
200 yards
VICTORIA COACH STATION
Eccleston Square
Rd

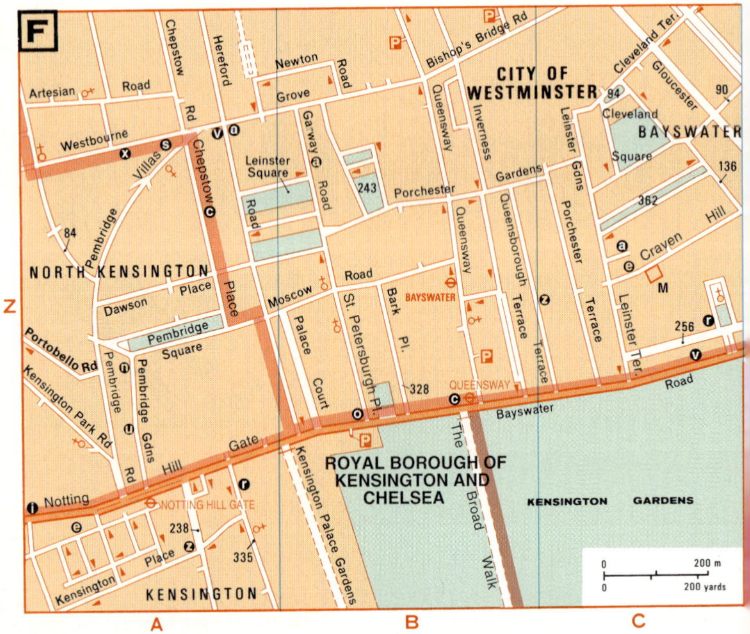
F
Chepstow Rd
Hereford Rd
Newton Road
Bishop's Bridge Rd
Cleveland Ter.
Gloucester
Artesian Road
Grove
Queensway
CITY OF WESTMINSTER
94
90
Inverness
Cleveland
BAYSWATER
Westbourne
Chepstow
Garway Road
Leinster Square
Leinster Gdns
Square
Villas
Road
243
Porchester
Gardens
136
362
84
Pembridge
Hill
Craven
NORTH KENSINGTON
Queensway
Queensborough
Porchester
Dawson Place
Place
Moscow Road
Road
M
BAYSWATER
Pembridge Square
St. Petersburgh Pl.
Bark Pl.
Terrace
Terrace
Terrace
Leinster Ter.
256
Portobello Rd
Palace
Pembridge
Pembridge Gdns
Court
Kensington Park Rd
328
QUEENSWAY
Bayswater Road
Rd
Gate
The Broad Walk
Hill
Kensington Palace Gardens
ROYAL BOROUGH OF KENSINGTON AND CHELSEA
KENSINGTON GARDENS
Notting
NOTTING HILL GATE
238
335
Place
Kensington
KENSINGTON
0
200 m
0
200 yards
A
B
C
Z

Artillery Row CVX 8	Eccleston Bridge BY 157	Orme Court BZ 328
Bream's Buildings EV 47	Great Cumberland Place EZ 191	Oxford Square EZ 332
Bressenden Place BX 48	Guildhouse Street BY 201	Palace Gardens Terrace AZ 335
Buckingham Gate CV 56	Henrietta Street DX 217	Queen's Gardens CZ 362
Cambridge Square EZ 67	Hyde Park Square EZ 234	St. Giles High Street DV 377
Chepstow Crescent AZ 84	Kensington Church Street AZ 238	Sardinia Street EV 381
Chester Square AX 88	Kensington Gardens Square BZ 243	Southampton Street DX 388
Chilworth Street CZ 90	Lancaster Gate CDZ 256	South Eaton Place AY 389
Clarendon Place EZ 93	Lancaster Terrace DZ 257	Stanhope Place EZ 400
Cleveland Gardens CZ 94	Lower Grosvenor Place BX 274	Sussex Square DZ 404
Connaught Square EZ 103	Museum Street DV 294	Terminus Place BX 412
Cranbourn Street DX 115	New Oxford Street DV 308	Thirleby Road CX 416
Devonshire Terrace CZ 136	Newton Street DV 309	Upper St. Martin's Lane DX 430
Duke of Wellington Place AV 142	Norfolk Crescent EZ 310	Westbourne Crescent DZ 448
Duncannon Street DY 147	Norfolk Square DZ 313	Westbourne Street DZ 450
Earlham Street DV 153		William IV Street DY 467

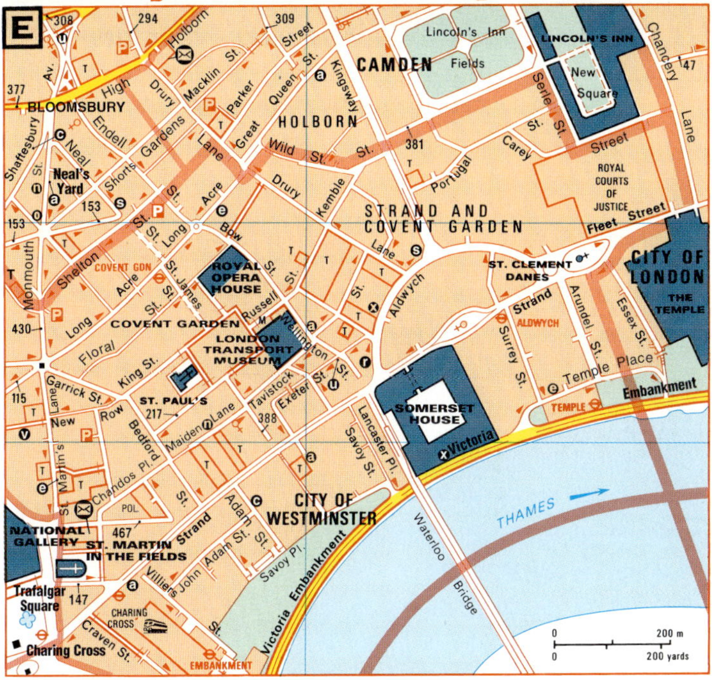

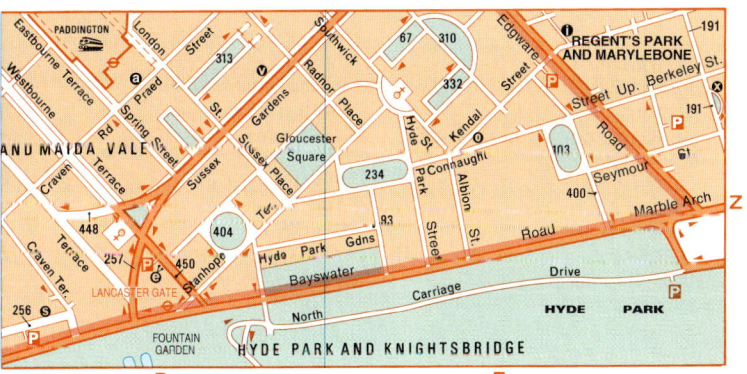

Alphabetical list of hotels and restaurants
Liste alphabétique des hôtels et restaurants
Elenco alfabetico degli alberghi e ristoranti

A

B

C

D

E

F

G

H

I

U - V - W

X - Y - Z

Starred establishments in London

Les établissements à étoiles de Londres

Gli esercizi con stelle a Londra

127 *Chelsea*   ჯჯჯჯ Gordon Ramsay

123 *Chelsea*	🏛 Capital	171 *Mayfair*	ჯჯჯჯჯ Le Gavroche
181 *Regent's Park & Marylebone*	ჯჯჯჯჯ John Burton-Race	94 *Bloomsbury*	ჯჯჯ Pied à Terre
		172 *Mayfair*	ჯჯჯ The Square

Good food at moderate prices
Repas soignés à prix modérés
Pasti accurati a prezzi contenuti

 "Bib Gourmand"

Particularly pleasant hotels and restaurants
Hôtels et restaurants agréables
Alberghi e ristoranti ameni

165 *Belgravia*	The Berkeley	166 *Hyde Park & Knightsbridge*	Mandarin Oriental Hyde Park
168 *Mayfair*	Claridge's	185 *St James's*	Ritz
167 *Mayfair*	Dorchester	193 *Strand & Covent Garden*	Savoy

169 *Mayfair*   Connaught

140 *South Kensington*	Blakes	196 *Victoria*	The Goring
123 *Chelsea*	Capital	165 *Belgravia*	The Halkin
178 *Regent's Park & Marylebone*	Charlotte Street	135 *Kensington*	The Milestone
124 *Chelsea*	Cliveden Town House	193 *Strand & Covent Garden*	One Aldwych
92 *Bloomsbury*	Covent Garden	140 *South Kensington*	The Pelham
124 *Chelsea*	Durley House		

186 *St. James's*   22 Jermyn Street

187 *St. James's*   The Restaurant (at Ritz H.)

171 *Mayfair*   Grill Room (at Dorchester H.)

181 *Regent's Park & Marylebone*	Orrery	154 *Southwark*	Oxo Tower
		151 *Bermondsey*	Le Pont de la Tour

188 *St. James's*	Le Caprice	187 *St. James's*	Quaglino's
194 *Strand & Covent Garden*	J. Sheekey	194 *Strand & Covent Garden*	Rules

Restaurants classified according to type
Restaurants classés suivant leur genre
Ristoranti classificati secondo il loro genere

Bangladeshi

164 *Bayswater & Maida Vale* X Ginger

Chinese

171 *Mayfair*	XXXX The Oriental	129 *Chelsea*	XX Mao Tai
174 *Mayfair*	XXX Kai	111 *Fulham*	XX Mao Tai
89 *Mill Hill*	XX Good Earth	107 *Ealing*	XX Maxim
131 *Chelsea*	XX Good Earth	136 *Kensington*	XX Memories of China
95 *Bloomsbury*	XX ✿ Hakkasan	167 *Hyde Park & Knightsbridge*	XX Mr Chow
148 *South Woodford*	XX Ho-Ho	91 *Orpington*	XX Xian
104 *City of London*	XX Imperial City	98 *Hampstead*	XX ZeNW3
200 *Victoria*	XX Ken Lo's Memories of China	189 *St James's*	X China House
		192 *Soho*	X Fung Shing
		106 *Croydon*	X Tai Tung

Danish

142 *South Kensington* XX Lundum's

English

171 *Mayfair*	XXXX Grill Room (at Dorchester H.)	199 *Victoria*	XXX Shepherd's
174 *Mayfair*	XXX Scotts	194 *Strand & Covent Garden*	XX Rules

Filipino

96 *Bloomsbury* X Josephine's

French

181 *Regent's Park & Marylebone*	XXXXX ✿✿ John Burton-Race	183 *Regent's Park & Marylebone*	XX L'Aventure
171 *Mayfair*	XXXX ✿✿ (Le) Gavroche	188 *St. James's*	XX 🍤 Brasserie Roux
138 *North Kensington*	XXX Chez Moi	129 *Chelsea*	XX (La) Chaumière
122 *Islington*	XX Almeida	103 *City of London*	XX ✿ Club Gascon
113 *Crouch End*	XX (Les) Associés	130 *Chelsea*	XX (Le) Colombier
		95 *Bloomsbury*	XX Mon Plaisir

85

149	Hampton Hill	XX ✿ Monsieur Max	144	Surbiton	X (The) French Table
129	Chelsea	XX Poissonnerie de l'Avenue (Seafood)	145	Kennington	X Lobster Pot (Seafood)
129	Chelsea	XX 🙂 Racine	200	Victoria	X (La) Poule au Pot
166	Belgravia	XX Vong (French Thai)	109	Dalston	X Soulard
			191	Soho	X (La) Trouvaille

Greek

110	Hoxton	X Mezedopolio	109	Hoxton	X Real Greek

Indian

142	South Kensington	XXX Bombay Brasserie	182	Regent's Park & Marylebone	XX Rasa Samudra (Seafood) (Vegetarian)
128	Chelsea	XXX Chutney Mary	159	Southfields	XX 🙂 Sarkhel's
198	Victoria	XXX (The) Cinnamon Club	145	Herne Hill	XX 3 Monkeys
190	Soho	XXX Red Fort	130	Chelsea	XX Vama
173	Mayfair	XXX ✿ Tamarind	175	Mayfair	XX Yatra
198	Victoria	XXX Quilon	135	Kensington	XX ✿ Zaika
152	Bermondsey	XX Bengal Clipper	160	Wandsworth	X Bombay Bicycle Club
157	Spitalfields	XX Bengal Trader	143	South Kensington	X Café Lazeez
190	Soho	XX Café Lazeez	120	Finsbury	X Café Lazeez City
157	Whitechapel	XX 🙂 Cafe Spice Namaste	159	Tooting	X Kastoori (Vegetarian)
175	Mayfair	XX Chor Bizarre	137	Kensington	X 🙂 Malabar
131	Chelsea	XX Haandi	96	Bloomsbury	X Mela
143	South Kensington	XX Khan's of Kensington	118	Archway	X 🙂 (The) Parsee
95	Bloomsbury	XX Malabar Junction	110	Stoke Newington	X Rasa (Vegetarian)
143	South Kensington	XX Memories of India	90	Willesden Green	X 🙂 Sabras (Vegetarian)
99	Primrose Hill	XX Okra	192	Soho	X Soho Spice
105	Addington	XX Planet Spice	143	South Kensington	X Star of India
182	Regent's Park & Marylebone	XX (La) Porte des Indes	176	Mayfair	X Veeraswamy
			132	Chelsea	X Zaika Bazaar

Italian

173	Mayfair	XXX Cecconi's	183	Regent's Park & Marylebone	XX Bertorelli's
127	Chelsea	XXX Floriana	182	Regent's Park & Marylebone	XX Caldesi
199	Victoria	XXX (L') Incontro	130	Chelsea	XX Caraffini
167	Hyde Park & Knightsbridge	XXX Isola	199	Victoria	XX (Il) Convivio
181	Regent's Park & Marylebone	XXX ✿ Locanda Locatelli	159	Putney	XX Enoteca Turi
			122	Islington	XX 🙂 Metrogusto
199	Victoria	XXX Santini	128	Chelsea	XX Montes
173	Mayfair	XXX Sartoria	110	Stoke Newington	XX Muranco
128	Chelsea	XXX Toto's	95	Bloomsbury	XX Neal Street
174	Mayfair	XX Alloro	129	Chelsea	XX Pellicano
163	Bayswater & Maida Vale	XX Al San Vincenzo	139	North Kensington	XX (Il) Posto
136	Kensington	XX (The) Ark	111	Hammersmith	XX ✿ River Café

Japanese

Lebanese

Moroccan

North African

Polish

Pubs

97 *Bloomsbury*   (The) Perseverance

100 *Primrose Hill*   (The) Queens

118 *Archway*   St John's

111 *Fulham*   (The) Salisbury Tavern

185 *Regents Park & Marylebone*   (The) Salt House

133 *Chelsea*   Swag and Tails

164 *Bayswater & Maida Vale*   (The) Waterway

Scottish

200 *Victoria*   XX Boisdale

Seafood

128 *Chelsea*   XXX One-O-One

157 *St. Katherine's Dock*   XX (The) Aquarium

175 *Mayfair*   XX Bentley's

105 *Bloomsbury*   XX Chamberlain's

163 *Bayswater & Maida Vale*   XX Jason's

194 *Strand & Covent Garden*   XX J. Sheekey

128 *Chelsea*   XX Poissonnerie de l'Avenue (French)

182 *Regent's Park & Marylebone*   XX Rasa Samudra (Indian) (Vegetarian)

142 *South Kensington*   XX (The) Restaurant at One Ninety

132 *Chelsea*   X Bibendum Oyster Bar

156 *Canary Wharf*   X Fish !

155 *Southwark*   X Fish !

117 *Chiswick*   X Fish Hoek

139 *North Kensington*   X Livebait

154 *Southwark*   X Livebait

195 *Strand & Covent Garden*   X Livebait

145 *Kennington*   X Lobster Pot

South African

117 *Chiswick*   X Dumela

South East Asian

104 *City of London*   XX Pacific Oriental

Spanish

120 *Clerkenwell*   XX Gaudi

143 *South Kensington*   XX Cambio De Tercio

96 *Bloomsbury*   X Cigala

Thai

110 *Fulham*   XX Blue Elephant

158 *Battersea*   XX Chada

166 *Belgravia*   XX Mango Tree

166 *Belgravia*   XX ❀ Nahm

163 *Bayswater & Maida Vale*   XX Nipa

166 *Belgravia*   XX Vong (French Thai)

144 *Kingston*   X Ayudhya

143 *South Kensington*   X Bangkok

184 *Regent's Park & Marylebone*   X Chada Chada

159 *Tooting*   X Oh Boy

191 *Soho*   X Sri Siam Soho

Turkish

182 *Regent's Park & Marylebone*   XX Ozer

Vegetarian

110 *Stoke Newington*   X Rasa (Indian)

182 *Regent's Park & Marylebone*   XX Rasa Samudra (Indian) (Seafood)

159 *Tooting*   XX Kastoori (Indian)

90 *Willesden Green*   X ❀ Sabras (Indian)

Vietnamese

121 *Highbury*   X Au Lac

Boroughs and areas

Greater London *is divided, for administrative purposes, into 32 boroughs plus the City : these sub-divide naturally into minor areas, usually grouped around former villages or quarters, which often maintain a distinctive character.*

BARNET *Gtr London.*

Brent Cross *Gtr London –* ✉ *NW2.*

 Holiday Inn London Brent Cross   p. 9 **DU** **n**
Tilling Rd, NW2 1LP, ℰ (020) 8201 8686, *Fax (020) 8455 4660*
⚡, ⇔ rm, 🖥 📺 ☎ ⅃ 🅿 – 🔥 50. 🆑 🆒 🔘 *VISA* ⌨, ⋙
Meals (bar lunch)/dinner 15.00 and a la carte 15.30/29.15 **s.** – ⌻ 13.95 –
153 rm 160.00.
♦ A ten storey purpose-built group hotel, usefully located at the foot of the M1. Well-equipped bedrooms are triple-glazed and business rooms are available. Informal restaurant and all-day open bar.

Child's Hill *Gtr London –* ✉ *NW2.*

XX **Philpott's Mezzaluna**   p. 9 **DU** **c**
 424 Finchley Rd, NW2 2HY, ℰ (020) 7794 0455, *Fax (020) 7794 0452*
🍴 – 🖥. 🆒 🆑 *VISA*
closed 25-26 December, 1 January, Saturday lunch and Monday – **Meals** -
Italian influences - 19.00/23.00.
♦ Homely Italian restaurant, affably run by patrons. Huge lunar artefacts complement the plain walls. Weekly changing menus offer tasty, modern cuisine at moderate prices.

Golders Green *Gtr London –* ✉ *NW11.*

XX **The Villa**   p. 9 **DU** **e**
38 North End Rd, NW11 7PT, ℰ (020) 8458 6344, *Fax (020) 8458 6344*
🖥. 🆑 🆒 🔘 *VISA*
closed 1 January and Monday – **Meals** - Italian - 14.50/18.00 and a la carte 20.80/27.70.
♦ A long-standing Italian restaurant with a loyal local following. Contemporary in style with terracotta tiles and modern prints. Menu offers a mix of traditional and modern.

Mill Hill *Gtr London –* ✉ *NW7.*

🚇 *100 Barnet Way, Mill Hill* ℰ *(020) 8959 2282* **CT.**

XX **Good Earth**   p. 9 **CT** **a**
143 The Broadway, NW7 4RN, ℰ (020) 8959 7011, *Fax (020) 8959 1464*
🖥. 🆑 🆒 *VISA* ⌨
closed 23-30 December – **Meals** - Chinese - a la carte 21.80/29.80.
♦ Smart, formal Chinese restaurant set slightly back from the busy A1 outside. Spacious and comfortable with neatly attired staff. Authentic menu; extensive vegetarian choice.

BEXLEY *Gtr London.*

Bexley *Kent – ⊠ Kent.*

 Holiday Inn   p. 15   JX   e
Black Prince Interchange, Southwold Rd, DA5 1ND, on A 2, ✆ (0870) 4009006, *Fax (01322) 526113*
⊞, ✝ rm, TV ⅙ P – ⚒ 70. ⓜ AE ⓪ VISA
Meals *(closed Saturday lunch and dinner 31 December)* 13.00/15.00 and a la carte 20.85/24.85 **s.** – ⊇ 13.95 – **108 rm** 89.00/125.00.
♦ A commercial hotel with mock Tudor exterior, convenient for Bexleyheath town centre. Modern, well-equipped bedrooms in a Scandinavian style. Rustic public bar. Busy, informal restaurant.

Bexleyheath *Kent – ⊠ Kent.*

 Bexleyheath Marriott   p. 15   JX   c
1 Broadway, DA6 7JZ, ✆ (020) 8298 1000, *bexleyheath@marriott.co.uk, Fax (020) 8298 1234*
I₅, ⊠ – ⊞, ✝ rm, ▤ TV ⅙ P – ⚒ 250. ⓜ AE ⓪ VISA JCB
Copper *:* **Meals** (carvery rest.) 19.75 (dinner) and a la carte 20.00/33.00 – ⊇ 13.95 – **142 rm** 109.00.
♦ A group hotel offering extensive conference facilities as well as a leisure club in a Greco-Roman theme. Comfortable and spacious bedrooms with marble bathrooms. Popular carvery restaurant.

BRENT *Gtr London.*

Wembley *Middx – ⊠ Middx.*

 Premier Lodge   p. 9   CU   z
151 Wembley Park Drive, HA9 8HQ, ✆ (0870) 7001446, *wembleypremierlodge @snr.co.uk, Fax (0870) 7001447*
⊞ ✝ ▤ TV ✆ ⅙ P. ⓜ AE ⓪ VISA JCB. ✿
Meals (grill rest.) (dinner only) a la carte 9.90/24.20 – **153 rm** 54.95.
♦ Lodge offering good value accommodation. All of the spacious modern bedrooms are carefully planned and feature king size beds. Bright, colourful restaurant.

Willesden Green *Middx – ⊠ Middx.*

✗ **Sabras**   p. 9   CU   e
263 High Rd, NW10 2RX, ✆ (020) 8459 0340, *Fax (020) 8459 0541*
ⓜ AE ⓪ VISA JCB
closed 25-26 December and Monday – **Meals** - Indian Vegetarian - (dinner only) a la carte 17.50/24.50.
♦ Inexpensive Indian vegetarian food served in modest, but friendly, surroundings. Framed awards and write-ups garnered since opening in 1973 bear testament to its popularity.

✗ **Sushi-Say**   p. 9   CU   a
33B Walm Lane, NW2 5SH, ✆ (020) 8459 2971, *Fax (020) 8907 3229*
ⓜ AE VISA JCB
closed 25-26 December, 1 January, Easter, 1 week August and Monday – **Meals** - Japanese - (dinner only and lunch Saturday and Sunday)/dinner 18.10/28.30 and a la carte 13.70/36.35.
♦ Friendly service provided by the owner in traditional dress. From bare wooden tables, watch her husband in the open-plan kitchen carefully prepare authentic Japanese food.

BROMLEY *Gtr London.*

☖₁₈, ☖₉ *Cray Valley, Sandy Lane, St. Paul's Cray, Orpington* ✆ *(01689) 837909* **JY**.

Bromley *Kent –* ✉ *Kent.*

☖₉ *Magpie Hall Lane* ✆ *(020) 8462 7014* **HY**.

🏨 **Bromley Court**   p. 15   **HY**   **Z**

Bromley Hill, BR1 4JD, ✆ (020) 8464 5011, *bromleyhotel@btinternet.com, Fax (020) 8460 0899*

🌲, ⅙, ⩶, 🛋 – 🛗, 🌬 rm, ▤ rest, 📺 ☎ [P] – 🔼 150. 🔟 AE ⓪ *VISA*

Meals *(closed Saturday lunch)* 14.95/17.95 (dinner) and a la carte 23.15/27.45 **s.** – **113 rm** � 105.00/118.00, 2 suites.

◆ A grand neo-Gothic mansion in three acres of well-tended garden. Popular with corporate guests for the large conference space, and the bedrooms with modems and voicemail. Conservatory or terrace dining available.

Farnborough *Kent –* ✉ *Kent.*

※※※ **Chapter One**   p. 15   **HZ**   **a**

❀ Farnborough Common, Locksbottom, BR6 8NF, ✆ (01689) 854848, *info@chapterrestaurants.com, Fax (01689) 858439*

▤ [P]. 🔟 AE ⓪ *VISA* JCB

closed 2-8 January – **Meals** 19.50/24.95 �.

◆ The mock Tudor exterior belies the stylish, light and contemporary interior. Precise and well executed modern European menu. West End sophistication without the prices.

Spec. Lobster ravioli, cauliflower purée. Saddle of rabbit with pancetta, leg confit, Gewurztraminer sauce. Apple tart, thyme ice cream, caramel sauce.

Orpington *Kent –* ✉ *Kent.*

☖₁₈ *High Elms, High Elms Rd, Downe, Orpington* ✆ *(01689) 858175.*

※※ **Xian**   p. 15   **JY**   **a**

324 High St, BR6 0NG, ✆ (01689) 871881

▤, 🔟 AE ⓪ *VISA*

closed 1 week August,3 days Christmas and Sunday lunch – **Meals** - Chinese (Peking, Szechuan) - 9.00/13.00 and a la carte 13.50/18.90.

◆ Modern, marbled interior with oriental artefacts make this personally run Chinese restaurant a firm favourite with locals. Specialises in the hotter dishes of Peking.

Penge *Gtr London –* ✉ *SE20.*

🏠 **Melrose House**   p. 14   **GY**   **a**

89 Lennard Rd, SE20 7LY, ✆ (020) 8776 8884, *melrose.hotel@virgin.net, Fax (020) 8325 7636*

without rest., 🌬 – 🌬 📺 ₺ [P]. 🔟 *VISA*. 🍽

closed 20 December-3 January – **6 rm** ⊃ 40.00/70.00.

◆ An imposing Victorian house with a conservatory sitting room. Breakfast is taken "en famille" and the older bedrooms still have their original fireplaces.

The rates shown may be revised if the cost of living changes to any great extent.
Before making your reservations,
confirm with the hotelier the exact price that will be charged.

Bloomsbury *Gtr London –* ✉ *NW1/W1/WC1.*

Le Meridien Russell p. 26 **LU** o
Russell Sq, WC1B 5BE, ☎ (020) 7837 6470, *reservations@lemeridien.com,*
Fax (020) 7837 2857
⑂, ✂ rm, ▤ TV 📞 – ⚒ 400. **MO AE O** *VISA* JCB. ⅍
Meals a la carte 22.95/32.40 – **369 rm** � 190.00/245.00, 2 suites.
♦ An impressive Victorian building dominating the charming Russell Square. Boasts many original features including the imposing marbled lobby and staircase. Choice of dining areas.

Holiday Inn Kings Cross p. 26 **MT** a
1 Kings Cross Rd, WC1X 9HX, ☎ (020) 7833 3900, *sales@holidayinnlondon.dem on.co.uk, Fax (020) 7917 6163*
⑂₆, ⌾, 🖂 – ⑂, ✂ rm, ▤ TV 📞 ₺ – ⚒ 220. **MO AE O** *VISA*. ⅍
Simply Spice : **Meals** - Indian - *(closed Saturday lunch)* a la carte 17.35/39.15
Carriages : **Meals** a la carte 18.50/27.00 **s.** – districts 13.95 – **403 rm** 190.00/210.00, 2 suites.
♦ In a fast developing part of town and close to Kings Cross station. Comfortable bedrooms with all mod cons. Clubby lobby bar with deep leather armchairs and sofas. Simply Spice offers bold surroundings. Carriages is half lounge, half restaurant.

Marlborough p. 26 **LU** i
9-14 Bloomsbury St, WC1B 3QD, ☎ (020) 7636 5601, *resmarl@radisson.com, Fax (020) 7240 0532*
⑂, ✂ rm, ▤ rest, TV 📞 ₺ – ⚒ 200. **MO AE O** *VISA* JCB. ⅍
Glass : **Meals** 19.50/30.00 **s.** – districts 15.00 – **171 rm** 229.00/260.85, 2 suites.
♦ A Victorian building around the corner from the British Museum. The lobby has been restored to its original marbled splendour and bedrooms offer modern and stylish comforts. Glass, unsurprisingly, offers a plethora of mirrors.

Mountbatten p. 37 **DV** o
20 Monmouth St, WC2H 9HD, ☎ (020) 7836 4300, *Fax (020) 7240 3540*
⑂₆ – ⑂, ✂ rm, ▤ TV 📞 – ⚒ 90. **MO AE O** *VISA* JCB. ⅍
Dial : **Meals** 22.50/45.00 **s.** – districts 15.00 – **121 rm** 301.90/334.80, 7 suites.
♦ Photographs and memorabilia of the eponymous Lord Louis adorn the walls and corridors. Ideally located in the heart of Covent Garden. Compact but comfortable bedrooms. Chic, stylish restaurant.

Covent Garden p. 37 **DV** n
10 Monmouth St, WC2H 9HB, ☎ (020) 7806 1000, *covent@firmdale.com, Fax (020) 7806 1100*
⑂₆ – ⑂ ▤ TV 📞 – ⚒ 50. **MO AE** *VISA*. ⅍
Brasserie Max : **Meals** (booking essential) a la carte 31.50/38.00 ⋎ – districts 17.50 – **56 rm** 229.00/381.00, 2 suites.
♦ Individually designed and stylish bedrooms, with CDs and VCRs discreetly concealed. Boasts a very relaxing first floor oak-panelled drawing room with its own honesty bar. Informal restaurant.

Grafton p. 26 **KU** n
130 Tottenham Court Rd, W1P 9HP, ☎ (020) 7388 4131, *resgraf@radisson. com, Fax (020) 7387 7394*
⑂₆ – ⑂, ✂ rm, ▤ rest, TV 📞 – ⚒ 100. **MO AE O** *VISA* JCB. ⅍
Aston's : **Meals** 19.50/30.00 **s.** – districts 12.00 – **320 rm** 229.10/260.80, 4 suites.
♦ Just yards from Warren Street tube. Discreet Edwardian charm that belies its location in one of London's busier streets. Hallmark bedrooms are particularly well-equipped. Restaurant enhanced by deep leather sofas.

Kenilworth
p. 26 LU **a**

97 Great Russell St, WC1B 3LB, ℘ (020) 7637 3477, *resmarl@radisson.com, Fax (020) 7631 3133*

ƙ – |♦|, ⇆ rm, 🖂 📺 ✆ ⚹ – 🅰 100. ⓄⓄ AE Ⓞ VISA JCB. ✖

Meals 19.50/35.00 **s.** – ⌾ 12.00 – **186 rm** 229.00/260.80.

♦ Usefully placed for the shops of Oxford Street. Stylish interiors echo ornate Edwardian themes. Comfortable bedrooms equipped to meet the needs of the corporate traveller. Dining room with glass wall exudes smart, modern style.

Jurys Gt Russell St
p. 26 LU **n**

16-22 Gt Russell St, WC1B 3NN, ℘ (020) 7347 1000, *Fax (020) 7347 1001*

|♦|, ⇆ rm, 🖂 📺 ✆ ⚹ – 🅰 220. ⓄⓄ AE Ⓞ VISA. ✖

Lutyens *:* **Meals** 25.00/40.00 **s.** and a la carte – ⌾ 20.00 – **168 rm** 220.00/250.00, 1 suite.

♦ Neo-Georgian building by Edward Lutyens, built for YMCA in 1929. Smart comfortable interior decoration from the lounge to the bedrooms. Facilities include a business centre. Restaurant has understated traditional style.

Montague
p. 26 LU **c**

15 Montague St, WC1B 5BJ, ℘ (020) 7637 1001, *bookmt@rchmail.com, Fax (020) 7637 2516*

🌿, ƙ, ⇌, 🚗 – |♦|, ⇆ rm, 🖂 📺 ✆ ⚹ – 🅰 120. ⓄⓄ AE Ⓞ VISA. ✖

Blue Door Bistro *:* **Meals** a la carte 15.50/35.00 ♀ – ⌾ 16.50 – **98 rm** 205.60/235.00, 6 suites.

♦ A period townhouse with pretty hanging baskets outside. The hushed conservatory overlooks a secluded garden. The clubby bar has a Scottish golfing theme. Rich bedroom décor. Restaurant divided into two small, pretty rooms.

Thistle Bloomsbury
p. 26 LU **r**

Bloomsbury Way, WC1A 2SD, ℘ (020) 7242 5881, *bloomsbury@thistle.co.uk, Fax (020) 7831 0225*

|♦|, ⇆ rm, 🖂 rest, 📺 ⚹ – 🅰 100. ⓄⓄ AE Ⓞ VISA JCB. ✖

Meals *(closed lunch Saturday and Sunday)* 19.95 and a la carte 30.70/50.30 **s.** – ⌾ 12.95 – **138 rm** 196.23/224.43.

♦ Established over 100 years ago and retains much charm. Quiet and discreet lobby. An old fashioned lift leads up to the bedrooms that have a very English feel. Edwardian bar and dining room.

Holiday Inn London Bloomsbury
p. 26 LT **c**

Coram St, WC1N 1IIT, ℘ (0870) 4009222, *reservations-bloomsbury@6c.com, Fax (020) 7837 5374*

|♦|, ⇆ rm, 🖂 📺 ✆ ⚹ – 🅰 300. ⓄⓄ AE Ⓞ VISA JCB. ✖

Meals *(closed Saturday and Sunday dinner and Bank Holiday lunch)* 15.00 and a la carte 19.65/28.85 **s.** – ⌾ 14.95 – **312 rm** 179.00/189.00.

♦ Bright, modern bedrooms in warm, neutral tones. Choose between stylish bar with leather chairs and glass top tables and Callaghans Irish themed bar. Relaxed dining on comfortable leather chairs.

Blooms
p. 26 LU **c**

7 Montague St, WC1B 5BP, ℘ (020) 7323 1717, *blooms@mermaid.co.uk, Fax (020) 7636 6498*

🚗 – |♦| 📺 ✆. ⓄⓄ AE Ⓞ VISA JCB. ✖

Meals a la carte 17.95/30.20 – ⌾ 10.00 – **26 rm** 135.00/225.00.

♦ An 18C townhouse in an area steeped in literary history. Individually designed bedrooms, some with themes such as Dickens or Lords. Small but secluded walled garden. Cosy basement restaurant and library bar.

🏨 Myhotel
p. 26 **KU** **a**

11-13 Bayley St, Bedford Sq, WC1B 3HD, ✆ (020) 7667 6000, *guest-services@myhotels.co.uk, Fax (020) 7667 6001*

🔥🛁 – |📶| ❌ 🖿 📺 📞 – 🚡 40. 🆒 AE VISA

Yo! Sushi : **Meals** - Japanese - a la carte 18.00/21.50 ⚲ – ☕ 16.00 – **78 rm** 199.75/246.75.

◆ The minimalist interior is designed on the principles of feng shui; even the smaller bedrooms are stylish and uncluttered. Mybar is a fashionable meeting point. Diners can enjoy Japanese food from conveyor belt.

🏨 Bonnington in Bloomsbury
p. 26 **LU** **s**

92 Southampton Row, WC1B 4BH, ✆ (020) 7242 2828, *sales@bonnington.com, Fax (020) 7831 9170*

|📶| ❌ rm, 🖿 📺 📞 & – 🚡 250. 🆒 AE ① VISA JCB. ✍

Meals *(closed Sunday)* (bar lunch)/dinner 20.75 – **243 rm** ☕ 125.00/159.00.

◆ Built in 1911 and providing easy access to a number of tourist attractions. Functional, but well-kept, bedrooms offer traditional comforts with many modern extras. Classically decorated dining room.

🏨 The Academy
p. 26 **KLU** **v**

21 Gower St, WC1E 6HG, ✆ (020) 7631 4115, *res_academy@theetongroup.com, Fax (020) 7636 3442*

without rest., 🚗 – ❌ 🖿 📺 📞. 🆒 AE ① VISA JCB

closed 25-26 December – **49 rm** ☕ 140.00/225.00.

◆ Boutique hotel made up of five Georgian townhouses joined together. The cosy sitting rooms, and many of the well-appointed bedrooms, overlook a secluded rear garden.

🍴🍴🍴 179 Shaftesbury Avenue
p. 37 **DV** **c**

179 Shaftesbury Ave, WC2H 8JR, ✆ (020) 7836 3111, *info@onesevennine.com, Fax (020) 7836 3888*

🖿. 🆒 AE VISA

closed 25 December, Saturday lunch, Sunday and Bank Holidays – **Meals** 18.95 (lunch) and a la carte 29.50/38.25 ⚲.

◆ Stylish venue with a distinctive contemporary feel. Immaculate place settings and formal service amidst rich leather and tonal lighting. Modern cuisine with a classic base.

🍴🍴🍴 Pied à Terre
p. 26 **KU** **e**

❀❀ 34 Charlotte St, W1P 1HJ, ✆ (020) 7636 1178, *p-a-t@dircon.co.uk, Fax (020) 7916 1171*

❌ 🖿. 🆒 AE VISA

closed last week December, first week January, Sunday and lunch Monday and Saturday – **Meals** 23.00/42.50 ⚲.

◆ Frosted glass front hints at the understated, cool interior. The kitchen offers an elaborate and adventurous, yet refined take on modern French cuisine. Well-chosen wine list.

Spec. Seared and poached foie gras in a Sauternes consommé. Roasted sea bass with braised fennel, green olive and vanilla sauce. Bitter chocolate tart with stout ice cream.

🍴🍴 Incognico
p. 33 **GK** **a**

117 Shaftesbury Ave, WC2H 8AD, ✆ (020) 7836 8866, *Fax (020) 7240 9525*

🖿. 🆒 AE ① VISA

closed 4 days Easter, 10 days Christmas, Sunday and Bank Holidays – **Meals** 12.50 (lunch) and a la carte 29.00/42.50 ⚲.

◆ Opened in 2000 with its robust décor of wood panelling and brown leather chairs. Downstairs bar has a window into the kitchen, from where French based dishes are produced.

XX **Neal Street**   p. 37   DV   S
26 Neal St, WC2H 9QW, ℘ (020) 7836 8368, *reserve@nealstreet.co.uk,
Fax (020) 7240 3964*
⓪⓪ AE ⓪ VISA
closed 25 December-2 January and Sunday – **Meals** - Italian - a la carte 25.50/
42.50 ♈.
♦ Light, bright and airy; tiled flooring and colourful pictures. Dishes range
from the simple to the more complex. Mushrooms a speciality. Has its own
shop next door.

XX **Sardo**   p. 26   KU   C
45 Grafton Way, W1P 5LA, ℘ (020) 7387 2521, *info@sardo-restaurant.com,
Fax (020) 7387 2559*
⓪⓪ AE ⓪ VISA JCB
closed Sunday and Bank Holiays – **Meals** - Italian (Sardinian specialities) -
a la carte 22.90/32.80.
♦ Simple, stylish interior run in a very warm and welcoming manner with
very efficient service. Rustic Italian cooking with a Sardinian character and a
modern tone.

XX **Hakkasan**   p. 26   KU   O
✿
8 Hanway Pl, W1P 9DH, ℘ (020) 7907 1888, *mail@hakkasan.com,
Fax (020) 7907 1889*
▤ . ⓪⓪ AE VISA
closed 25 December – **Meals** - Chinese (Canton) - a la carte 25.00/
50.00 **s.** ♈.
♦ A distinctive, modern interpretation of Cantonese cooking in an appropri-
ately contemporary and cavernous basement. The lively, bustling bar is an
equally popular nightspot.
Spec. Stir-fry scallop and prawn cake. Pan-fried rib-eye of beef, sweet soya
and almonds. Jasmine tea smoked chicken.

XX **Mon Plaisir**   p. 37   DV   a
21 Monmouth St, WC2H 9DD, ℘ (020) 7836 7243, *eatafrog@mail.com,
Fax (020) 7240 4774*
⓪⓪ AE ⓪ VISA JCB
closed Christmas-New Year, Saturday lunch, Sunday and Bank Holidays –
Meals - French - 15.95 (lunch) and a la carte 24.75/36.50 ♈.
♦ London's oldest French restaurant and family-run for over fifty years.
Divided into four rooms, all with a different feel but all proudly Gallic in their
decoration.

XX **Archipelago**   p. 26   KU   C
110 Whitfield St, W1T 5ED, ℘ (020) 7383 3346, *Fax (020) 7383 7181*
⓪⓪ AE VISA JCB
closed 25 December, Saturday lunch and Sunday – **Meals** 20.50/38.50.
♦ Eccentric in both menu and décor and not for the faint hearted. Crammed
with knick-knacks from cages to Buddhas. Menu an eclectic mix of influences
from around the world.

XX **Malabar Junction**   p. 26   LU   X
107 Great Russell St, WC1B 3NA, ℘ (020) 7580 5230, *Fax (020) 7436 9942*
▤ . ⓪⓪ AE VISA
closed 25-26 December – **Meals** - South Indian - a la carte 25.00/30.00.
♦ Specialising in dishes from southern India. Bright restaurant with a small
fountain in the centre of the room below a large skylight. Helpful and
attentive service.

✕ Passione
p. 26 **KU** u

10 Charlotte St, W1T 2LT, ✆ (020) 7636 2833, *Liz@passione.co.uk*, *Fax (020) 7636 2889*

MO **AE** **①** **VISA** **JCB**

closed 1 week Christmas, Saturday lunch, Sunday and Bank Holidays – **Meals** - Italian - (booking essential) a la carte 22.50/32.00.

◆ Compact but light and airy. Modern Italian cooking served in informal surroundings, with friendly and affable service. Particularly busy at lunchtime.

✕ Alfred
p. 37 **DV** u

245 Shaftesbury Ave, WC2H 8EH, ✆ (020) 7240 2566, *Fax (020) 7497 0672*

🍴 – 🍽. **MO** **AE** **①** **VISA** **JCB**

closed Saturday lunch, Sunday and Bank Holidays – **Meals** 13.90/20.45 and a la carte 20.45/25.45 ⬚.

◆ Double-aspect views of the busy streets. Simple laminated tabletops and wooden chairs. No-nonsense cooking with specialities from around the British Isles.

✕ Cigala
p. 26 **LU** z

54 Lamb's Conduit St, WC1N 3LW, ✆ (020) 7405 1717, *tasty@cigala.co.uk*, *Fax (020) 7242 9949*

MO **AE** **①** **VISA** **JCB**

closed 24-27 December and Bank Holidays – **Meals** - Spanish - 18.00 (lunch) and a la carte approx. 26.50 ⬚.

◆ Spanish restaurant on the corner of attractive street. Simply furnished with large windows and open-plan kitchen. Robust Iberian cooking. Informal tapas bar downstairs.

✕ Josephine's
p. 26 **KU** s

4 Charlotte St, W1T 2LP, ✆ (020) 7580 6551, *jones4@aol.com*, *Fax (020) 7580 1514*

MO **AE** **①** **VISA** **JCB**

closed 25 December, 1 January and Sunday lunch – **Meals** - Filipino - a la carte 12.20/26.40.

◆ Good value, authentic Filipino cooking served in simple, unpretentious surroundings. A large mural depicting scenes from the Philippines dominates one wall.

✕ Paolo
p. 26 **KU** i

16 Percy St, W1T 1DT, ✆ (020) 7637 9900, *percystreet16@aol.com*, *Fax (020) 7580 9055*

🍽. **MO** **①** **VISA**

closed Sunday – **Meals** - Italian - 14.50/17.50 ⬚.

◆ Wood floored restaurant with intimate basement and brighter ground floor dining rooms. Authentic, rustic Italian dishes with a predominately Northern Italian style.

✕ Mela
p. 33 **GK** c

152-156 Shaftesbury Ave, WC2H 6HL, ✆ (020) 7836 8635, *info@melarestaurant .co.uk, Fax (020) 7379 0527*

MO **AE** **①** **VISA**

closed 25 December – **Meals** - Indian - 10.95/34.95 and a la carte 16.45/19.15.

◆ Vibrantly decorated dining room with a simple style in a useful location close to Theatreland. Enjoy thoroughly tasty Indian food in a bustling, buzzy environment.

✗ Abeno
p. 26 LU e

47 Museum St, WC1A 1LY, ☏ (020) 7405 3211, *okonomi@abeno.co.uk, Fax (020) 7405 3212*

▤ 🗺 AE ⓪ *VISA* ᴊᴄʙ

closed 25-26 December – **Meals** - Japanese (Okonomi-Yaki) - 6.50/16.50 (lunch) and a la carte 10.55/27.80.

♦ Specialises in Okonomi-yaki: little Japanese "pancakes" cooked on a hotplate on each table. Choose your own filling and the size of your pancake.

🏠 The Perserverance
p. 26 LU z

63 Lambs Conduit St, WC1 3NB, ☏ (020) 7405 8278, *Bdlondon@btopenworld. com, Fax (020) 7831 0031*

🗺 AE *VISA*

closed Saturday lunch and Sunday dinner – **Meals** a la carte 22.00/30.00 ♀.

♦ A corner pub decorated in classic London pub style. Interesting modern menus served downstairs for lunch and in a slightly more formal upper dining room in the evening.

Dartmouth Park *Gtr London* – ✉ NW5.

🏠 Bull & Last
p. 24 EU n

168 Highgate Rd, NW5 1QS, ☏ (020) 7267 3641, *Fax (020) 7482 6366*

🗺 *VISA*

closed 25 December – **Meals** a la carte 14.25/24.25 ♀.

♦ Log fires and locals in the ground floor bar and the dining room upstairs. Modern menu with daily changing specials. Friendly service by T-shirted staff.

🏠 Lord Palmerston
p. 24 EU x

33 Dartmouth Park Hill, NW5 1HU, ☏ (020) 7485 1578

🗺 *VISA*

Meals (bookings not accepted) a la carte approx. 17.00.

♦ Find space in the busy bar favoured by the locals, or the small conservatory behind. Blackboard menu offers a range from sandwiches to full meals.

Euston *Gtr London* – ✉ WC1.

🏛 Shaw Park Plaza
p. 26 LI í

100-110 Euston Rd, NW1 2AJ, ☏ (020) 7666 9000, *sppres@parkplazahotels.co. uk, Fax (020) 7666 9100*

🛗, ⟳ – ▤, ✳ rm, ▤ 📺 ☏ ♿ – 🔬 450. 🗺 AE ⓪ *VISA* ·🖵·, ⊀

Meals 17.00 (lunch) and dinner a la carte 23.00/33.00 ♀ – ⊂ 14.50 – **312 rm** 217.30.

♦ Extensive conference facilities that include the redeveloped Shaw theatre. Large marbled lobby. Modern bedrooms that offer views of London's rooftops from the higher floors. Lobby-based restaurant and bar look onto busy street.

🏛 Euston Plaza
p. 26 KLT e

17-18 Upper Woburn Pl, WC1H 0HT, ☏ (020) 7943 4500, *info@euston-plaza-hotel.com, Fax (020) 7943 4501*

🛗, ⟳ – ▤, ✳ rm, ▤ 📺 ☏ ♿ – 🔬 150. 🗺 AE ⓪ *VISA* ᴊᴄʙ. ⊀

***Three Crowns : *** Meals *(closed Saturday)* (dinner only) 18.95/30.00 **s.** ♀

***Terrace : *** **Meals** 18.95 (dinner) and a la carte 15.00/19.00 **s.** ♀ – ⊂ 12.95 – **150 rm** 169.00/239.00.

♦ Nearby transport links make this a useful location. Scandinavian owned, which is reflected in the style of the bedrooms. Executive rooms are particularly well-equipped. Three Crowns has smart basement location. Terrace conservatory restaurant with plants.

🏨 London Euston Travel Inn Capital
p. 26 **LT s**

141 Euston Rd, WC1H 9PJ, ✆ (020) 7554 3400, *Fax (020) 7554 3419*

|⬧|, ✻ rm, ▤ rest, 📺 ⓑ. ⓦ AE ⓪ *VISA*. ✗

Meals (grill rest.) (dinner only) – **220 rm** 79.95.

◆ Budget accommodation with clean and spacious bedrooms, all with a large workspace. Double glazed but still ask for a quieter room at the back.

Hampstead *Gtr London –* ✉ *NW3.*

🏌 *Winnington Rd, Hampstead* ✆ *(020) 8455 0203.*

🏨 Holiday Inn
p. 24 **ES r**

215 Haverstock Hill, NW3 4RB, ✆ (0870) 4009037, *reservations-hampstead@6c.com, Fax (020) 7435 5586*

|⬧|, ✻ rm, 📺 ✆ 🅿. ⓦ AE ⓪ *VISA* 🇯CB

Meals a la carte 18.85/31.85 – ⌷ 14.95 – **140 rm** 160.00/185.00.

◆ A well-equipped group hotel adjacent to a petrol station. Convenient for the boutiques and cafés of Hampstead. Bright, modern bedrooms. Formula menus.

🏨 Langorf
p. 24 **ES c**

20 Frognal, NW3 6AG, ✆ (020) 7794 4483, *langorf@aol.com, Fax (020) 7435 9055*

without rest. – |⬧| 📺. ⓦ AE ⓪ *VISA*. ✗

31 rm ⌷ 82.00/110.00, 5 suites.

◆ Converted Edwardian house in a quiet residential area. Bright breakfast room overlooks secluded walled garden. Fresh bedrooms, many of which have high ceilings.

✕✕ ZeNW3
p. 24 **ES a**

83-84 Hampstead High St, NW3 1RE, ✆ (020) 7794 7863, *Fax (020) 7794 6956*

▤. ⓦ ⓪ *VISA*

closed 24-25 December – **Meals** - Chinese - 13.80/33.50 and a la carte 22.40/33.50.

◆ Contemporary interior provided by the glass topped tables and small waterfall feature on the stairs. Professional service. Carefully prepared Chinese food.

✕ Cucina
p. 24 **ES x**

45a South End Rd, NW3 2QB, ✆ (020) 7435 7814, *enquiries@cucina.uk.com, Fax (020) 7435 7147*

▤. ⓦ AE *VISA*

closed Sunday dinner and Bank Holidays – **Meals** 17.50/21.50 ⅌.

◆ The small deli at the front gives few clues to the large room inside. Eclectic mix of artwork scattered around the room. Modern menu with influences from around the globe.

✕ Base
p. 24 **ES e**

71 Hampstead High St, NW3 1QP, ✆ (020) 7431 2224, *Fax (020) 7433 1262*

▤. ⓦ AE ⓪ *VISA*

Meals - North African specialities - a la carte 10.50/18.95 ⅌.

◆ Narrow, informal restaurant offering a menu of North African specialities with the emphasis on Algeria and Morocco. Front half of the room is given over to an all day café.

🍺 The Magdala
p. 24 **ES i**

2A South Hill Park, NW3 2SB, ✆ (020) 7435 2503, *Fax (020) 7435 6167*

ⓦ AE *VISA*

closed 25 December – **Meals** a la carte 15.70/21.75 ⅌.

◆ A large pub on the edge of the Heath - ideally placed for walking off any lunchtime excesses. Informal ground floor bar; first floor dining room. Traditional cuisine.

Hatton Garden *Gtr London* – ✉ *EC1.*

XX **Bleeding Heart** p. 27 **NU e**

Bleeding Heart Yard, EC1N 8SJ, off Greville St, ☏ (020) 7242 2056, *bookings@bleedingheart.co.uk, Fax (020) 7831 1402*

🍴 – ⬤ AE ① VISA

closed 23 December-2 January, Saturday, Sunday and Bank Holidays – **Meals** a la carte 25.20/33.45 ⍴.

◆ Wood panelling, candlelight and a heart motif; a popular romantic dinner spot. By contrast, a busy City restaurant at lunchtime. French influenced menu. Weighty wine list.

Holborn *Gtr London* – ✉ *WC2.*

🏨 **Renaissance London Chancery Court** p. 26 **MU a**

252 High Holborn, WC1V 7EN, ☏ (020) 7829 9888, *sales.chancerycourt@renaissancehotels.com, Fax (020) 7829 9889*

🍴, ⛾s – 🛗, ✳ rm, 🖳 TV ☏ ㅤ – 🏛 400. ⬤ AE ① VISA JCB. ⌖

Meals – (see *QC* below) – ⌕ 16.95 – **356 rm** 323.10/528.75.

◆ Striking building built in 1914 with an impressive marbled lobby area and a grand central courtyard. Bedrooms are all very large and feature comprehensive modern facilities.

🏨 **Kingsway Hall** p. 37 **EV a**

Great Queen St, WC2B 5BX, ☏ (020) 7309 0909, *kingswayhall@compuserve.com, Fax (020) 7309 9696*

🍴 – 🛗, ✳ rm, 🖳 TV ☏ ㅤ – 🏛 150. ⬤ AE ① VISA JCB. ⌖

Harlequin : Meals 16.50/22.00 and a la carte 22.00/33.90 **s.** – ⌕ 15.25 – **168 rm** 230.00/240.00, 2 suites.

◆ Large, corporate-minded hotel. Striking glass-framed and marbled lobby. Stylish ground floor bar. Well-appointed bedrooms with an extensive array of mod cons. Relaxing restaurant in warm pastel colours.

XXX **QC** (at Renaissance London Chancery Court H.) p. 26 **MU a**

252 High Holborn, WC1V 7EN, ☏ (020) 7829 7000, *Fax (020) 7829 9889*

⬤ AE ① VISA JCB

closed Sunday – **Meals** 16.50/20.50 and dinner a la carte 29.50/46.50 ⍴.

◆ Impressive dining room with walls clad in Italian marble and Corinthian columns. Well-spaced tables contribute intimate atmosphere; original menus.

Primrose Hill *Gtr London* ✉ *NW1.*

XX **Odette's** p. 25 **HS i**

130 Regent's Park Rd, NW1 8XL, ☏ (020) 7586 5486, *Fax (020) 7586 0508*

⬤ AE ① VISA

closed 10 days Christmas-New Year and Sunday dinner – **Meals** 12.50/15.00 (lunch) and a la carte 29.00/36.00 ⍴ – (see also *Odette's Wine Bar* below).

◆ Identified by the pretty hanging baskets outside. A charming interior with mirrors of various sizes covering the walls. Detailed service. Contemporary cuisine.

XX **Okra** p. 25 **HIS c**

40 Chalcot Rd, NW1 8LS, ☏ (020) 7483 0077, *Fax (020) 266 5522*

🍽. ⬤ AE VISA

Meals - Indian - (dinner only and Sunday lunch) 15.00/25.00 and a la carte 16.00/23.50 **s.**

◆ The smaller ground floor room overlooks the larger lower level. Stone flooring and chocolate brown tones all add to the up-to-the-minute feel. Modern Indian cooking.

✗ **Odette's Wine Bar** (at Odette's)   p. 25   HS   i
130 Regent's Park Rd, NW1 8XL, ☎ (020) 7586 5486, *Fax (020) 7586 0508*
🅜🅢 AE ⓞ VISA
closed 10 days Christmas-New Year and Sunday dinner – **Meals** (booking
essential) a la carte 15.50/23.00 ⚏.
◆ In a basement below the main restaurant. Walls adorned with assorted
photographs and pictures. Inexpensive modern menu, served informally by
friendly young staff.

🍽 **The Queens**   p. 25   HS   a
49 Regent's Park Rd, NW1 8XD, ☎ (020) 7586 0408, *Fax (020) 7586 5677*
🌳 – 🅜🅢 VISA
Meals a la carte 14.00/24.00 ⚏.
◆ One of the original "gastropubs". Very popular balcony overlooking
Primrose Hill and the high street. Robust and traditional cooking from the
blackboard menu.

🍽 **The Engineer**   p. 25   IS   z
65 Gloucester Ave, NW1 8JH, ☎ (020) 7722 0950, *info@the-eng.com,
Fax (020) 7483 0592*
🌳 – 🅜🅢 VISA
closed 25-26 December – **Meals** a la carte 17.75/29.00 ⚏.
◆ Small but busy front bar with hatch allowing views into the kitchen. Rear
dining room decorated with modern pictures leads onto an attractive
terrace. Modern cuisine.

🍽 **The Lansdowne**   p. 25   IS   r
90 Gloucester Ave, NW1 8HX, ☎ (020) 7483 0409, *admin@thelandsowne.free
serve.co.uk, Fax (020) 7586 1723*
🅜🅢 VISA
closed 25 and 31 December, 1 January, Monday and Sunday dinner – **Meals**
(dinner only and Sunday lunch) a la carte 21.50/30.50 ⚏.
◆ Informal ground floor with blackboard menu; orders are taken at the bar.
For those seeking a quieter evening, try the upstairs room. Robust cooking
with generous portions.

Swiss Cottage *Gtr London* – ✉ *NW3.*

🏨 **Marriott Regents Park**   p. 25   GS   a
128 King Henry's Rd, NW3 3ST, ☎ (020) 7722 7711, *Fax (020) 7586
5822*
🎗, ⊜s, ⬜ – 🛗, ⇸ rm, ▤ TV ☏ & P – 🔼 300. 🅜🅢 AE ⓞ VISA.
⊗
Meals (bar lunch)/dinner a la carte 25.00/30.00 **s.** – ⊑ 16.45 – **298 rm** 176.25,
5 suites.
◆ Large writing desks and technological extras attract the corporate market
to this purpose-built group hotel. The impressive leisure facilities appeal to
weekend guests. Large, open-plan restaurant and bar.

🏨 **Swiss Cottage**   p. 25   GS   n
4 Adamson Rd, NW3 3HP, ☎ (020) 7722 2281, *reservations@swisscottage
hotel.co.uk, Fax (020) 7483 4588*
without rest. – 🛗 TV – 🔼 35. 🅜🅢 AE ⓞ VISA JCB, ⊗
53 rm ⊑ 65.00/115.00, 6 suites.
◆ Made up of four Victorian houses in a residential conservation area. Bedrooms vary in size and shape, reflecting the age of the house. Basement
breakfast room.

XX Bradley's
p. 25 GS e

25 Winchester Rd, NW3 3NR, ✆ (020) 7722 3457, *Fax (020) 7435 1392*
▤. MC AE VISA
closed 25 December-3 January and Saturday lunch – **Meals** 14.00/27.00 ♀.
◆ Warm pastel colours and modern artwork add a Mediterranean touch to this neighbourhood restaurant. The theme is complemented by the cooking of the chef patron.

XX Benihana
p. 25 GS o

100 Avenue Rd, NW3 3HF, ✆ (020) 7586 9508, *benihana@dircon.co.uk, Fax (020) 7586 6740*
▤. MC AE DC VISA
closed 25 December – **Meals** - Japanese (Teppan-Yaki) - 8.75/17.00 and a la carte 25.00/50.00.
◆ An entertaining experience where Japanese chefs chop, juggle and cook in front of you. Be prepared to talk with strangers as guests are seated in groups around the counters.

X Globe
p. 25 GS v

100 Avenue Rd, NW3 3HF, ✆ (020) 7722 7200, *globerella@aol.com, Fax (020) 7722 2772*
▤. MC AE VISA
closed lunch Saturday and Sunday – **Meals** a la carte 20.00/28.00.
◆ Next to the Hampstead theatre so this airy, conservatory establishment tends to be busier earlier and later in the evening. Modern menu with the occasional oriental twist.

In this guide
a symbol or a character,
printed in red or black, in light or bold type
does not have the same meaning.
Pay particular attention to the explanatory pages.

CITY OF LONDON *Gtr London.*

Great Eastern
p. 27 PU o

Liverpool St, EC2M 7QN, ✆ (020) 7618 5000, *sales@great-eastern-hotel.co.uk, Fax (020) 7618 5011*
Iδ – |♦|, ⇸ rm, ▤ TV ✆ ♿ – 🏔 250. MC AE DC VISA
Fishmarket : **Meals** - Seafood - *(closed Saturday lunch and Sunday)* a la carte 26.00/52.00 ♀
Miyabi : **Meals** - Japanese - *(closed Saturday, Sunday and Bank Holidays)* 23.50 (lunch) and a la carte 20.50/32.50 – (see also ***Aurora*** below) – ☕ 22.00 – **264 rm** 264.30/334.80, 3 suites.
◆ A contemporary and stylish interior hides behind the classic Victorian façade of this railway hotel. Bright and spacious rooms with state-of-the-art facilities and hi-fi's. Fishmarket based within original hotel lobby. Miyabi is compact Japanese restaurant

Threadneedles
p. 27 PV o

5 Threadneedle St, EC2R 8AY, ✆ (020) 7657 8080, *res_threadneedles@etontownhouse.com, Fax (020) 7657 8100*
|♦| ⇸ ▤ TV ✆ ♿ – 🏔 35. MC AE DC VISA JCB. ✂
Meals – (see ***Bonds*** below) – ☕ 19.95 – **69 rm** 311.40/464.10, 1 suite.
◆ A converted banking hall, dating from 1856, with a stunning stained-glass cupola. Bedrooms are very stylish and individual featuring CD players and Egyptian cotton sheets.

The Chamberlain
p. 27 **PV** n

130-135 Minories, EC3 1NU, ☎ (020) 7680 1500, *thechamberlain@fullers.co.uk, Fax (020) 7702 2500*

✆✕ rm, 🖥 📺 📞 ♿ – 🛗 40. 🆖 AE ① *VISA*

Meals (in bar Saturday and Sunday) a la carte 14.00/16.00 ♀ – ☜ 10.95 – **64 rm** 149.00.

◆ Modern hotel aimed at business traveller, two minutes from the Tower of London. Warmly decorated bedrooms with writing desks. All bathrooms have inbuilt TV sets.

Novotel London Tower Bridge
p. 27 **PV** n

10 Pepys St, EC3N 2NR, ☎ (020) 7265 6000, *h3107@accor-hotels.com, Fax (020) 7265 6060*

📠, ☎s – 🛗, ✆✕ rm, 🖥 rest, 📺 📞 ♿ – 🛗 80. 🆖 AE ① *VISA*. ✄

The Garden Brasserie : **Meals** 18.95 (lunch) and a la carte approx. 25.00 **s**. ♀ – ☜ 12.95 – **199 rm** 155.00/175.00, 4 suites.

◆ Modern, purpose-built hotel with carefully planned, comfortable bedrooms. Useful City location and close to Tower of London which is visible from some of the higher rooms. Informally styled brasserie.

Travelodge
p. 27 **PU** s

1 Harrow Pl, E1 7DB, ☎ (08700) 850950, *Fax (020) 7626 1105*

without rest. – 🛗 ✆✕ 📺 📞 ♿. 🆖 AE ① *VISA* JCB. ✄

142 rm 79.95.

◆ Suitable for both corporate travellers and families alike. Spacious, carefully designed, bright and modern rooms with sofa beds and ample workspace.

Aurora (at Great Eastern H.)
p. 27 **PU** o

Liverpool St, EC2M 7QN, ☎ (020) 7618 7000, *restaurants@great-eastern-hotel.co.uk, Fax (020) 7618 7001*

🖥. 🆖 AE ① *VISA*

closed Saturday, Sunday and Bank Holidays – **Meals** 28.00/38.00 and a la carte 33.80/50.50 ♀.

◆ Vast columns, ornate plasterwork and a striking glass dome feature in this imposing dining room. Polished and attentive service of an elaborate and modern menu.

City Rhodes
p. 27 **NU** u

1 New Street Sq, EC4A 3BF, ☎ (020) 7583 1313, *city.rhodes@sodexho.co.uk, Fax (020) 7353 1662*

🖥. 🆖 AE ① *VISA*

closed 25 December-2 January, Saturday, Sunday and Bank Holidays – **Meals** a la carte 29.50/49.00 **s**. ♀.

◆ The discreet entrance belies this bright and spacious first floor restaurant. Approachable and slick service of inspired modern British cooking. Notable wine list.

Spec. Hot smoked salmon, mashed potato and truffle veal jus. Roast loin of pork, caramelised apple and girolles. Bread and butter pudding.

Coq d'Argent
p. 27 **PV** c

No 1 Poultry, EC2R 8EJ, ☎ (020) 7395 5000, *Fax (020) 7395 5050*

🌳 – 🛗 🖥. 🆖 AE ① *VISA*

closed Saturday lunch and Sunday dinner – **Meals** (booking essential) 25.00 (lunch) and a la carte 43.00/50.00 ♀.

◆ Take the dedicated lift to the top of this modern office block. Some tables on the rooftop terrace have city views. Modern British cooking and oyster bar. Busy atmosphere.

XXX **Twentyfour** p. 27 PU v
24th floor, Tower 42, 25 Old Broad St, EC2N 1HQ, ℘ (020) 7877 2424, Fax (020) 7877 7788
London – closed Christmas and New Year, Saturday, Sunday and Bank Holidays – **Meals** (booking essential) 26.00 (lunch) and a la carte approx 35.50.
♦ Modern restaurant on the 24th floor of the former Natwest building affords panoramic views of the city. Extensive menu of contemporary British dishes. Attentive service.

XXX **Tatsuso** p. 27 PU u
32 Broadgate Circle, EC2M 2QS, ℘ (020) 7638 5863, Fax (020) 7638 5864
closed 25 December, Saturday, Sunday and Bank Holidays – **Meals** - Japanese - (booking essential) 28.00/43.00 and a la carte approx. 26.50/66.00.
♦ Dine in the busy teppan-yaki bar or in the more formal restaurant. Approachable staff in traditional costume provide attentive service of authentic and precise dishes.

XXX **1 Lombard Street (Restaurant)** p. 27 PV r
1 Lombard St, EC2V 9AA, ℘ (020) 7929 6611, hb@1lombardstreet.com, Fax (020) 7929 6622 –
closed 10 days Christmas, Saturday, Sunday and Bank Holidays – **Meals** (lunch booking essential) 32.00/34.00 and a la carte 50.00/58.50 – (see also ***1 Lombard Street (Brasserie)*** below).
♦ A haven of tranquillity behind the forever busy brasserie. Former bank provides the modern and very comfortable surroundings in which to savour the accomplished cuisine.
Spec. Carpaccio of tuna with Oriental spices, ginger and lime vinaigrette. Caramelised lobster and scallops in Sauternes, lime-spiced carrot tagliatelle. Fillet of lamb, sautéed vegetables, tomato and basil velouté.

XXX **Prism** p. 27 PV u
147 Leadenhall, EC3V 4QT, ℘ (020) 7256 3875, prism@harveynichols.co.uk, Fax (020) 7256 3876
closed 24 December-6 January, Saturday, Sunday and Bank Holidays – **Meals** a la carte 40.00/45.00.
♦ Enormous Corinthian pillars and a busy bar feature in this capacious and modern restaurant. Efficient service of an eclectic menu. Quieter tables in covered courtyard.

XXX **Bonds** (at Threadneedles H.) p. 27 PV o
5 Threadneedle St, EC2R 8AY, ℘ (020) 7657 8088, bonds@theetongroup.com, Fax (020) 7657 8089 –
closed Saturday and Sunday – **Meals** a la carte 33.75/40.50.
♦ Modern interior juxtaposed with the grandeur of a listed city building. Vast dining room with high ceiling and tall pillars. Attentive service of hearty, contemporary food.

XX **Club Gascon** (Aussignac) p. 27 OU z
57 West Smithfield, EC1A 9DS, ℘ (020) 7796 0600, Fax (020) 7796 0601
closed 23 December-5 January, Saturday lunch, Sunday and Bank Holidays – **Meals** - French (Gascony specialities) - (booking essential) 35.00 and a la carte 25.00/40.00.
♦ Intimate and rustic restaurant on the edge of Smithfield Market. Specialises in both the food and wines of Southwest France. Renowned for the foie gras tasting dishes.
Spec. Grilled foie gras with grapes. Cappuccino of black pudding, lobster and asparagus. Roasted leg of rabbit, prune chutney.

Searcy's at The Barbican
p. 27   OU   n

Level 2, The Barbican, Silk St, EC2Y 8DS, ℰ (020) 7588 3008, *searcys@barbican. org.uk, Fax (028) 7382 7247*

▤, ⓂⒸ ⒶⒺ ⓪ VISA

closed 24-25 December, Saturday lunch and Sunday – **Meals** 22.50 and a la carte 32.50/36.00 ⅀.

◆ Stylish modern surroundings, smooth effective service and seasonal modern British cooking. Unique location ideal for visitors to Barbican's multi-arts events.

The Don
p. 27   PV   s

The Courtyard, 20 St Swithins Lane, EC4N 8AD, ℰ (020) 7626 2606, *bookings@ thedonrestaurant.co.uk, Fax (020) 7626 2616*

▤, ⓂⒸ ⒶⒺ ⓪ VISA

closed 24 December-2 January, Saturday, Sunday and Bank Holidays – **Meals** (lunch booking essential) a la carte 24.85/32.20 ⅀.

◆ Characterful former premises of Sandeman Port, tucked away on tiny courtyard. Formal air in high ceilinged main room, lighter style in original cellars. Modern British fare.

1 Lombard Street (Brasserie)
p. 27   PV   r

1 Lombard St, EC2V 9AA, ℰ (020) 7929 6611, *Fax (020) 7929 6622*

▤, ⓂⒸ ⒶⒺ ⓪ VISA JCB

closed Saturday, Sunday and Bank Holidays – **Meals** (lunch booking essential) a la carte 23.20/37.50 ⅀.

◆ Impressive former banking hall with neo-classical décor and cupola above the feature central bar. Well-drilled service of modern European dishes. Lively atmosphere.

Brasserie Rocque
p. 27   PU   u

37 Broadgate Circle, EC2M 2QS, ℰ (020) 7638 7919, *Fax (020) 7628 5899*

🌤 – ▤, ⓂⒸ ⒶⒺ VISA

closed Saturday, Sunday and Bank Holidays – **Meals** (booking essential) (lunch only) a la carte 18.70/32.40 ⅀.

◆ Bright and modern restaurant with an appealing pavement terrace. The classically based menu and efficient service are appreciated by the City clientele.

Pacific Oriental
p. 27   PV   x

first floor, 1 Bishopsgate, EC2N 3AB, ℰ (020) 7929 6888, *Fax (020) 7929 7227*

▤, ⓂⒸ ⒶⒺ VISA

closed Saturday, Sunday and Bank Holidays – **Meals** - South East Asian influences - a la carte approx 33.50 ⅀.

◆ Watch the chefs prepare authentic South East Asian dishes in the first floor restaurant and micro-brewery. Bustling basement bar/brasserie offers more informal surroundings.

Imperial City
p. 27   PV   a

Royal Exchange, Cornhill, EC3V 3LL, ℰ (020) 7626 3437, *enquiries@orgplc. co.uk, Fax (020) 7338 0125*

▤, ⓂⒸ ⒶⒺ ⓪ VISA

closed 25-26 December, Saturday, Sunday and Bank Holidays – **Meals** - Chinese - 17.00 and a la carte 14.70/23.45 ⅀.

◆ Vaulted basement restaurant with large water feature; originally Royal Exchange wine cellars. Smart, friendly service of an authentic menu covering all regions of China.

✕✕ Chamberlain's
p. 27 **PV** v

23-25 Leadenhall Market, EC3V 1LR, ℰ (020) 7648 8690, *info@chamberlains. org, Fax (020) 7648 8691*

⓪⓪ 💳 ⓪ VISA

closed Saturday lunch and Sunday – **Meals** - Seafood - 17.00 (dinner) and a la carte 29.00/37.00.

♦ Bright, modern restaurant in ornate Victorian indoor market. Top quality seafood from fish and chips to mousse of lobster. There's even a fish tank in the lavatories

---

CROYDON *Gtr London.*

Addington – ✉ *Surrey.*

🏌₁₈ , 🏌₁₈ , 🏌₉ *Addington Court, Featherbed Lane* ℰ *(020) 8657 0281* GZ – 🏌₁₈ *The Addington, 205 Shirley Church Rd* ℰ *(020) 8777 1055* GZ.

✕✕ Planet Spice
p. 14 GZ c

88 Selsdon Park Rd, CR2 8JT, ℰ (020) 8651 3300, *Fax (020) 8651 4400*

▤ P. ⓪⓪ 💳 ⓪ VISA JCB

closed 25-26 December – **Meals** - Indian - a la carte 15.90/23.15 ♈.

♦ Brasserie style Indian restaurant with fresh, vibrant décor and a modern feel. Attentive and helpful service. Traditional cooking with some innovative touches.

Coulsdon *Surrey* – ✉ *Surrey.*

🏛 Coulsdon Manor
Coulsdon Court Rd, via Stoats Nest Rd, CR5 2LL, ℰ (020) 8668 0414, *coulsdon manor@marstonhotel.com, Fax (020) 8668 3118*

👣, ≼, 🏊, ≘s, 🏌₁₈, ✕, squash – 🛗 ✻ 📺 ☎ P. – 🔼 180. ⓪⓪ 💳 ⓪ VISA, ✗

Manor House : **Meals** *(closed Saturday lunch)* 19.50/27.00 and dinner a la carte approx. 38.00 **s.** ♈ – 🍵 11.00 – **35 rm** 108.00/130.00.

♦ A secluded Victorian country house, extended over the years. Set in 140 acres, much of which is taken up by the popular golf course. Smart bedrooms, restful sitting room. Softly-lit dining room with cocktail bar.

Croydon *Surrey* – ✉ *Surrey.*

🈺 *Croydon Clocktower, Katharine St* ℰ *(020) 8253 1009.*

🏛 Hilton Croydon
p. 14 FZ e

Waddon Way, Purley Way, CR9 4HH, ℰ (020) 8680 3000, *Fax (020) 8681 6171*

🏊, ≘s, 🗖 – 🛗 ✻ ▤ 📺 ☎ 👣 P. – 🔼 400. ⓪⓪ 💳 ⓪ VISA, ✗

Meals a la carte approx. 18.00 **s.** ♈ – 🍵 14.50 – **168 rm** 110.00/150.00.

♦ A modern hotel where the relaxing café in the open-plan lobby is open all day. Internet access is available in all bedrooms, which are decorated to a good standard. Open-plan dining room and adjacent bar.

🏛 Croydon Park
p. 14 FZ u

7 Altyre Rd, CR9 5AA, ℰ (020) 8680 9200, *reservations@croydonparkhotel.co. uk, Fax (020) 8760 0426*

🏊, ≘s, 🗖, squash – 🛗 ✻ rm, ▤ 📺 ☎ P. – 🔼 300. ⓪⓪ 💳 ⓪ VISA, ✗

Oscars : **Meals** 16.95/20.95 and a la carte 22.50/40.00 ♈ – **211 rm** 🍵 125.00/160.00.

♦ Ideally placed for Croydon's business district and with good transport links. Bustling lobby, comprehensive leisure facilities and good-sized bedrooms. Capacious restaurant with gas-lit bar.

🏨 Aerodrome
p. 14 **FZ** **o**

Purley Way, CR9 4LT, ℰ (020) 8680 1999, *info@aerodrome-hotel.co.uk,*
Fax (020) 86888 7247

🍴 – ↩ , ▤ rest, 📺 🅿 – 🏋 120. 🐵 🄰🄴 🅾 𝗩𝗜𝗦𝗔

Meals 9.95/15.00 a la carte 20.85/24.50 ♀ – ⌑ 11.95 – **83 rm** 75.00/120.00.

♦ Originally housed locally based RAF pilots; now a busy group hotel geared predominantly to the corporate market. Some small bedrooms but all with the appropriate mod cons. Informally stylish restaurant.

🏨 Travel Inn Metro
p. 14 **GZ** **s**

104 Coombe Rd, CR0 5RB, on A 212, ℰ (020) 8686 2030, *Fax (020) 8686 6435*

🚗 – ↩ rm, 📺 & 🅿, 🐵 🄰🄴 🅾 𝗩𝗜𝗦𝗔 . ✂

Meals (grill rest.) – **39 rm** 54.95.

♦ Surprisingly pleasant country setting for this purpose-built lodge-style hotel; surrounded by woodland with an adjacent mock-rustic pub serving traditional cuisine.

🏨 Premier Lodge
p. 14 **FZ** **e**

619 Purley Way, CR0 4RJ, ℰ (020) 8225 1909, *Fax (020) 8680 9109*

📶 ↩ 📺 & 🅿, 🐵 🄰🄴 🅾 𝗩𝗜𝗦𝗔 . ✂

Meals (grill rest.) a la carte 10.35/24.20 – **82 rm** 54.95.

♦ Located in an out-of-town leisure park with assorted fast food outlets and children's play area. Uniform lodge accommodation, competitively priced. Bright, popular dining room.

✗ Mario
p. 14 **FZ** **s**

299 High St, CR0 1QL, ℰ (020) 8686 5624, *Fax (020) 8636 5624*

🐵 🄰🄴 𝗩𝗜𝗦𝗔

closed 1 week Spring, 2 weeks September, 25-26 December, Saturday lunch, Sunday, Monday and Bank Holidays – **Meals** - Italian - 16.00 (lunch) and a la carte 16.75/32.25.

♦ Guests can be in no doubt as to the nationality of this cosy, personally run establishment; walls are adorned with Italian pictures and knick-knacks. Traditional menu.

✗ Tai Tung
p. 14 **FZ** **v**

Unit 1A, Wing Yip Centre, 550 Purley Way, CR0 4RF, ℰ (020) 8688 3668, *Fax (020) 8688 0116*

▤ 🅿, 🐵 🄰🄴 𝗩𝗜𝗦𝗔

closed 24 to 26 December – **Meals** - Chinese (Canton) - 11.00/15.50 and a la carte 10.00/16.50.

♦ Part of an oriental complex that includes a Chinese supermarket and bakery. The lunchtime dim sum is particularly popular. Attentive and efficient service.

Sanderstead *Surrey* – ✉ *Surrey*.

🏨 *Selsdon Park Hotel, Addington Rd, Sanderstead* ℰ *(020) 8657 8811* **GZ**.

🏰 Le Meridien Selsdon Park
p. 14 **GZ** **n**

Addington Rd, CR2 8YA, ℰ (020) 8657 8811, *reservation.selsdonpark@lemeridien.com, Fax (020) 8651 6171*

≤ , ₪, ⌂ , ⌑ heated, 🔲, 🏨 , 🚗 , 🎿 , ✗ , squash – 📶 ↩ , ▤ rest, 📺 📞 🅿 – 🏋 150. 🐵 🄰🄴 🅾 𝗩𝗜𝗦𝗔 𝗝𝗖𝗕 . ✂

Meals (dancing Saturday evening) (buffet lunch Monday-Saturday) 19.95/27.00 a la carte 27.00/39.00 **s.** – ⌑ 12.95 – **200 rm** 129.00/190.00, 4 suites.

♦ An imposing Victorian stately home in 200 acres. Enough leisure facilities inside and out to appeal to all. Despite its size, retains much character. Vast dining room overlooking the grounds.

Ealing *Gtr London –* ✉ *W5.*

📍18 *West Middlesex, Greenford Rd, Southall* ℘ *(020) 8574 3450* BV – 📍9 *Horse-nden Hill, Woodland Rise, Greenford* ℘ *(020) 8902 4555* BU.

🏨 Ramada Jarvis London West
p. 9   CV   **v**

Ealing Common, W5 3HN, ℘ (020) 8896 8400, *sales.londonwest@ramadajarvis. co.uk, Fax (020) 8992 7082*

|💲|, ⇆ rm, 🍽 rest, 📺 ☎ 🅿 – 🏊 250. 🐵 🆎 ⓪ 𝗩𝗜𝗦𝗔, ⚡

Meals (buffet lunch Monday-Friday) (bar lunch Saturday) a la carte 17.25/ 22.85 ♀ – ⬛ 11.95 – **189 rm** 140.00/160.00.

♦ On the edge of the Common, a commercial hotel refurbished in 2000. Smart, modern interior in contrast to the rather uninspiring façade. Warmly decorated bedrooms. Restaurant or bar dining options.

🏠 Travel Inn Metro
p. 8   BU   **c**

Western Ave, Greenford, UB6 8TR, off A 40, ℘ (020) 8998 8820, *Fax (020) 8998 8823*

⇆ rm, 🍽 rest, 📺 ⚙ 🅿. 🐵 🆎 ⓪ 𝗩𝗜𝗦𝗔 ᴊᴄʙ, ⚡

Meals (grill rest.) – **39 rm** 54.95.

♦ Modern, purpose-built lodge offering good value accommodation with bright and carefully planned bedrooms. Children's play area and popular grill restaurant adjacent.

🏠 Travelodge
p. 13   CV   **x**

Western Ave, W3 0TE, ℘ (08700) 850950, *Fax (020) 8752 1134* without rest. – |💲| ⇆ 📺 ⚙ 🅿. 🐵 🆎 ⓪ 𝗩𝗜𝗦𝗔, ⚡

64 rm 69.95.

♦ Modern lodge-style accommodation with clean and spacious bedrooms at an affordable price. Convenient for the A40. All rooms double glazed but those at the back are quieter.

🍴🍴 Parade
p. 13   CV   **s**

18-19 The Mall, W5 2PJ, ℘ (020) 8810 0202, *Fax (020) 8810 0303*

🍽. 🐵 🆎 𝗩𝗜𝗦𝗔

closed Sunday dinner and Bank Holidays – **Meals** 15.00 (lunch) and a la carte 19.50/29.50 ♀.

♦ Front café and bar area leads into a stylish yet relaxing room, with contemporary pictures and wood flooring. Menu uses many European influences. Structured service.

🍴🍴 Maxim
p. 8   BV   **a**

153-155 Northfield Ave, W13 9QT, ℘ (020) 8567 1719, *Fax (020) 8932 0717*

🍽. 🐵 🆎 𝗩𝗜𝗦𝗔 ᴊᴄʙ

closed 25 to 28 December and Sunday lunch – **Meals** - Chinese (Peking) - 12.90/27.90 and a la carte 15.00/29.00.

♦ Decorated with assorted oriental ornaments and pictures. Well-organised service from smartly attired staff. Authentic Chinese cooking from the extensive menu.

South Ealing.

🍴 Ealing Park Tavern
p. 8   BV   **e**

222 South Ealing Rd, W5 4RL, ℘ (020) 8758 1879, *Fax (020) 8560 5269*

🌳 –🐵 🆎 𝗩𝗜𝗦𝗔

closed 25 December, 1 January and Monday lunch (except Bank Holidays) – **Meals** a la carte 17.50/20.50 ♀.

♦ Victorian building with an atmospheric, cavernous interior. Characterful beamed dining room and an open-plan kitchen serving modern dishes from a daily changing menu.

ENFIELD *Gtr London – pop. 566.*

📐 *Lee Valley Leisure, Picketts Lock Lane, Edmonton* ℰ *(020) 8803 3611* GT.

Enfield *Middx – ✉ Middx.*

📐 *Whitewebbs, Beggars Hollow, Clay Hill* ℰ *(020) 8363 2951, N : 1 m.* FT.

🏨 **Royal Chace**   p. 10   ET   **a**
The Ridgeway, EN2 8AR, ℰ *(020) 8884 8181, royal.chace@dial.pipex.com, Fax (020) 8884 8150*
🏊 heated, 🌲 – ⤫ 📺 ♿ 🅿 – 🍴 270. 🆗 ᴀᴇ 𝘝𝘐𝘚𝘈. ⊗
closed 25-26 December and 1 January – **Meals** *(closed Sunday dinner)* (bar lunch Monday to Saturday)/dinner a la carte 17.75/25.50 **s. – 92 rm** � 99.00/115.00.
 ♦ A corporate-minded hotel, privately owned and convenient for the M25. Many of the uniformly decorated bedrooms look out over the large gardens and parkland at the rear. Restaurant is popular for private functions.

🏠 **Oak Lodge**   p. 10   FT   **a**
80 Village Rd, Bush Hill Park, EN1 2EU, ℰ *(020) 8360 7082, oaklodge@fsmail.net*
🌳, 🌲 – ⤫ 📺 ♿. 🆗 ᴀᴇ ⓞ 𝘝𝘐𝘚𝘈 ᴊᴄʙ
Meals (dinner only) a la carte 20.50/29.00 – **6 rm** � 79.50/110.00.
 ♦ An Edwardian house personally run by the hospitable owner and located in a residential area. Individually decorated bedrooms are compact but well-equipped. Cosy dining room overlooks secluded rear garden.

Hadley Wood *Herts. – ✉ Herts.*

🏰 **West Lodge Park**   p. 10   ET   **i**
off Cockfosters Rd, EN4 0PY, ℰ *(020) 8216 3900, info@westlodgepark.com, Fax (020) 8216 3937*
🐾, ≤, 🌳, 🌲, ♨ – 📶 ⤫, ▤ rest, 📺 📞 ♿ 🅿 – 🍴 80. 🆗 ᴀᴇ ⓞ 𝘝𝘐𝘚𝘈. ⊗
The Cedar : **Meals** 22.00/32.25 **s.** ♀ – � 13.50 – **59 rm** 108.00/150.00.
 ♦ Family owned for over half a century, a country house in sweeping grounds with arboretum. Comfortable sitting rooms; neat, spacious bed-rooms. Use of nearby leisure centre. Dining room boasts large windows and exposed brick walls.

Winchmore Hill *Gtr London – ✉ N21.*

🍴 **The Kings Head**   p. 10   FT   **e**
1 The Green, N21 1BB, ℰ *(020) 8886 1988, Fax (020) 8882 3881*
🅿. 🆗 𝘝𝘐𝘚𝘈
Meals a la carte 23.10/31.70 ♀.
 ♦ Large scrubbed pine tables, leather sofas and wall tapestries decorate this contemporary inn. Modern, eclectic cooking with supplementary blackboard specials.

GREENWICH *Gtr London.*

Blackheath *Gtr London – ✉ SE3.*

🍴🍴 **Chapter Two**   p. 15   HX   **c**
43-45 Montpelier Vale, SE3 0TJ, ℰ *(020) 8333 2666, fiona.chapter2@talk21.com, Fax (020) 8355 8399*
⤫ ▤. 🆗 ᴀᴇ ⓞ 𝘝𝘐𝘚𝘈 ᴊᴄʙ
closed 2-4 January – **Meals** 18.50/22.50.
 ♦ Smart and contemporary interior. Decorated in primary colours, with pine flooring. Formal service of a well-priced, well-judged European-influenced modern menu.

Greenwich *Ctr London –* ✉ *SE10.*

🖼 *Pepys House, Old Royal Naval College, King William Walk ☎ (0870) 6082000.*

XX **Spread Eagle** p. 14 **GV** c
1-2 Stockwell St, SE10 9JN, ☎ (020) 8853 2333, *goodfood@spreadeagle.org,*
Fax (020) 8305 0447
▤, 🅲🅾 AE ⑩ VISA JCB
closed 25-26 December and Sunday dinner – **Meals** 13.00/16.75 (lunch)
and a la carte 23.75/28.75 ⵣ.
◆ This converted pub is something of an institution. Cosy booth seating,
wood panelling and a further upstairs room. Traditional French-influenced
menu with attentive service.

X **North Pole** p. 14 **GV** u
131 Greenwich High Rd, SE10 8JA, ☎ (020) 8853 3020, *Fax (020) 8853 3501*
🅲🅾 AE VISA
Meals (dinner only and lunch December and Sunday)/dinner 17.50
and a la carte 22.00/25.00 ⵣ.
◆ Former corner pub with popular ground floor bar. Upstairs dining room
benefits from high ceilings, large windows and bright colours. Relaxed service, robust cooking.

The rates shown may be revised if the cost of living changes to any great extent.
Before making your reservations,
confirm with the hotelier the exact price that will be charged.

HACKNEY *Ctr London.*

Dalston *Ctr London –* ✉ *N1.*

X **Soulard** p. 27 **PS** e
113 Mortimer Rd, N1 4JY, ☎ (020) 7254 1314, *Fax (020) 7254 1314*
🅲🅾 VISA
closed 3 weeks August-September, between Christmas-New Year, Sunday and
Monday – **Meals** - French - (dinner only and lunch December) 21.00.
◆ Proudly French in both the decoration and the fixed price bistro-style
cooking, with blackboard specials. Friendly owner knows his regulars. Cosy
and unpretentious.

Hoxton *Ctr London* ✉ *N1.*

🏨 **Express by Holiday Inn** p. 27 **PT** a
275 Old St, EC1V 9LN, ☎ (020) 7300 4300, *reservationstc@holidayinnlondon.*
com, Fax (020) 7300 4400
⬦, ✦ rm, ▤ rest, 📺 ☎ ♿ – 🔥 80. 🅲🅾 AE ⑩ VISA JCB. ✻
Meals (dinner only) a la carte approx. 23.00 – **224 rm** 110.00.
◆ Large purpose-built property close to the tube and the financial district.
Brightly decorated bedrooms are all generously sized and offer good value
accommodation. Open-plan dining room.

XX **Real Greek** p. 27 **PT** v
15 Hoxton Market, N1 6HG, ☎ (020) 7739 8212, *admin@therealgreek.co.uk,*
Fax (020) 7739 4910
🅲🅾 VISA
closed Christmas, Easter, Sunday and Bank Holidays – **Meals** - Greek -
a la carte approx 31.00 ⵣ.
◆ A former Victorian pub in a pleasant square. Plain wooden tables with
open-plan kitchen. Very tasty, wholly Greek menu and wine list with unaffected and pleasant service.

※ **Mezedopolio** p. 27 **PT** V
15 Hoxton Market, N1 6HG, ✆ (020) 7739 8212, *admin@therealgreek.demon.c o.uk, Fax (020) 7739 4910*
M© **VISA**
closed 25 December, Sunday and Bank Holidays – **Meals** - Greek meze - (bookings not accepted) a la carte approx. 20.00 ♀.
◆ Greek meze bar, part of The Real Greek, though with a more informal style. High ceilings, marble memorials. Large menu of authentic dishes from Greece and the Aegean.

Stoke Newington *Gtr London* – ✉ *N16.*

※※ **Mesclun** p. 10 **FU** C
24 Stoke Newington Church St, N16 0LU, ✆ (020) 7249 5029, *Fax (020) 7275 8448*
M© **AE** **①** **VISA** **JCB**
Meals 10.50 (lunch) a la carte 19.75/21.75.
◆ A local following and vivid modern artwork create a pleasant, convivial atmosphere. Service is never less than friendly whilst the menu is modern and eclectic in its range.

※※ **Muranco** p. 10 **FU** C
10 Stoke Newington Church St, N16 0LU, ✆ (020) 7275 7867
▤. **M©** **VISA**
closed 25-26 December, 1 January and Monday – **Meals** - Italian - (dinner only and lunch Saturday and Sunday)/dinner a la carte 16.25/24.45.
◆ This smart, modern restaurant has an intimate atmosphere and friendly, efficent service. Offers regularly changing menus of authentic Italian dishes classically prepared.

※ **Rasa** p. 10 **FU** C
55 Stoke Newington Church St, N16 0AR, ✆ (020) 7249 0344
▤ **M©** **AE** **VISA**
closed 25 Decmber and 1 January – **Meals** - Indian Vegetarian - (booking essential)(dinner only and lunch Saturday and Sunday) 15.00 and a la carte 8.85/10.25.
◆ Busy Indian restaurant, an unpretentious environment in which to sample authentic, sometimes unusual, dishes. The "Feast" offers a taste of the range of foods on offer.

HAMMERSMITH and FULHAM *Gtr London.*

Fulham *Gtr London* – ✉ *SW6.*

🏠 **London Putney Bridge Travel Inn Capital** p. 16 **AQ** C
3 Putney Bridge Approach, SW6 3JD, ✆ (020) 7471 8300, *Fax (020) 7471 8315*
|$|, ✲ rm, ▤ rest, **TV** ᕦ. **M©** **AE** **①** **VISA**. ✲
Meals (grill rest.) (dinner only) – **154 rm** 74.95.
◆ A longer name for a larger lodge. Converted office block offering clean, well-priced accommodation. All rooms have sofa beds and large worktops.

※※ **Blue Elephant** p. 28 **EZ** Z
4-6 Fulham Broadway, SW6 1AA, ✆ (020) 7385 6595, *london@blueelephant. com, Fax (020) 7386 7665*
▤. **M©** **AE** **①** **VISA**
closed Christmas and Saturday lunch – **Meals** - Thai - (booking essential) 32.00/37.00 and a la carte 27.50/39.50.
◆ Elaborately ornate, unrestrained décor: fountains, bridges, orchids and ponds with carp. Authentic Thai food served by attentive staff in national costumes.

XX Mao Tai
p. 16 BQ e

58 New Kings Rd, Parsons Green, SW6 4LS, *(020) 7731 2520, mbmaotai@aol. com, Fax (020) 7471 8992*

▤ ◑❺ ᴀᴇ *VISA*

closed 25-26 December – **Meals** - Chinese (Szechuan) - 12.50/24.70 and a la carte 22.70/31.35 ₤.

♦ A light and modern interior with wood flooring and framed artwork with an eastern theme. Well organised service. Chinese cuisine with Szechuan specialities.

The Salisbury Tavern
p. 28 EZ e

21 Sherbrooke Rd, SW6 7HX, *(020) 7381 4005, longshot@dial.pipex.com, Fax (020) 7381 1002*

▤ ◑❺ ᴀᴇ *VISA*

closed 24-26 December – **Meals** (live jazz Monday evening) 15.00 (lunch) and a la carte 21.35/27.85 ₤.

♦ Its residential location attracts a local crowd to the stylish bar. Separate, and equally à la mode, dining room with pleasant young staff. Wide ranging traditional menu.

Hammersmith *Gtr London –* ⊠ *W6/W12/W14.*

XX River Café *(Ruth Rogers/Rose Gray)*
p. 13 DV r

❀ Thames Wharf, Rainville Rd, W6 9HA, *(020) 7386 4200, info@rivercafe.co.uk, Fax (020) 7386 4201*

 ⟨⟩ –◑❺ ᴀᴇ ◐ *VISA* ᴊᴄʙ

closed Christmas-New Year, Sunday dinner and Bank Holidays – **Meals** - Italian - (booking essential) a la carte 38.00/55.50 ₤.

♦ Warehouse conversion with full length windows on one side, open plan kitchen the other. Canteen-style atmosphere. Accomplished rustic Italian cooking, using the finest produce.

Spec. Crab tagliatelle. Roast turbot with capers, oregano and wood-roasted beetroot. "Chocolate nemesis".

X Snows on the Green
p. 13 DV x

166 Shepherd's Bush Rd, Brook Green, W6 7PB, *(020) 7603 2142, Fax (020) 7602 7553*

▤ ◑❺ ᴀᴇ ◐ *VISA*

closed 4 days Christmas, Saturday lunch, Sunday and Bank Holidays – **Meals** 13.00 (lunch) and a la carte 21.95/25.95 ₤.

♦ Name refers to the chef patron, not the inclement weather found in west London. Mediterranean influenced decoration matched by the style of the cooking.

X Maquis
p. 13 DV n

⟨⟩ 111 Hammersmith Grove, W6 0NQ, *(020) 8846 3850, Fax (020) 8846 3855*
◑❺ ᴀᴇ ◐ *VISA*

closed Saturday lunch, Sunday dinner, 25 December-1 January and Bank Holidays – **Meals** 18.00 (lunch) and a la carte 21.94/31.00 **s.** ₤.

♦ Modern restaurant in a parade of shops tucked away in centre of Hammersmith. Pleasant, informal atmosphere. Simple, good quality British classics using quality ingredients.

X The Brackenbury
p. 13 CV a

129-131 Brackenbury Rd, W6 0BQ, *(020) 8748 0107, brack@placement.fsnet. co.uk, Fax (020) 8741 0905*

 ⟨⟩ –◑❺ ᴀᴇ ◐ *VISA*

closed Easter, Christmas, Saturday lunch and Sunday dinner – **Meals** 12.50 (lunch) and a la carte 23.00/28.50 ₤.

♦ The closely set wooden tables, pavement terrace and relaxed service add to the cosy, neighbourhood feel. Cooking is equally unfussy; modern yet robust.

✕ Azou
p. 13 **CV** u

375 King St, W6 9NJ, ✆ (020) 8536 7266, *Fax (020) 8748 1009*
▤. **M⊚** **⓪** **VISA**
closed lunch Saturday, Sunday and Bank Holidays – **Meals** - North African - (lunch booking essential) a la carte 13.65/16.50.

• The North African theme is not confined to the menu; the room is decorated with hanging lanterns, screens and assorted knick-knacks. Friendly service and well priced dishes.

▐⊡ Anglesea Arms
p. 13 **CV** c

35 Wingate Rd, W6 0UR, ✆ (020) 8749 1291, *fievans@aol.com, Fax (020) 8749 1254*
� – **M⊚** **VISA**
closed 1 week Christmas – **Meals** (bookings not accepted) a la carte 17.00/20.20 ℤ.

• The laid-back atmosphere and local feel make this pub a popular venue. Worth arriving early as bookings are not taken. Modern cooking from blackboard menu.

Olympia *Gtr London* – ✉ W14.

✕✕ Cotto
p. 28 **EY** i

44 Blythe Rd, W14 0HA, ✆ (020) 7602 9333, *bookings@cottorestaurant.co.uk, Fax (020) 7602 5003*
▤. **M⊚** **AE** **VISA** **JCB**
closed 25-26 December, Saturday lunch, Sunday and Bank Holidays – **Meals** 15.50/18.00 and dinner a la carte 18.00/29.00 ℤ.

• On two floors, with vivid abstract paintings on white walls, chrome-framed chairs and music. Efficient service from black-clad staff. Modern cooking with some originality.

Shepherd's Bush *Gtr London* – ✉ W12/W14.

⛪ K West
p. 13 **DV** c

Richmond Way, W14 0AX, ✆ (020) 7674 1000, *bookit@k-west.co.uk, Fax (020) 7674 1050*
I₆, ⇌S – ▥ ⤢ ▤ TV ✆ ⅙ – ⛟ 60. **M⊚** **AE** **⓪** **VISA** **JCB**. ⅍
Meals a la carte 17.00/27.00 ℤ – � 17.00 – **222 rm** 176.25/308.00.

• Former BBC offices, the interior now decorated in smart, contemporary style. Bedrooms in understated modern style, deluxe rooms with work desks and DVD and CD facilities.

✕✕ Chinon
p. 13 **DV** c

23 Richmond Way, W14 0AS, ✆ (020) 7602 5968, *johnchinon@hotmail.com, Fax (020) 7602 4082*
▤. **M⊚** **AE** **⓪** **VISA** **JCB**
closed 12 August-2 September, Sunday and Monday – **Meals** (dinner only) 25.00.

• The warm, bohemian style interior compensates for the sometimes rather tortuous act of finding a place to park. Casually relaxed service from the owner. Modern cooking.

✕ Onami
p. 13 **DV** a

236 Blythe Rd, W14 0HJ, ✆ (020) 7603 7267
Meals - Japanese - a la carte approx. 15.00.

• Glass-fronted restaurant in residential area. Simple interior with stripped wood floors and walls hung with framed war banners. Authentic Japanese cooking and a sushi bar.

🖾 Havelock Tavern
p. 13 DV e

57 Masbro Rd, W14 0LS, ✆ (020) 7603 5374, *Fax (020) 7602 1163*

🌦 – ▣

closed 22-26 December – **Meals** (bookings not accepted) a la carte approx. 20.00 s. ♀.

• Typical new wave London pub where the kitchen produces generously portioned modern food. Pine tables and chairs, and a large central bar. Privately owned.

HARINGEY *Gtr London.*

Crouch End *Gtr London* – ✉ *N8.*

♤ Mountview
p. 10 EU r

31 Mount View Rd, N4 4SS, ✆ (020) 8340 9222, *mountviewbb@aol.com, Fax (020) 8342 8494*

without rest., 🛋 – ᵗ⊁ 📺. ⓦⓞ 𝗩𝗜𝗦𝗔. 🛇

3 rm ⊑ 40.00/70.00.

• Redbrick Victorian house with a warm and stylish ambience engendered by the homely décor. One bedroom features an original fireplace and two overlook the quiet rear garden.

✗✗ Les Associés
p. 10 EU e

172 Park Rd, N8 8JT, ✆ (020) 8348 8944, *Fax (020) 8340 7499* – ⓦⓞ 𝗩𝗜𝗦𝗔

closed Sunday dinner and Monday – **Meals** - French - (dinner only and Sunday lunch)/dinner a la carte 19.00/26.70.

• Its relaxed ambience and polite, friendly service make this a popular local spot. Traditional and reliable French cooking in comfortable surroundings.

✗ Florians
p. 10 EU c

4 Topsfield Par, Middle Lane, N8 8RP, ✆ (020) 8348 8348, *Fax (020) 8292 2092*

🌦 – ▣. ⓦⓞ 𝗩𝗜𝗦𝗔

closed 25-26 December and 1 January – **Meals** - Italian - 15.95 (lunch) and a la carte 17.75/23.50.

• Light room with tiled flooring and large paintings, nestling behind a busy front bar. Italian menu with blackboard daily specials. Efficient and obliging service.

HARROW *Gtr London.*

Harrow Weald *Middx* – ✉ *Middx.*

🏛 Grim's Dyke
p. 8 BT a

Old Redding, HA3 6SH, ✆ (020) 8385 3100, *reservations@grimsdyke.com, Fax (020) 8954 4560*

🐟, 🛋, ♨ – ᵗ⊁ rm, 📺 🅿 – 🔥 70. ⓦⓞ 🅰🅴 ⓞ 𝗩𝗜𝗦𝗔

Meals *(closed Saturday lunch)* 19.95/25.95 and a la carte 29.25/43.25 ♀ –

44 rm ⊑ 125.00/170.00.

• Victorian mansion, former country residence of W.S.Gilbert. Rooms divided between main house and lodge, the former more characterful. Over 40 acres of garden and woodland. Restaurant with ornately carved fireplace.

Kenton *Middx* – ✉ *Middx.*

🏨 Travel Inn Metro
p. 8 BU e

Kenton Rd, HA3 8AT, ✆ (020) 8907 4069, *Fax (020) 8909 1604*

🛗, ᵗ⊁ rm, 📺 🔥 🅿. ⓦⓞ 🅰🅴 ⓞ 𝗩𝗜𝗦𝗔. 🛇

Meals (grill rest.) – **70 rm** 54.95.

• Lodge hotel providing clean, comfortable and affordable accommodation. Adjacent Beefeater pub offers a menu specialising in popular grill-based dishes.

Pinner *Middx –* ✉ *Middx.*

Friends
p. 8 **BU** **a**

11 High St, HA5 5PJ, 𝄢 (020) 8866 0286, *info@friendsrestaurant.co.uk, Fax (020) 8866 0286*

✻ 🔲. ⓶ 🆎 ⓪ *VISA*

closed 25-26 December, Sunday dinner and Monday – **Meals** 16.50/25.00 ℥.

♦ Pretty beamed cottage, with some parts dating back 400 years. Inside, a welcoming glow from the log fire; personal service from owners and a fresh, regularly-changing menu.

HAVERING *Gtr London.*

Romford *Essex –* ✉ *Essex.*

 ₁₈ , ₉ *Risebridge, Risebridge Chase, Lower Bedfords Rd* 𝄢 *(01708) 741429,* **JT.**

Travel Inn Metro
p. 11 **JU** **a**

Mercury Gdns, RM1 3EN, 𝄢 (01708) 760548, *Fax (01708) 760456*

⌷, ✻ rm, 📺 ♿ 🅿. ⓶ 🆎 ⓪ *VISA*

Meals (grill rest.) – **40 rm** 54.95.

♦ Clean and well-maintained lodge-style accommodation, with the nearby M25 providing easy road links. Adjacent pub-restaurant specialises in popular, grilled dishes.

Write us...

If you have any comments on the contents of this Guide. Your praise as well as your criticisms will receive careful consideration and, with your assistance, we will be able to add to our stock of information and, where necessary, amend our judgments.

Thank you in advance!

HILLINGDON *Gtr London.*

 ₁₈ *Haste Hill, The Drive, Northwood* 𝄢 *(01923) 825224* **AU.**

Hayes *–* ✉ *Middx.*

Travel Inn Metro
p. 8 **AV** **a**

362 Uxbridge Rd, UB4 0HF, 𝄢 (020) 8573 7479, *Fax (020) 8569 1204*

✻ rm, 🔲 rest, 📺 ♿ 🅿. ⓶ 🆎 ⓪ *VISA*. ⌗

Meals (grill rest.) – **62 rm** 54.95.

♦ Functional lodge accommodation, offering spacious and clean bedrooms, all with sofa beds. Family orientated adjacent pub serves a popular grill-based menu.

Heathrow Airport *Middx –* ✉ *Middx.*

Radisson Edwardian
p. 12 **AX** **e**

140 Bath Rd, Hayes, UB3 5AW, 𝄢 (020) 8759 6311, *busctr@radissonedwardian. com, Fax (020) 8759 4559*

🔏, ≋s, 🔲 – ⌷, ✻ rm, 🔲 📺 📞 🅿 – 🔼 550. ⓶ 🆎 ⓪ *VISA* JCB. ⌗

Henleys : Meals 25.00/50.00 **s.**

Brasserie : Meals 30.00 **s.** – ⌑ 15.00 – **442 rm** 233.80/257.30, 17 suites.

♦ Capacious group hotel with a huge atrium over the leisure facilities. Plenty of comfortable lounges, well-appointed bedrooms and attentive service. Henleys boasts oil paintings and cocktail bar. Informal, slim leather-chaired Brasserie.

Crowne Plaza London Heathrow
p. 8   AV   v

Stockley Rd, West Drayton, UB7 9NA, ℘ (01895) 445555, *sales.cplhr@6c.com,*
Fax (01895) 445122

⅃₆, ⇌s, ⌷, ᵣ₉ – 🛗, ⤨ rm, ▤ 📺 📞 🚹 ⬇, 🅟 – 🔀 200. ⑩ AE ① *VISA* ᴊᴄʙ. ⚔

Concha Grill *:* Meals 13.75/23.50 and a la carte 27.40/39.40 Ⴘ – (see also
Simply Nico Heathrow below) – ⊐ 15.00 – **457 rm** 195.00, 1 suite.

♦ Extensive leisure, aromatherapy and beauty salons make this large hotel a
popular stop-over for travellers. Club bedrooms are particularly well-
equipped. Bright, breezy Concha Grill with juice bar.

Sheraton Skyline
p. 12   AX   u

Bath Rd, Hayes, UB3 5BP, ℘ (020) 8759 2535, *res268_skyline@sheraton.com,*
Fax (020) 8750 9150

⅃₆, ⌷ – 🛗, ⤨ rm, ▤ 📺 📞 🅟 – 🔀 500. ⑩ AE ① *VISA* ᴊᴄʙ

Sage *:* Meals a la carte 22.00/40.00 s. Ⴘ – ⊐ 16.00 – **347 rm** 186.00/211.00,
3 suites.

♦ At the quieter end of the airport. Well known for its unique indoor pool
surrounded by a tropical garden; overlooked by many of the bedrooms.
Business centre available. Classically decorated dining room.

Hilton London Heathrow Airport
p. 12   AX   n

Terminal 4, TW6 3AF, ℘ (020) 8759 7755, *gm_heathrow@hilton.com,*
Fax (020) 8759 7579

⅃₆, ⇌s, ⌷ – 🛗, ⤨ rm, ▤ 📺 📞 ⬇, 🅟 – 🔀 240. ⑩ AE ① *VISA* ᴊᴄʙ

Brasserie *:* Meals 23.50/29.50 and dinner a la carte 19.10/29.80 s. Ⴘ
Zen Oriental *:* Meals - Chinese - 28.80/38.50 and a la carte 19.70/42.20 –
⊐ 18.50 – **390 rm** 176.25/287.80, 5 suites.

♦ Group hotel with a striking modern exterior and linked to Terminal 4
by a covered walkway. Good sized bedrooms, with contemporary styled
suites. Spacious Brasserie in vast atrium. Zen Oriental offers formal Chinese
experience.

London Heathrow Marriott
p. 12   AX   z

Bath Rd, Hayes, UB3 5AN, ℘ (020) 8990 1100, *Fax (020) 8990 1110*

⅃₆, ⇌s, ⌷ – 🛗, ⤨ rm, ▤ 📺 📞 ⬇, 🅟 – 🔀 540. ⑩ AE ① *VISA.* ⚔

Tuscany *:* Meals - Italian -*(closed Sunday)* (dinner only) a la carte 25.00/
37.00

Allie's grille *:* Meals a la carte 22.00/31.40 Ⴘ – ⊐ 16.45 **388 rm** 160.00/
200.00, 2 suites

♦ A recent addition to the airport, built in 1999. Modern and comfortable,
centred around a large atrium, with lounges. Tuscany's is bright and convivial.
Allie's a grill room.

Le Meridien Heathrow
p. 12   AX   x

Bath Rd, West Drayton, UB7 0DU, ℘ (020) 8759 6611, *reservations.heathrow@
lemeridien.com, Fax (020) 8759 3421*

⅃₆, ⌷ – 🛗, ⤨ rm, ▤ 📺 ⬇, 🅟 – 🔀 700. ⑩ AE ① *VISA* ᴊᴄʙ. ⚔

Meals *(closed Saturday lunch)* (carvery) 22.95

Snappers *:* Meals *(closed July and August)* a la carte 31.80/44.80 Ⴘ – ⊐ 14.95
– **525 rm** 146.80/182.10, 10 suites.

♦ One of the airport's larger hotels, with extensive banqueting and leisure
facilities. Bedrooms are spacious and comfortable, especially the modern
Royal Club rooms. Large, traveller-friendly carvery. Snappers is smart, long-
standing restaurant.

Holiday Inn London Heathrow
p. 8 AV C

Sipson Rd, West Drayton, UB7 0JU, ℘ (0870) 4008595, *Fax (020) 8897 8659*

|⬆|, � rm, 🖳 📺 &. P – 🏃 140. 🆖 🆎 ⓪ *VISA* JCB. ✍

Sampans *:* **Meals** - Chinese - (dinner only) 8.95/19.00 and a la carte 25.45/29.45 **s.**

Rotisserie *:* **Meals** 8.95/19.00 and a la carte 25.45/29.45 **s.** – ⌒ 15.95 – **604 rm** 170.00, 6 suites.

♦ Busy group hotel where the Academy conference suite attracts the business community. Bedrooms come in a variety of styles. Popular Irish bar. Sampans offers regional Chinese dishes. Spacious Rotisserie with chef carving to order.

Renaissance London Heathrow
p. 12 AX C

Bath Rd, TW6 2AQ, ℘ (020) 8897 6363, *ihrrenaissance@aol.com, Fax (020) 8897 1113*

ⅠჇ, ⊜S – |⬆|, � rm, 🖳 📺 ☎ &. P – 🏃 550. 🆖 🆎 ⓪ *VISA* JCB. ✍

Meals 18.50/21.50 and a la carte 20.40/25.40 **s.** ♀ – ⌒ 13.95 – **644 rm** 189.00, 5 suites.

♦ Low level façade belies the size of this easily accessible hotel. Large lounge and assorted shops in the lobby. Some of the soundproofed bedrooms have views of the runway. Open-plan restaurant with buffet or à la carte.

Sheraton Heathrow
p. 12 AVX a

Colnbrook bypass, West Drayton, UB7 0HJ, ℘ (020) 8759 2424, *res293.heathrow@sheraton.com, Fax (020) 8759 2091*

ⅠჇ – |⬆|, � rm, 🖳 📺 ☎ P – 🏃 70. 🆖 🆎 ⓪ *VISA*. ✍

Meals 17.50/19.75 and a la carte 18.15/32.95 **s.** ♀ – ⌒ 14.50 – **421 rm** 210.00, 3 suites.

♦ International group hotel where corporate travellers benefit from the business centre, open 24 hours a day. Large work areas and good mod cons in all the bedrooms. Airy, bright dining room with live entertainment.

Holiday Inn Heathrow Ariel
p. 12 AX i

118 Bath Rd, Hayes, UB3 5AJ, ℘ (0870) 400 9040, *reservations-heathrow@posthouse-hotels.com, Fax (020) 8564 9265*

|⬆|, � rm, 🖳 rest, 📺 P – 🏃 55. 🆖 🆎 ⓪ *VISA*

Meals (bar lunch Saturday) (buffet lunch) 13.95 – ⌒ 14.95 – **186 rm** 159.00.

♦ Usefully located hotel, in a cylindrical shape. Bedrooms decorated in a modern, Scandinavian style with light woods and warm colours. Several conference rooms available. Subtly-lit, relaxing restaurant.

Travelodge
p. 12 AX x

Sipson Rd, West Drayton, UB7 0UD, ℘ (08700) 850950, *Fax (020) 8897 6381*

|⬆| ✍ 🖳 📺 &. P. 🆖 🆎 ⓪ *VISA* JCB. ✍

Meals (grill rest.) – **289 rm** 49.95.

♦ Modern lodge-style budget hotel offering clean and spacious accommodation. All bedrooms benefit from having a large work area and an extra sofa-bed.

Simply Nico Heathrow (at Crowne Plaza London Heathrow H.)

Stockley Rd, West Drayton, UB7 9NA, ℘ (01895) 437564, *heathrow@simplynico.co.uk, Fax (01895) 437565*
p. 12 AV v

🖳 P. 🆖 🆎 ⓪ *VISA*

closed Sunday and Bank Holidays – **Meals** 12.95 (lunch) and a la carte 24.95/29.40 ♀.

♦ Located within the hotel but with its own personality. Mixes modern with more classically French dishes. Professional service in comfortable surroundings.

If you are held up on the road - from 6pm onwards -
confirm your hotel booking by telephone.
It is safer and quite an accepted practice.

HOUNSLOW *Gtr London.*

🏌 *Wyke Green, Syon Lane, Isleworth* ✆ *(020) 8560 8777* **BV** – 🏌 *Airlinks, Southall Lane* ✆ *(020) 8561 1418* **ABV** – 🏌 *Hounslow Heath, Staines Rd* ✆ *(020) 8570 5271* **BX**.

🏛 *24 The Treaty Centre, High St* ✆ *(020) 8572 8279 (closed Sunday).*

Chiswick *Middx –* ✉ *W4.*

XX La Trompette   p. 13   CV   Z
5-7 Devonshire Rd, W4 2EU, ✆ *(020) 8747 1836, latrompette@btconnect. com, Fax (020) 8995 8097*
🏛 – 🍽. **①②** **AE** **VISA**
closed 24-26 December – **Meals** 19.50/30.00 ⚲.
♦ Terraced property on smart residential street. Open-plan restaurant with linen laid tables and a bustling atmosphere. Daily menus of French influenced robust modern dishes.

X Dumela   p. 13   CV   Z
42 Devonshire Rd, W4 2HD, ✆ *(020) 8742 3149, info@springbokcafecusine. com, Fax (020) 8742 8541*
①② **VISA**
closed Sunday – **Meals** - South African - (dinner only) a la carte 22.00/ 38.50 ⚲.
♦ The open-plan kitchen lets diners feel involved in the cooking of the South African menu. Chef owner has created a relaxed environment, with his home-land-inspired décor.

X Fish Hoek   p. 13   CV   r
W4 1PE, ✆ (020) 8742 0766, *info@springbokcafecuisine.com, Fax (020) 8742 3374*
①② **VISA**
closed 10 days Christmas-New Year – **Meals** - Seafood - a la carte 19.00/ 31.00.
♦ Smart interior with tiled floor and fishing photos on the walls. Menu offers a wide selection of seafood from around the world, prepared with care and competence.

X The Chiswick   p. 13   CV   e
131 Chiswick High Rd, W4 2ED, ✆ *(020) 8994 6887, thechiswick@aol.com, Fax (020) 8994 5504*
🏛 – 🍽. **①②** **AE** **VISA**
closed 25-26 December, 1 January, Saturday lunch, Sunday dinner and Bank Holidays – **Meals** 12.95 and a la carte 20.50/30.50 **s**. ⚲.
♦ Bare wooden tables and chairs and T-shirted staff add to the informal atmosphere. Usually busy and bustling with locals. Various European influen-ces on the modern menu.

X Pug   p. 13   CV   n
68 Chiswick High Rd, W4 1SY, ✆ *(020) 8987 9988, Fax (020) 8987 9911*
🏛 – 🍽. **①②** **AE** **VISA**
Meals 14.95 and a la carte 21.00/29.00 ⚲.
♦ Wood-floored restaurant with simple décor and dark wood tables, adjoins leather furnished bar and lounge area. Daily changing modern menus with Mediterranean influences.

*If you are held up on the road - from 6pm onwards -
confirm your hotel booking by telephone.
It is safer and quite an accepted practice.*

Feltham *Middx* – ⊠ *Middx*.

 ### St Giles
p. 12 **AX** v
Hounslow Rd, TW14 9AD, ✆ (020) 8817 7000, book@stgiles.com, *Fax (020) 8817 7001*
≤, ƒₛ – ⃝, ⊱⊰ rm, ▤ TV ⅗ P – ⌖ 120. ⊕ AE ⊙ VISA. ⊱
closed 24-26 December – **Meals** - Italian - *(closed lunch Saturday and Sunday)* a la carte 22.00/28.00 **s.** – ☕ 9.95 – **292 rm** 119.00/129.00, 8 suites.
♦ Modern, purpose-built hotel, providing useful accommodation near Heathrow. Large marbled lobby; brightly coloured bedrooms. Higher floors boast good views. Dining room, bar and lounge merge into one.

Heston Service Area *Middx* – ⊠ *Middx*.

 ### Travelodge
p. 12 **ABV** e
TW5 9NB, on M 4 (between junctions 2 and 3 westbound carriageway), ✆ (08700) 850950, *Fax (020) 8580 2006*
without rest. – ⊱⊰ TV ⅗ P. ⊕ AE ⊙ VISA JCB. ⊱
145 rm 49.95.
♦ Convenient for Heathrow airport, lodge accommodation in a busy service area. Bedrooms all have work desks and family rooms will sleep four people.

Travelodge
p. 12 **AV** s
TW5 9NA, on M 4 (between junctions 3 and 2 on eastbound carriageway), ✆ (08700) 850950, *Fax (020) 8580 2128*
⊱⊰ rm, TV ⅗ P. ⊕ AE ⊙ VISA JCB. ⊱
Meals (grill rest.) – **66 rm** 49.95.
♦ Lodge hotel providing clean, comfortable and affordable accommodation. Little Chef restaurant adjacent offers an all-day family-oriented menu.

Prices
For notes on the prices quoted in this Guide, see the explanatory pages.

ISLINGTON *Gtr London*.

Archway – ⊠ *N19*.

 ### The Parsee
p. 10 **EU** a
34 Highgate Hill, N19 5NL, ✆ (020) 7272 9091, dining@theparsee.co.uk, *Fax (020) 7687 1139*
▤. ⊕ AE ⊙ VISA
closed 25-26 December, 1 January and Sunday – **Meals** - Indian (Parsee) - (dinner only) 20.00/30.00 and a la carte 21.00/24.70 ⓩ.
♦ Two brightly painted rooms, one non smoking and featuring a painting of a Parsee Angel. Good value, interesting, carefully spiced cuisine, Persian and Indian in inspiration.

 ### St John's
p. 10 **EU** s
91 Junction Rd, N19 5QU, ✆ (020) 7272 1587, stjohnsarchway@virgin.net, *Fax (020) 7272 8023*
⊕ AE VISA
closed 25-26 December, 1 January and Monday lunch – **Meals** a la carte 18.00/24.50 ⓩ.
♦ Busy front bar enjoys a lively atmosphere; dining room in a large rear room. Log fire at one end, open hatch into kitchen the other. Blackboard menu; rustic cooking.

Barnsbury *Gtr London –* ✉ *N1.*

✕ **The Dining Room** p. 26 **MS** **a**
169 Hemingford Rd, N1 1DA, ✆ (020) 7609 3009
closed 1 week Christmas, Sunday dinner and Monday – **Meals** (dinner only
and Sunday lunch) a la carte 17.00/25.50.
◆ Simple, attractive and cosy neighbourhood restaurant with dark blue walls
and mirrors. Open hatch into kitchen. Well-balanced, robust, honest cooking
at a fair price.

Canonbury *Gtr London –* ✉ *N1.*

🍴 **Centuria** p. 10 **FU** **v**
100 St Paul's Rd, N1 2QP, ✆ (020) 7704 2345
M◉ **VISA** **JCB**
closed lunch Monday-Friday – **Meals** a la carte 17.00/22.70 ♀.
◆ Large pub in a residential area, with the dining room separate from the
busy bar. Open-plan kitchen produces a modern menu, with a subtle Italian
twist. Leisurely service.

Clerkenwell *Gtr London –* ✉ *EC1.*

🏠 **The Rookery** p. 27 **NU** **O**
12 Peters Lane, Cowcross St, EC1M 6DS, ✆ (020) 7336 0931, *reservations@
rookery.co.uk, Fax (020) 7336 0932*
without rest. – **TV** **☎** **M◉** **AE** **①** **VISA** **JCB**
closed 24-25 December – ☕ 8.95 – **32 rm** 235.00/282.00, 1 suite.
◆ A row of charmingly restored 18C houses. Wood panelling, stone-flagged
flooring, open fires and antique furniture. Highly individual bedrooms, with
Victorian bathrooms.

✕✕ **Maison Novelli** p. 27 **NU** **a**
29 Clerkenwell Green, EC1R 0DU, ✆ (020) 7251 6606, *jcnovelli@wslrestaurants.
co.uk, Fax (020) 7490 1083*
▤ , **M◉** **AE** **①** **VISA**
closed Saturday lunch, Sunday and Bank Holidays – **Meals** a la carte 28.50/
34.00 ♀.
◆ Brightly decorated restaurant on two floors, with earnest and keen
young waiting staff. Kitchen produces skilled cuisine with a degree of
originality.

✕✕ **Smiths of Smithfield** p. 27 **NU** **S**
Top Floor, 67-77 Charterhouse St, EC1M 6HJ, ✆ (020) 7251 7950, *smiths@
smithfield.co.uk, Fax (020) 7236 5666*
≤, 🌣 – ♦ ▤. **M◉** **AE** **①** **VISA**
closed 25-26 December, 1 January and Saturday lunch – **Meals** a la carte
30.50/44.00 ♀
The Dining Room : **Meals** *closed Saturday lunch and Sunday* a la carte 19.25/
20.25 ♀.
◆ On three floors where the higher you go the more formal it becomes.
Busy, bustling atmosphere and modern menu. Good views of the market
from the top floor terrace. The Dining Room with mirrors and dark blue
walls.

XX **Gaudi** p. 27 NU z

63 Clerkenwell Rd, EC1M 5PT, ✆ (020) 7608 3220, *gaudi@turnmills.co.uk, Fax (020) 7250 1057*

🖃, 🕝 AE ① VISA

closed 25-31 December, Saturday lunch, Sunday and Bank Holiday Monday – **Meals** - Spanish - 15.00/35.00 and a la carte 24.90/36.00 ℤ.

♦ Tiled restaurant where the Art Nouveau decoration is inspired by the great architect. Inventive Spanish cooking, on view from the open-plan kitchen.

X **St John** p. 27 OU c

26 St John St, EC1M 4AY, ✆ (020) 7251 0848, *reservations@stjohnrestaurant. co.uk, Fax (020) 7251 4090*

🖃, 🕝 AE ① VISA JCB

closed 24 December, 1 January, Easter, Saturday lunch and Sunday – **Meals** a la carte 29.50/38.00 ℤ.

♦ Deservedly busy converted 19C former smokehouse. Popular bar, simple comforts. Menu specialises in offal and an original mix of traditional and rediscovered English dishes.

🍴 **The Bear** p. 27 NU c

No 2 St Johns Sq, EC1M 4DE, ✆ (020) 7608 2117, *Fax (020) 7608 2116*

🖃, 🕝 VISA

closed Saturday and Sunday – **Meals** a la carte 16.85/21.85 ℤ.

♦ Well-run modern pub in a quiet square on edge of the City. Busy ground floor bar and tranquil first floor drinking and dining area. Eclectic menu of mainly European dishes.

Finsbury *Gtr London* – ✉ *WC1/EC1/EC2.*

XX **The Clerkenwell Dining Room** p. 26 NOU i

69-73 St John St, EC1M 4AN, ✆ (020) 7253 9000, *Fax (020) 7253 3322*

🖃, 🕝 AE ① VISA JCB

closed 24-26 December, Saturday lunch and Sunday – **Meals** 15.50 (lunch) and a la carte 24.75/33.00 **s.**

♦ Former pub, now a stylish modern restaurant with etched glass façade. Three adjoining dining areas. Good value, contemporary British cooking.

X **Café Lazeez City** p. 27 OU e

88 St John St, EC1M 4EH, ✆ (020) 7253 2224, *clerkenwell@cafelazeez.com, Fax (020) 7253 2112*

🖃, 🕝 AE ① VISA JCB

closed Sunday and Bank Holidays – **Meals** - North Indian - 12.00 (lunch) and a la carte 18.45/28.05 ℤ.

♦ Past the busy bar into this modern Indian restaurant. Has a certain warehouse feel, with a high ceiling and wood flooring. North Indian cooking from the open-plan kitchen.

X **Quality Chop House** p. 26 MT n

94 Farringdon Rd, EC1R 3EA, ✆ (020) 7837 5093, *qualitychophouse@clara.co. uk, Fax (020) 7833 8748*

✂ 🖃, 🕝 AE VISA

closed 24 December-2 January and Saturday lunch – **Meals** a la carte 21.25/ 32.25.

♦ On the window is etched "Progressive working class caterers". This is borne out with the individual café-style booths and a menu ranging from jellied eels to caviar.

Moro
p. 27   NT   a

34-36 Exmouth Market, EC1R 4QE, ℰ (020) 7833 8336, *info@moro.co.uk,
Fax (020) 7833 9338*

📠, 🅼🅲 🄰🄴 🅾 𝗩𝗜𝗦𝗔

closed 22 December-2 January, Saturday lunch and Sunday – **Meals** (booking
essential) a la carte 24.50/27.00 ♀.

◆ Daily changing menu an eclectic mix of Mediterranean, Moroccan and
Spanish. Friendly T-shirted staff. Informal surroundings with bare tables and a
large zinc bar.

The Peasant
p. 27   NT   e

240 St John St, EC1V 4PH, ℰ (020) 7336 7726, *eat@thepeasant.co.uk,
Fax (020) 7490 1089*

🅼🅲 🄰🄴 𝗩𝗜𝗦𝗔

closed 1 week Christmas-New Year, Saturday lunch and Sunday – **Meals**
(booking essential) 14.00 (lunch) and a la carte 19.00/23.00 ♀.

◆ Large, busy pub with half of the ground floor given over as a bar. Dining
continues in the high-ceilinged room upstairs. Robust and rustic cooking
with generous portions.

Highbury *Gtr London* – ✉ N7.

Au Lac
p. 10   FU   a

82 Highbury Park, N5 2XE, ℰ (020) 7704 9187, *Fax (0207) 704 9187*

📠, 🅼🅲 🅾 𝗩𝗜𝗦𝗔

closed lunch Saturday and Sunday – **Meals** - Vietnamese - a la carte approx.
17.50.

◆ Cosy Vietnamese restaurant, with brightly coloured walls and painted fans.
Large menus with Vietnamese dishes usefully highlighted. Fresh flavours;
good value.

Islington *Gtr London* – ✉ N1.

Hilton London Islington
p. 27   NS   s

53 Upper St, N1 0UY, ℰ (020) 7354 7700, *reservations@islington.stakis.co.uk,
Fax (020) 7354 7711*

🏠, 🖐, 🛄 – 🛗, ↦ rm, 📺 ✆ 👍 – 🕍 35. 🅼🅲 🄰🄴 🅾 𝗩𝗜𝗦𝗔 🄹🄲🄱.
🕸

Meals *(closed Sunday lunch)* a la carte 22.50/29.00 ♀ – ⊇ 16.00 – **178 rm**
160.90, 6 suites.

◆ Benefits from its location adjacent to the Business Design Centre. A
purpose-built hotel with all bedrooms enjoying the appropriate creature
comforts. Open-plan brasserie with small bar.

Jurys Inn London
p. 26   MT   e

60 Pentonville Rd, N1 9LA, ℰ (020) 7282 5500, *jurysinnlondon@jurysdoyle.
com, Fax (020) 7282 5511*

🛗, ↦ rm, 📺 ✆ 👍 – 🕍 40. 🅼🅲 🄰🄴 🅾 𝗩𝗜𝗦𝗔. 🕸

closed 24-26 December – **Meals** (bar lunch)/dinner 18.00 **s.** and a la carte –
⊇ 10.00 – **229 rm** 99.00.

◆ A corporate group hotel with good local transport links. Large lobby leads
off the characterful Irish themed pub. Uniform-sized bedrooms, all well-
equipped.

XX **Lola's**   p. 27 NS n
The Mall, 359 Upper St, N1 0PD, ℘ (020) 7359 1932, *lolas@lolas.co.uk,*
Fax (020) 7359 2209
📧. 🆖 AE ⓪ VISA
closed 25-26 December, 1 January and Bank Holidays – **Meals** 17.75 (lunch)
and a la carte 27.25/39.75 �.
♦ On the first floor of a converted tram shed, with 'wine flight' menu. Bright
and airy, with glass ceiling and pieces of art. Modern British cooking; urbane
service.

XX **Frederick's**   p. 27 NS c
Camden Passage, N1 8EG, ℘ (020) 7359 2888, *eat@fredericks.co.uk,*
Fax (020) 7359 5173
🏡, 🌿 – 📧. 🆖 AE ⓪ VISA JCB
closed Sunday and Bank Holidays – **Meals** 15.50 (lunch) and a la carte 28.00/
32.50 ℨ.
♦ Long-standing restaurant among the antique shops of Camden Passage.
Attractive garden and al fresco dining; main room with large, plant-filled
conservatory.

XX **Almeida**   p. 26 NS r
30 Almeida St, N1 1AD, ℘ (020) 7354 4777, *oliviere@conran-restaurants.*
co.uk, Fax (020) 7354 2777
📧. 🆖 AE ⓪ VISA JCB
closed 25-26 December and 1-2 January – **Meals** - French - 17.50 (lunch)
and a la carte 19.50/37.50 ℨ.
♦ Spacious, open plan restaurant with pleasant contemporary styling
adjacent to Almeida Theatre. Large à la carte: a collection of classic French
dishes.

XX **Metrogusto**   p. 27 NS e
13 Theberton St, N1 0QY, ℘ (020) 7226 9400, *Fax (020) 7226 9400*
✦✕ 📧. 🆖 AE VISA
closed Bank Holidays and lunch Monday-Thursday – **Meals** - Italian - 14.50
(lunch) and a la carte 19.45/26.50 ℨ.
♦ Stylish and smart with a contemporary feel. Dining in two rooms with art
on the walls and a relaxed atmosphere. Modern Italian food using flair and
fine ingredients.

X **Granita**   p. 27 NS a
127 Upper St, N1 1QP, ℘ (020) 7226 3222, *Fax (020) 7226 4833*
📧. 🆖 ⓪ VISA
Meals 12.50 (lunch) and a la carte 21.00/29.50 ℨ.
♦ Boldly minimalist, well-established restaurant with a cosmopolitan
clientele. Pleasant and attentive service from young team. Modern menu
with global influences.

🏠 **Drapers Arms**   p. 26 NS x
44 Barnsbury St, N1 1ER, ℘ (020) 7619 0348, *Fax (020) 7619 0413*
🏡 – 🆖 VISA
closed 24-27 December – **Meals** a la carte 17.00/28.50 ℨ.
♦ Real presence to the façade of this Georgian pub tucked away in a quiet
residential area. Spacious modern interior where competent, contemporary
dishes are served.

🍸 The Northgate
p. 27 **PS** a

113 Southgate Rd, N1 3JS, ☏ (020) 7359 7392, *Fax (020) 7359 7393*

🛜 – 🆎 *VISA* **JCB**

closed 24-26 December and 1 January – **Meals** (dinner only and lunch Saturday and Sunday) a la carte 19.80/23.50 ☨.

♦ Corner pub with wood flooring and modern art on display. Rear dining area with a large blackboard menu offering a cross section of internationally influenced modern dishes.

KENSINGTON and CHELSEA (Royal Borough of) *Gtr London*.

Chelsea *Gtr London* – ✉ SW1/SW3/SW10.

🏨 Carlton Tower
p. 35 **FR** n

Cadogan Pl, SW1X 9PY, ☏ (020) 7235 1234, *contact@carltontower.com, Fax (020) 7235 9129*

≤, 🛁, ⊆s, 🔲, 🐎, ℅ – ⬆, ⟴ rm, 🖥 📺 ☏ 🚗 – 🔒 400. 🆎 **AE** ⓪ *VISA* **JCB**. ℅

Rib Room : **Meals** 40.00/52.00 and a la carte 30.00/49.00

Grissini : **Meals** - Italian - *(closed Saturday lunch and Sunday dinner)* 27.00 (lunch) and a la carte 27.00/38.00 ☨ – ⊑ 19.50 – **191 rm** 346.60/376.00, 29 suites.

♦ Imposing international hotel overlooking a leafy square. 'The Peak' health club is particularly well-equipped. Generously proportioned rooms have every conceivable facility. Rib Room restaurant has a clubby atmosphere. Grissini boasts domed glass canopy

🏨 Conrad London
p. 17 **CQ** i

Chelsea Harbour, SW10 0XG, ☏ (020) 7823 3000, *Fax (020) 7351 6525*

≤, 🛁, ⊆s, 🔲 – ⬆, ⟴ rm, 🖥 📺 ☏ 🔥 🚗 – 🔒 200. 🆎 **AE** ⓪ *VISA* **JCB**

Meals – (see *Aquasia* below) – ⊑ 18.50, **160 suites** 282.00/329.00.

♦ Modern, all-suite hotel within an exclusive marina and retail development. Many of the spacious and well-appointed rooms have balconies and views across the Thames.

🏨 Sheraton Park Tower
p. 35 **FQ** v

101 Knightsbridge, SW1X 7RN, ☏ (020) 7235 8050, *central.london.reservations@sheraton.com, Fax (020) 7235 8231*

≤, 🛁 – ⬆, ⟴ rm, 🖥 📺 ☏ 🔥 🚗 – 🔒 100. 🆎 **AE** ⓪ *VISA* **JCB**. ℅

Meals – (see *One-O-One* below) – ⊑ 21.75 – **258 rm** 446.50/470.00, 22 suites.

♦ Built in the 1970s in a unique cylindrical shape. Well-equipped bedrooms are all identical in size. Top floor executive rooms have commanding views of Hyde Park and City.

🏛 Capital
p. 35 **ER** a

ॐॐ 22-24 Basil St, SW3 1AT, ☏ (020) 7589 5171, *reservations@capitalhotel.co.uk, Fax (020) 7225 0011*

⬆, ⟴ rm, 🖥 📺 ☏ 🚗 – 🔒 25. 🆎 **AE** ⓪ *VISA* **JCB**. ℅

Meals (booking essential) 27.50/54.00 ☨ – ⊑ 16.50 – **48 rm** 229.00/440.00.

♦ Discreet and privately owned town house with distinct English charm. Individual, opulently decorated rooms with plenty of thoughtful touches. Elegant and intimate restaurant.

Spec. Seared langoustines, deep-fried chorizo, red pepper bruschetta. Pot-roast pigeon, potato and bacon galette, truffle jus. Iced coffee parfait, chocolate fondant.

The Cadogan
p. 35 **FR** e

75 Sloane St, SW1X 9SG, ℘ (020) 7235 7141, *info@cadogan.com, Fax (020) 7245 0994*

🚗, ✗ – |♦|, ✗ rm, ▤ rest, 📺 ☏ – ♨ 40. ⓜ ⅢⒺ 𝘝𝘐𝘚𝘈
Meals *(closed Saturday lunch)* 18.90/28.50 and a la carte 38.50/47.50 **s.** ♀ –
⚏ 16.50 – **61 rm** 164.50/282.00, 4 suites.
♦ A true English hotel retaining many Edwardian features: Oscar Wilde was arrested here. Charming wood panelled drawing room. Smart bedrooms in a country house style. Discreet, cosy wood panelled restaurant.

Chelsea Village
p. 28 **FZ** n

Fulham Rd, SW6 1HS, ℘ (020) 7565 1400, *reservations@chelseavillage.com, Fax (020) 7565 1450*

🛁, ⬆, ▤ – |♦|, ✗ rm, ▤ 📺 ☏ ♿ Ⓟ – ♨ 600. ⓜ ⅢⒺ ⓞ 𝘝𝘐𝘚𝘈, ✗
***Fishnets :* Meals** - Seafood - a la carte 22.00/28.00
***Kings brasserie :* Meals** a la carte 25.00/29.00 – ⚏ 14.00 – **288 rm** 160.00,
3 suites.
♦ Modern, corporate hotel beside, and owned by, Chelsea Football Club. Bright and spacious bedrooms split between main hotel and adjacent Court. Capacious Fishnets restaurant has nautical theme. Kings a modern brasserie.

Durley House
p. 35 **FS** e

115 Sloane St, SW1X 9PJ, ℘ (020) 7235 5537, *info@durleyhouse.com, Fax (020) 7259 6977*

🚗, ✗ – |♦| 📺 ☏. ⓜ ⅢⒺ 𝘝𝘐𝘚𝘈, ✗
Meals (room service only) – ⚏ 18.50, **11 suites** 423.00/616.80.
♦ Exclusive, all-suite Georgian town house overlooking an attractive square. Charming drawing room with honesty bar. Individual, richly furnished rooms. Attentive service.

Basil Street
p. 35 **FQ** o

8 Basil St, SW3 1AH, ℘ (020) 7581 3311, *info@thebasil.com, Fax (020) 7581 3693*

|♦|, ✗ rm, 📺 ☏ – ♨ 30. ⓜ ⅢⒺ 𝘝𝘐𝘚𝘈 ᴊᴄʙ, ✗
Meals 21.00/25.00 – ⚏ 15.00 – **80 rm** 170.30/240.80.
♦ Classic English hotel in a pleasant residential road between Harrods and Harvey Nichols. Exclusive ladies only lounge. Traditionally furnished rooms with modern amenities. Dining room boasts rich style of a bygone era.

Cliveden Town House
p. 35 **FS** c

26 Cadogan Gdns, SW3 2RP, ℘ (020) 7730 6466, *reservations@clivedentown house.co.uk, Fax (020) 7730 0236*

🚗 – |♦|, ✗ rm, ▤ rm, 📺 ☏. ⓜ ⅢⒺ ⓞ 𝘝𝘐𝘚𝘈
Meals (room service only) – ⚏ 18.50 – **31 rm** 200.00/340.00, 4 suites.
♦ Charming Victorian house in an exclusive residential area. Elegant sitting room overlooks the tranquil communal garden. Individually decorated rooms in a country house style.

Millennium Knightsbridge
p. 35 **FR** r

17-25 Sloane St, SW1X 9NU, ℘ (020) 7235 4377, *reservations-knightsbridge@ mill-cop.com, Fax (020) 7235 3705*

|♦| ✗ ▤ 📺 ☏ ♿ – ♨ 120. ⓜ ⅢⒺ ⓞ 𝘝𝘐𝘚𝘈, ✗
Meals – (see ***Mju*** below) – ⚏ 17.50 – **218 rm** 211.50/329.50, 4 suites.
♦ Modern, corporate hotel in the heart of London's most fashionable shopping district. Bedrooms are well-appointed and equipped with the latest technology.

Franklin
p. 35 DS e

22-28 Egerton Gdns, SW3 2DB, ℰ (020) 7584 5533, *bookings@franklinhotel.co .uk, Fax (020) 7584 5449*

🛏 – 🛗 ▤ TV 📞 ⬛ AE ⓪ VISA . ✗

Meals (room service only) a la carte 24.50/32.50 **s.** ♀ – ⊑ 16.50 – **47 rm** 188.00/380.00.

♦ Attractive Victorian town house in an exclusive residential area. Charming drawing room overlooks a tranquil communal garden. Well-furnished rooms in a country house style.

Knightsbridge
p. 35 ER s

10 Beaufort Gdns, SW3 1PT, ℰ (020) 7584 6300, *knightsbridge@firmdale.com, Fax (020) 7584 6355*

🛗 ▤ TV 📞 ⬛ AE VISA . ✗

Meals (room service only) – **44 rm** ⊑ 135.00/165.00.

♦ Attractively furnished town house with a very stylish, discreet feel. Every bedroom is immaculately appointed and has an individuality of its own; fine detailing throughout.

The London Outpost of the Carnegie Club
p. 35 FS r

69 Cadogan Gdns, SW3 2RB, ℰ (020) 7589 7333, *info@londonoutpost.co.uk, Fax (020) 7581 4958*

without rest., 🛏 – 🛗 ⬥ ▤ TV . ⬛ AE ⓪ VISA JCB

closed 24-26 December – ⊑ 16.95 – **11 rm** 188.00/317.25.

♦ Classic town house in a most fashionable area. Relaxed and comfy lounges full of English charm. Bedrooms, named after local artists and writers, full of thoughtful touches.

The Sloane
p.35 ET c

29 Draycott Pl, SW3 2SH, ℰ (020) 7581 5757, *reservations@sloanehotel.com, Fax (020) 7584 1348*

🛗 ⬥ rm, ▤ TV 📞 . ⬛ AE ⓪ VISA JCB . ✗

Meals (room service) – ⊑ 12.00 – **22 rm** 176.20/282.00.

♦ Intimate and discreet Victorian town house with an attractive rooftop terrace. Individually styled and generally spacious rooms with antique furniture and rich fabrics.

Eleven Cadogan Gardens
p. 35 FS u

11 Cadogan Gdns, SW3 2RJ, ℰ (020) 7730 7000, *reservations@number-eleven .co.uk, Fax (020) 7730 5217*

ⓘ, ⇔, 🛏 – 🛗 TV 📞 . ⬛ AE ⓪ VISA JCB . ✗

Meals (room service) – ⊑ 13.00 – **56 rm** 168.00/298.00, 4 suites.

♦ Occupying four Victorian houses, one of London's first private town house hotels. Traditionally appointed bedrooms vary considerably in size. Genteel atmosphere.

Egerton House
p. 35 DR e

17-19 Egerton Terr, SW3 2BX, ℰ (020) 7589 2412, *bookings@egertonhouseho tel.co.uk, Fax (020) 7584 6540*

🛗 ▤ TV 📞 . ⬛ AE ⓪ VISA JCB . ✗

Meals (room service only) – ⊑ 16.00 – **29 rm** 188.00/293.00.

♦ Stylish redbrick Victorian town house close to the exclusive shops. Relaxed drawing room popular for afternoon tea. Antique furnished and individually decorated rooms.

Beaufort p. 35 **ER** **n**

33 Beaufort Gdns, SW3 1PP, ℰ (020) 7584 5252, *enquiries@thebeaufort.co.uk, Fax (020) 7589 2834*

without rest. – 📶 ⤢ ▤ 📺 ☎. ⓜⓞ ΛΕ ⓞ *VISA* . ⅍
28 rm 193.80/305.00.

♦ English floral watercolours adorn the walls throughout this elegant Victorian town house. Attractive and restful rooms. Tariff includes all drinks and continental breakfast.

 Parkes p. 35 **ER** **x**

41 Beaufort Gdns, SW3 1PW, ℰ (020) 7581 9944, *reception@parkeshotel.com, Fax (020) 7581 1999*

without rest. – 📶 ▤ 📺 ☎. ⓜⓞ ΛΕ ⓞ *VISA* Jᴄʙ. ⅍
⊟ 10.00 – **19 rm** 229.00/282.00, 14 suites 381.00/487.00.

♦ Behind the portico entrance one finds a well-kept private hotel. The generally spacious and high ceilinged rooms are pleasantly decorated. Friendly and personally run.

 Myhotel Chelsea p. 35 **DT** **z**

35 Ixworth Pl, SW3 3QX, ℰ (020) 7225 7500, *Fax (020) 7225 7555*
📶 ⤢ ▤ 📺 ☎ – ⩎ 80. ⓜⓞ ΛΕ ⓞ *VISA* Jᴄʙ
Meals a la carte 16.00/34.00 – ⊟ 12.50 – **41 rm** 170.30/217.30, 4 suites.

♦ Restored Victorian property in a fairly quiet and smart side street. Conservatory breakfast room. Modern and well-equipped rooms are ideal for the corporate traveller.

 57 Pont Street p. 35 **ER** **e**

57 Pont St, SW1X 0BD, ℰ (020) 7590 1090, *no57@no57.com, Fax (020) 7590 1099*

without rest. – 📶 ▤ 📺 ☎ – ⩎ 30. ⓜⓞ ΛΕ ⓞ *VISA* Jᴄʙ. ⅍
⊟ 10.00 – **20 rm** 146.00/205.00.

♦ Small, friendly, modern townhouse with discreet plaque at the end of Pont Street. Basement breakfast room and sitting room with deep brown suede chairs. Snug, modern rooms.

L'Hotel p. 35 **ER** **i**

28 Basil St, SW3 1AS, ℰ (020) 7589 6286, *reservations@lhotel.co.uk, Fax (020) 7823 7826*

📶, ▤ rest, 📺 ⇦. ⓜⓞ ΛΕ ⓞ *VISA* Jᴄʙ. ⅍
Le Metro : **Meals** *(closed 25 December, Sunday dinner and Bank Holidays)* a la carte 18.00/21.00 ♀ – **12 rm** 176.25/211.50.

♦ Discreet town house a short walk from Harrods. Wooden shutters, pine furniture and stencilled walls provide a subtle rural theme. Well-appointed, comfy and informally run. Basement café dining.

Sloane Square Moat House p. 35 **FST** **v**

Sloane Sq, SW1W 8EG, ℰ (020) 7896 9988, *cbdrl@queensmoat.co.uk, Fax (020) 7824 8381*

📶 ⤢ 📺 ☎ – ⩎ 40. ⓜⓞ ΛΕ ⓞ *VISA*
Meals – (see *Simply Nico* below) – ⊟ 8.50 – **105 rm** 173.00/213.00.

♦ Commercial hotel in two redbrick Victorian town houses in the heart of one of London's most fashionable areas. Busy and popular pub. Well-equipped and functional bedrooms.

🏠 **Claverley** p. 35 **ER** o

13-14 Beaufort Gdns, SW3 1PS, ✆ (020) 7589 8541, *reservations@claverleyhotel.co.uk, Fax (020) 7584 3410*

without rest. – 📶 ⛔ 📺. 🅰🅾 🆎 🅾 *VISA* JCB. ✂

30 rm ⬜ 100.00/195.00.

◆ Long-established private hotel in this quiet spot close to Harrods. The generally spacious rooms are individually decorated and some have four-poster beds.

XXXX **Gordon Ramsay** p. 35 **EU** c
❀❀❀

68-69 Royal Hospital Rd, SW3 4HP, ✆ (020) 7352 4441, *Fax (020) 7352 3334*

📇. 🅰🅾 🆎 🅾 *VISA* JCB

closed 2 week Christmas, Easter, Saturday, Sunday and Bank Holidays – **Meals** (booking essential) 35.00/65.00 ⬜.

◆ Elegant and sophisticated room. The eponymous chef creates some of Britain's finest, classically inspired cooking. Detailed and attentive service. Book one month in advance.

Spec. Mosaic of foie gras with smoked goose and marinated figs. Turbot with boulangère potato and cep velouté. Apricot parfait with pain d'épices and strawberry jus.

XXX **Aubergine** p. 34 **CU** r
❀

11 Park Walk, SW10 0AJ, ✆ (020) 7352 3449, *Fax (020) 7351 1770*

📇. 🅰🅾 🆎 🅾 *VISA*

closed 2 weeks August, 2 weeks Christmas, Easter, Saturday lunch, Sunday and Bank Holidays – **Meals** (booking essential) 25.00/48.00 **s**. ⬜.

◆ Intimate, refined restaurant where the keen staff provide well drilled service. French influenced menu uses top quality ingredients with skill and flair. Extensive wine list.

Spec. Seared scallops with pea purée, smoked bacon jus. Best end of lamb, braised sweetbreads, rosemary jus. Lime Chiboust with ginger purée and lime syrup.

XXX **Drones** p. 35 **FR** c

1 Pont St, SW1X 9EJ, ✆ (020) 7235 9555, *sales@whitestarline.org.uk, Fax (020) 7235 9566*

📇. 🅰🅾 🆎 🅾 *VISA*

closed 26 December and Sunday dinner – **Meals** 17.95/19.50 (lunch) and a la carte 31.95/53.50 ⬜.

◆ Smart exterior with etched plate-glass window. L-shaped interior with moody film star photos on walls. French and classically inspired tone to dishes.

XXX **Bibendum** p. 35 **DS** s

Michelin House, 81 Fulham Rd, SW3 6RD, ✆ (020) 7581 5817, *manager@bibendum.co.uk, Fax (020) 7823 7925*

📇. 🅰🅾 🆎 🅾 *VISA*

closed dinner 24-26 December – **Meals** 25.00 (lunch) and dinner a la carte 37.00/53.50.

◆ A fine example of Art Nouveau architecture; a London landmark. 1st floor restaurant with striking stained glass 'Michelin Man'. Attentive service of modern British cooking.

XXX **Floriana** p. 35 **ER** c

15 Beauchamp Pl, SW3 1NQ, ✆ (020) 7838 1500, *Fax (020) 7584 1464*

📇. 🅰🅾 🆎 🅾 *VISA* JCB

closed 25 December, 1 January, Easter Monday and Sunday – **Meals** - Italian - 19.50 (lunch) and a la carte 20.50/31.00 ⬜.

◆ Behind the busy bar is a refined and contemporary restaurant. Approachable service of an elaborate, modern Italian menu. 1st floor room, with atrium roof, is more relaxing.

XXX **The Fifth Floor** (at Harvey Nichols)   p. 35 FQ **a**
Knightsbridge, SW1X 7RJ, ✆ (020) 7235 5250, Fax (020) 7235 7856

🛗 ▤. 🆖 🆎 ⓪ VISA JCB

closed 25 December, 1 January and Sunday dinner – **Meals** 25.00 (lunch)
and dinner a la carte 29.00/45.00 ♀.
◆ Wander through this famous store or take the lift straight to the top floor.
Chic restaurant with comfy tub chairs overlooks a busy bar and the impressive delicatessen.

XXX **One-O-One** (at Sheraton Park Tower H.)   p. 35 FQ **v**
William St, SW1X 7RN, ✆ (020) 7290 7101, Fax (020) 7235 6196

▤. 🆖 🆎 ⓪ VISA JCB

Meals - Seafood - 21.50 (lunch) and a la carte 36.00/54.00 ♀.
◆ Modern and very comfortable restaurant overlooking Knightsbridge decorated in cool blue tones. Predominantly seafood menu offers traditional and
more adventurous dishes.

XXX **Toto's**   p. 35 ES **a**
Walton House, Walton St, SW3 2JH, ✆ (020) 7589 0075, Fax (020) 7581 9668

🏠 – 🆖 🆎 ⓪ VISA JCB

closed 3 days Christmas – **Meals** - Italian - 20.50 (lunch) and a la carte 33.50/
46.50 **s**. ♀.
◆ Converted mews house in tucked away location. Ornately decorated and
bright restaurant with additional balcony area. Professional service of an
extensive Italian menu.

XXX **Chutney Mary**   p. 28 FZ **v**
535 King's Rd, SW10 0SZ, ✆ (020) 7351 3113, action@realindianfood.com,
Fax (020) 7351 7694

▤. 🆖 🆎 ⓪ VISA JCB

Meals - Indian - (dinner only and lunch Saturday and Sunday) a la carte 23.50/
39.00 ♀.
◆ Striking murals of British India adorn the walls of this forever popular
restaurant. Extensive menu of specialities from all corners of India. Comple-
mentary wine list.

XX **Monte's**   p. 35 FR **s**
164 Sloane St, SW1X 9QB, ✆ (020) 7245 0896, Fax (020) 7235 3456

▤. 🆖 🆎 ⓪ VISA JCB

closed Sunday – **Meals** - Italian - (booking essential) (lunch only) 23.00
and a la carte 28.50/39.50 ♀.
◆ Next to the Carlton Tower hotel, among Sloane Street's boutiques. Tasty,
modern Italian menu with a clubby and fashionable feel.

XX **Aquasia** (at Conrad London H.)   p. 17 CQ **i**
Chelsea Harbour, SW10 0XG, ✆ (020) 7300 8443, Fax (020) 7351 6525

≤, 🏠 – ▤ 🅿. 🆖 🆎 ⓪ VISA JCB

Meals 19.50/27.00 and a la carte 26.00/29.00 ♀.
◆ Modern restaurant located within Conrad International hotel. Views over
Chelsea Harbour. Cuisine captures the essence of the Mediterranean and
Asia.

XX **Bluebird**   p. 34 CU **e**
350 King's Rd, SW3 5UU, ✆ (020) 7559 1000, Fax (020) 7559 1111

🛗 ▤. 🆖 🆎 ⓪ VISA

Meals 17.00 (lunch) and a la carte 27.00/37.00.
◆ A foodstore, café and homeware shop also feature at this impressive skylit
restaurant. Much of the modern British food is cooked in wood-fired ovens.
Lively atmosphere.

XX **Poissonnerie de l'Avenue** p. 35 **DS** u

82 Sloane Ave, SW3 3DZ, ✆ (020) 7589 2457, *info@poissonnerie.co.uk, Fax (020) 7581 3360*

▤. **MO AE O VISA**

closed 10 days Christmas, Sunday and Bank Holidays – **Meals** - French Seafood - 24.00 (lunch) and a la carte 34.00/46.00.

♦ Long-established and under the same ownership since 1965. Spacious and traditional French restaurant offering an extensive seafood menu. An institution favoured by locals.

XX **English Garden** p. 35 **ET** X

10 Lincoln St, SW3 2TS, ✆ (020) 7584 7272, *english.garden@ukgateway.net, Fax (020) 7584 1961*

▤. **MO AE VISA JCB**

closed 1 week August, 1 week Christmas and Monday lunch – **Meals** 19.50/ 27.50 ♀.

♦ Attractive mid-19C house in a stylish residential area. Relaxed restaurant with British slate covered walls. Conservatory to the rear. Detailed service, modern cooking.

XX **Racine** p. 35 **DR** i

239 Brompton Rd, SW3 2EP, ✆ (020) 7584 4477, *Fax (020) 7584 4900*

▤. **MO AE VISA**

closed 25-26 December – **Meals** - French - 15.00 (lunch) and a la carte 19.50/ 28.75 ♀.

♦ Dark leather banquettes, large mirrors and wood floors create the atmosphere of a genuine Parisienne brasserie. Good value, well crafted, regional French fare.

XX **Mao Tai** p. 35 **ES** i

96 Draycott Ave, SW3 3AD, ✆ (020) 7225 2500, *mbmaotai@aol.com, Fax (020) 7471 8992*

▤. **MO AE O VISA**

closed 25-26 December – **Meals** - Chinese (Szechuan) - 12.50/24.70 and a la carte 22.70/31.35 ♀.

♦ Spacious Chinese restaurant in the heart of Chelsea. Modern, stylish décor with distinctive Easten feel. Unique Szechuan menus, boasting some highly original dishes.

XX **La Chaumiere** p. 29 **GZ** a

50 Cheyne Walk, SW3 5LR, ✆ (020) 7376 8787, *Fax (020) 7376 5858*

MO AE VISA JCB

closed Monday – **Meals** - French - (dinner only and Sunday lunch) (booking essential) 45.00.

♦ The name translates as "rustic cottage" and very much describes the décor and menu style of this unique French restauant. Appealing menu and a central gas-fired grill.

XX **Pellicano** p. 35 **ET** a

19-21 Elystan St, SW3 3NT, ✆ (020) 7589 3718, *Fax (020) 7584 1789*

⛲ – ▤. **MO AE O VISA**

closed 1 week Christmas – **Meals** - Italian - 15.00 (lunch) and a la carte 20.00/ 35.50 ♀.

♦ Attractive neighbourhood restaurant with dark blue canopy over pavement terrace. Contemporary interior with wood floors. Tasty and interesting modern Italian dishes.

XX **Mju** (at Millennium Knightsbridge H.) p. 35 **FR** r
17-25 Sloane St, SW1X 9NU, *ℰ* (020) 7201 6330, *mju@mill-cop.com,*
Fax (020) 7235 3705
✦✕ ▤. **M0** **AE** **①**
closed Saturday lunch and Sunday – **Meals** - Japanese - 21.50/55.00 and dinner a la carte 32.00/45.00 ℒ.
♦ On the first floor of the Millennium Knightsbridge Hotel, a large glass
ceiling provides plenty of light. Original mix of flavours underpinned by
classical French base.

XX **Brasserie St Quentin** p. 35 **DR** a
243 Brompton Rd, SW3 2EP, *ℰ* (020) 7589 8005, *Fax (020) 7584 6064*
▤. **M0** **AE** **①** **VISA**
Meals 15.50 (lunch) and a la carte 22.95/30.95 ℒ.
♦ Authentic Parisien brasserie, with rows of closely set tables, banquettes
and ornate chandeliers. Attentive service and a lively atmosphere. French
classics aplenty.

XX **Benihana** p. 35 **EU** e
77 King's Rd, SW3 4NX, *ℰ* (020) 7376 7799, *benihana@dircon.co.uk,*
Fax (020) 7376 7377
▤. **M0** **AE** **①** **VISA**
closed 25 December – **Meals** - Japanese (Teppan-Yaki) - 8.75/17.00
and a la carte 25.00/50.00.
♦ Vast basement restaurant. Be prepared to share your table with other
guests; teppan-yakis sit up to eight. Theatrical preparation and service of
modern Japanese cooking.

XX **Caraffini** p. 35 **FT** a
61-63 Lower Sloane St, SW1W 8DH, *ℰ* (020) 7259 0235, *info@caraffini.co.uk,*
Fax (020) 7259 0236
🌤 – ▤. **M0** **AE** **VISA**
closed Sunday and Bank Holidays – **Meals** - Italian - a la carte 19.65/
32.25.
♦ The omnipresent and ebullient owner oversees the friendly service in this
attractive neighbourhood restaurant. Authentic and robust Italian cooking;
informal atmosphere.

XX **Vama** p. 29 **GZ** e
438 King's Rd, SW10 0LJ, *ℰ* (020) 7351 4118, *andy@vama.co.uk,*
Fax (020) 7565 8501
M0 **AE** **①** **VISA**
closed 25 December and 1 January – **Meals** - Indian - (booking essential) 13.00
(lunch) and a la carte 20.50/39.50 ℒ.
♦ Adorned with traditional artefacts, a modern and bright restaurant. Keen
and eager service of an elaborate and seasonally changing menu of North-
west Indian specialities.

XX **Le Colombier** p. 35 **DT** e
145 Dovehouse St, SW3 6LB, *ℰ* (020) 7351 1155, *colombier@compuserve.*
com, Fax (020) 7351 0077
🌤 – **M0** **AE** **①** **VISA**
Meals - French - 15.00 (lunch) and a la carte 22.90/28.90 ℒ.
♦ Proudly Gallic corner restaurant in an affluent residential area. Attractive
enclosed terrace. Bright and cheerful surroundings and service of traditional
French cooking.

XX **The Collection** p. 35 DS V

264 Brompton Rd, SW3 2AS, ✆ (020) 7225 1212, *Fax (020) 7225 1050*

📧 . 🔴 AE VISA

closed 25-26 December, 1 January and Bank Holidays – **Meals** (dinner only) 35.00 and a la carte 23.75/41.50 ♀.

♦ Beyond the impressive catwalk entrance one will find a chic bar and a vast split level, lively restaurant. The eclectic and global modern menu is enjoyed by the young crowd.

XX **Good Earth** p. 35 DR C

233 Brompton Rd, SW3 2EP, ✆ (020) 7584 3658, *goodearthgroup@aol.com, Fax (020) 7823 8769*

📧 . 🔴 AE VISA JCB

closed 23-30 December – **Meals** - Chinese - 9.95/25.00 and a la carte 17.30/29.80 ♀.

♦ Ornately decorated, long-established and comfortable restaurant. Polite and efficient service. Extensive and traditional Chinese menu.

XX **Dan's** p. 35 DU S

119 Sydney St, SW3 6NR, ✆ (020) 7352 2718, *Fax (020) 7352 3265*

🌿 – 🔴 AE VISA

closed 25-26 and 31 December, 1 January, Sunday dinner and Bank Holidays – **Meals** 25.00 and a la carte 19.50/34.40.

♦ The eponymous owner oversees the operation in this long established neighbourhood restaurant. Eclectic menu with global influences. Private dining available.

XX **Haandi** p. 35 ER V

136 Brompton Rd, SW3 1HY, ✆ (020) 7823 7373, *Fax (020) 7823 9696*

📧 . 🔴 AE VISA JCB

closed 25 December – **Meals** - Indian - 7.50/9.50 (lunch) and a la carte 14.65/38.20 ♀.

♦ Spacious basement restaurant, though with natural light in some sections. Live jazz in the bar and chefs very much on display. Flavoursome, succulent north Indian food.

X **Thierry's** p. 34 CU C

342 King's Rd, SW3 5UR, ✆ (020) 7352 3365, *eat@therrys-restaurant.co.uk, Fax (020) 7352 3365*

📧 . 🔴 AE ① VISA

closed 24-26 December, 1-2 January, 12-27 August, Sunday dinner, Monday and Bank Holidays – **Meals** - French - 9.95/12.45 (lunch) and a la carte 13.00/29.75 ♀.

♦ Keen service at this cosy and friendly French bistro. Favoured by local residents, the traditional menu features many of the classics.

X **Simply Nico** (at Sloane Square Moat House H.) p. 35 FST V

Sloane Sq, SW1W 8CG, ✆ (020) 7896 9909, *sloanesquare@simplynico.co.uk, Fax (020) 7896 9908*

📧 . 🔴 AE ① VISA

closed 24-25 December and dinner Bank Holidays – **Meals** a la carte 23.00/29.00 ♀.

♦ Relaxed and discreet restaurant with a certain bistro atmosphere can be found behind the café overlooking Sloane Square. Short, Anglo-French menu. Part of a small chain.

✗ Zaika Bazaar
p.35 **DT** **C**

2a Pond Pl, SW3 6QU, ✆ (020) 7584 6655, *info@zaika-bazaar.co.uk, Fax (020) 7584 6755*

▤ **⑯** **AE** **①** **VISA** **JCB**

closed 25-26 December and Sunday – **Meals** - Indian - (dinner only) a la carte 18.35/24.75 ₤.

◆ Modern, basement level Indian restaurant. Vivid walls and carved wooden tables: all furnishings are for sale. Indian style "tapas" with many tasty, individually priced dishes.

✗ Bibendum Oyster Bar
p. 35 **DS** **S**

Michelin House, 81 Fulham Rd, SW3 6RD, ✆ (020) 7589 1480, *manager@biben dum.co.uk, Fax (020) 7823 7148*

⑯ **AE** **①** **VISA**

closed dinner 24-26 December – **Meals** - Seafood specialities - (bookings not accepted) a la carte 18.00/34.50 ₤.

◆ Dine in either the busy bar, or in the light and relaxed foyer of this striking landmark. Concise menu of mainly cold dishes focusing on fresh seafood and shellfish.

✗ Tipico
p. 34 **BU** **Z**

351 Fulham Rd, SW10 9TW, ✆ (020) 7351 2939, *Fax (0200 7376 4619*

▤ . **⑯** **AE** **VISA**

Meals - Italian - 9.50 (lunch) and a la carte 16.00/20.50.

◆ Informal restaurant with lively local atmosphere, located on a busy stretch of the Fulham Road. Simple appointments match simple but fresh Italian food.

✗ itsu
p. 35 **DS** **a**

118 Draycott Ave, SW3 3AE, ✆ (020) 7590 2401, *cebsonetcomuk.co.uk, Fax (020) 7590 2403*

▤ . **⑯** **AE** **VISA**

closed 23 December-2 January – **Meals** - Japanese - (bookings not accepted) a la carte 12.00/18.00.

◆ Sit at the conveyor belt and select your dishes from it. Cosmopolitan 'euro sushi' selection with Asian specialities. Fashionable and willing staff. Busy bar upstairs.

🏚 Admiral Codrington
p. 35 **ES** **X**

17 Mossop St, SW3 2LY, ✆ (020) 7581 0005, *theadmiralcodrington@longshotlt d.com, Fax (020) 7589 2452*

⑯ **AE** **VISA**

Meals a la carte/approx 33.00 ₤.

◆ Aproned staff offer attentive, relaxed service in this busy gastropub. A retractable roof provides alfresco dining in the modern back room. Cosmopolitan menu of modern dishes.

🏚 Chelsea Ram
p. 28 **FZ** **r**

32 Burnaby St, SW10 0PL, ✆ (020) 7351 4008, *pint@chelsearam.com, Fax (020) 7349 0885*

⑯ **VISA** **JCB**

closed 24-31 December – **Meals** a la carte 15.85/22.85 ₤.

◆ Wooden floors, modern artwork and books galore feature in this forever popular pub. Concise menu of modern British cooking with daily changing specials. Friendly atmosphere.

Swag and Tails

p. 35   DR   **r**

10-11 Fairholt St, SW7 1EG, ☏ (020) 7584 6926, *swagandtails@mway.com, Fax (020) 7581 9935*

MB **AE** **①** **VISA** **JCB**

closed 25-26 December, Saturday lunch, Sunday dinner and Bank Holidays – **Meals** a la carte 18.45/26.70 ♀.

♦ Attractive Victorian pub close to Harrods and the fashionable Knightsbridge shops. Polite and approachable service of a blackboard menu of light snacks and seasonal dishes.

Builders Arms

p. 35   DU   **x**

13 Britten St, SW3 3TY, ☏ (020) 7349 9040, *Fax (020) 7357 3181*

▤. MB **VISA**

Meals (bookings not accepted) a la carte 25.75/35.90 ♀.

♦ Modern 'gastropub' favoured by the locals. Eclectic menu of contemporary dishes with blackboard specials. Polite service from a young and eager team.

Lots Road Pub & Dining Room

p. 29   FZ   **a**

114 Lots Rd, SW10 0RJ, ☏ (020) 7352 6645

▤. MB **AE** **VISA**

closed 25-26 December – **Meals** a la carte 17.00/26.00 ♀.

♦ Traditional corner pub with an open-plan kitchen, flowers at each table and large modern pictures on the walls. Contemporay menus change daily.

Earl's Court Gtr London – ✉ SW5/SW10.

K + K George

p. 28   EZ   **s**

1-15 Templeton Pl, SW5 9NB, ☏ (020) 7598 8700, *hotelgeorge@kkhotels. co.uk, Fax (020) 7370 2285*

☞ – ‖‡‖ ⸙✕ ▤ TV ☎ P – ⚘ 30. **MB** **AE** **①** **VISA** **JCB**. ⸜

Meals (in bar) a la carte 16.50/22.50 **s.** ♀ – **154 rm** ⊡ 170.00/200.00.

♦ Converted Victorian house overlooking its own secluded rear garden. Scandinavian style to the bedrooms with low beds, white walls and light wood furniture. Informal dining in the bar.

Twenty Nevern Square

p. 28   EZ   **u**

Nevern Sq, SW5 9PD, ☏ (020) 7565 9555, *hotel@twentynevernsquare.co.uk, Fax (020) 7565 9444*

‖‡‖ TV ☎ P. **MB** **AE** **①** **VISA** **JCB**. ⸜

Meals *(closed Sunday)* (residents only) (dinner only) a la carte 15.95/19.45 **s.** ♀ – ⊡ 9.00 – **19 rm** 110.00/190.00.

♦ In an attractive Victorian garden square, an individually designed, privately owned town house. Original pieces of furniture and some rooms with their own terrace.

Henley House

p. 34   AT   **e**

30 Barkston Gdns, SW5 0EN, ☏ (020) 7370 4111, *reservations@henleyhouse hotel.com, Fax (020) 7370 0026*

without rest. – ‖‡‖ TV. **MB** **AE** **①** **VISA** **JCB**. ⸜

⊡ 3.40 – **21 rm** 70.00/95.00.

♦ Located in a pleasant redbricked square, just yards from the high street. Bedrooms all styled similarly, with floral designs and good extras. Conservatory breakfast room.

Amsterdam

p. 28   EZ   **c**

7 and 9 Trebovir Rd, SW5 9LS, ☏ (020) 7370 2814, *reservations@amsterdam-hotel.com, Fax (020) 7244 7608*

without rest., ☞ – ‖‡‖ TV. **MB** **AE** **①** **VISA** **JCB**. ⸜

⊡ 2.75 – **19 rm** 68.00/88.00, 8 suites.

♦ Basement breakfast room leads out onto a small secluded garden. Boldly decorated bedrooms with vivid colour schemes, some with their own balcony.

⌂ Rushmore p. 28 EZ c
11 Trebovir Rd, SW5 9LS, ✆ (020) 7370 3839, *rushmore-reservations@london.com, Fax (020) 7370 0274*
without rest. – ⥙ 📺, 🅼🅾 AE ① VISA JCB. ⌘
22 rm ⊆ 59.00/79.00.
  ◆ Behind its Victorian façade lies an hotel popular with tourists. Individually decorated bedrooms in a variety of shapes and sizes. Piazza-styled conservatory breakfast room.

✗✗ Langan's Coq d'Or p. 34 AU e
254-260 Old Brompton Rd, SW5 9HR, ✆ (020) 7259 2599, *admin@langansrestaurant.co.uk, Fax (020) 7370 7735*
🌳 – ▤, 🅼🅾 AE ① VISA JCB
closed Monday and Bank Holidays – **Meals** (dinner only and lunch Saturday and Sunday) a la carte 21.20/26.25.
  ◆ Formal reception area leads into a modern, open-plan restaurant. Walls adorned with photographs of assorted celebrities. Smooth service and traditional British food.

Kensington *Gtr London* – ✉ *SW7/W8/W11/W14.*

🏨 Royal Garden p. 34 AQ c
2-24 Kensington High St, W8 4PT, ✆ (020) 7937 8000, *sales@royalgarden.co.uk, Fax (020) 7361 1991*
≤, 🛋, ⇔s – 🛗, ⥙ rm, ▤ 📺 📞 ⅙ 🅿 – 🔼 600. 🅼🅾 AE ① VISA JCB. ⌘
Park Terrace* : Meals** 14.50/18.50 (lunch) and a la carte 21.25/49.00 – (see also ***The Tenth below) – ⊆ 18.00 – **381 rm** 287.80/358.40, 15 suites.
  ◆ A tall, modern hotel with many of its rooms enjoying enviable views over the adjacent Kensington Gardens. All the modern amenities and services, with well-drilled staff. Bright, spacious, large-windowed restaurant.

🏨 Hilton London Kensington p. 28 EX s
179-199 Holland Park Ave, W11 4UL, ✆ (020) 7603 3355, *sales_kensington@hilton.com, Fax (020) 7602 9397*
🛗, ⥙ rm, ▤ 📺 📞 ⅙ 🅿 – 🔼 300. 🅼🅾 AE ① VISA JCB. ⌘
***Market* : Meals** *(closed lunch Saturday and Sunday)* 23.00 (dinner) and a la carte 26.75/42.95 **s.** ⊊
***Hiroko* : Meals** - Japanese - (closed Monday) 16.00/35.00 and a la carte 20.50/40.00 – ⊆ 15.00 – **602 rm** 139.80.
  ◆ The executive bedrooms and the nearby exhibition centres make this a popular business hotel. Equally useful spot for tourists; it has all the necessary amenities. Warm, pastel coloured Market. Discreet, stylish Hiroko.

🏨 Hilton London Olympia p. 28 EY a
380 Kensington High St, W14 8NL, ✆ (020) 7603 3333, *rm_olympia@hilton.com, Fax (020) 7603 4846*
🛗, ⥙ rm, ▤ 📺 📞 ⅙ 🅿 – 🔼 250. 🅼🅾 AE ① VISA
Meals *closed Saturday lunch* 18.50 and a la carte 16.50/25.00 ⊊ – ⊆ 16.50 – **395 rm** 210.30, 10 suites.
  ◆ Busy, corporate hotel, benefiting from being within walking distance of Olympia. Bedrooms of a good size, with light wood furniture and fully tiled bathrooms. Bright dining room with large windows.

🏛 Thistle Kensington Park
p. 34 BQ e

16-32 De Vere Gdns, W8 5AG, ℰ (0870) 333 9112, *kensingtonpark@thistle.co.uk, Fax (0870) 333 9212*

🔼, ✢ rm, ▤ 📺 ✆ – ♨ 120. ⓪ 🄰🄴 ⓪ *VISA* JCB, ⚅

Meals a la carte 19.00/26.00 **s.** ♈ – ⌲ 14.95 – **346 rm** 171.00/203.00, 6 suites.
♦ A row of adjoined period houses where joggers can enjoy its position opposite the park. Impressive marble lobby; spacious bedrooms in good order. Airy, popular brasserie-style restaurant.

🏛 The Milestone
p. 34 AQ u

1-2 Kensington Court, W8 5DL, ℰ (020) 7917 1000, *Fax (020) 7917 1010*
♨, ⬄ – 🔼, ✢ rm, ▤ 📺 ✆, ⓪ 🄰🄴 ⓪ *VISA* ⚅

Meals a la carte 23.75/41.00 ♈ – ⌲ 17.00 – **52 rm** 293.00/470.00, 5 suites.
♦ Elegant 'boutique' hotel with decorative Victorian façade and English feel. Charming oak panelled lounge and snug bar. Meticulously decorated bedrooms with period detail. Panelled dining room with charming little oratory for privacy seekers.

🏠 Holland Court
p. 28 EY e

31-33 Holland Rd, W14 8HJ, ℰ (020) 7371 1133, *reservations@hollandcourt.com, Fax (020) 7602 9114*
without rest., 🚗 – 🔼 ✢ 📺, ⓪ 🄰🄴 ⓪ *VISA* JCB, ⚅
22 rm ⌲ 59.00/69.00.
♦ Privately owned and run terraced house. Pretty little garden next to the conservatory extension of the breakfast room. Well-kept bedrooms benefit from the large windows.

🍴🍴🍴 The Tenth (at Royal Garden H.)
p. 34 AQ c

2-24 Kensington High St, W8 4PT, ℰ (020) 7361 1910, *Fax (020) 7361 1921*
≼ Kensington Palace and Gardens – ▤ 🄿, ⓪ 🄰🄴 ⓪ *VISA* JCB
closed Sunday and lunch Saturday – **Meals** (live music Saturday) 21.00 (lunch) and a la carte 28.00/40.50 ♈.
♦ Named after the hotel's top floor where this stylish yet relaxed room is situated. Commanding views of Kensington Palace and the Park. Well-structured service; modern menu.

🍴🍴🍴 Belvedere
p. 28 EY u

Holland House, off Abbotsbury Rd, W8 6LU, ℰ (020) 7602 1238, *sales@whitestarline.org.uk, Fax (020) 7610 4382*
🍽, ♣ – ▤, ⓪ 🄰🄴 ⓪ *VISA*
closed Sunday dinner in winter – **Meals** 17.95/27.50 and a la carte 36.75/51.00 ♈.
♦ Former 19C orangery in a delightful position in the middle of the Park. On two floors with a bar and balcony terrace. Huge vases of flowers. Modern take on classic dishes.

🍴🍴 Zaika
p. 34 AQ r

1 Kensington High St, W8 5NP, ℰ (020) 7795 6533, *info@zaika-restaurant.co.uk, Fax (020) 7937 8854*
▤, ⓪ 🄰🄴 *VISA* JCB
closed 25-26 December and Saturday lunch – **Meals** - Indian - 13.95 (lunch) and a la carte 29.00/46.50 ♈.
♦ A converted bank, sympathetically restored, with original features and Indian artefacts. Well organised service; careful and accomplished modern Indian cooking.
Spec. Hari Jalpari (lobster tail with curry leaf and broccoli risotto). Koh-e-roganjosh (lamb shank in onion and tomato sauce). Chocolate samosas, Indian tea ice cream.

XX **Clarke's** p. 28 **EX c**

124 Kensington Church St, W8 4BH, ☎ (020) 7221 9225, *restaurant@sally clarke.com, Fax (020) 7229 4564*

✗ ▤ 🆗 AE ⓪ VISA

closed 2 weeks August, 10 days Christmas-New Year, Sunday and Bank holidays – **Meals** (set menu only at dinner) 28.50/48.00 **s**. ♒.

♦ Open-plan kitchen, personally overseen by the owner, provides modern British cooking. No choice, set menu at dinner. Comfortable and bright, with a neighbourhood feel.

XX **Babylon** (at The Roof Gardens) p. 28 **FY u**

99 Kensington High St, W8 5ED, ☎ (020) 7368 3993, *babylon@roofgardens.virgin.co.uk, Fax (020) 7938 2774*

≤, 🏠 – ▤. 🆗 AE ⓪ VISA

closed Saturday lunch, Sunday dinner and Bank holidays – **Meals** 18.50 (lunch) and a la carte 23.50/37.25 ♒.

♦ Situated on the roof of this pleasant London building affording attractive veiws of the London skyline. Stylish modern décor in keeping with the contemporary, British cooking.

XX **Launceston Place** p. 34 **BR a**

1a Launceston Pl, W8 5RL, ☎ (020) 7937 6912, *LPR@place-restaurants.co.uk, Fax (020) 7938 2412*

▤. 🆗 AE ⓪ VISA JCB

closed Christmas, Easter, Saturday lunch and Bank Holidays – **Meals** 18.50 (lunch) and a la carte 30.50/34.50 ♒.

♦ Divided into a number of rooms, this corner restaurant is lent a bright feel by its large windows and gilded mirrors. Chatty service and contemporary cooking.

XX **Memories of China** p. 28 **EY v**

353 Kensington High St, W8 6NW, ☎ (020) 7603 6951, *Fax (020) 7603 0848*

▤. 🆗 AE ⓪ VISA

closed 25 December, 1 January and Sunday lunch – **Meals** - Chinese - (booking essential) a la carte 24.30/48.30 ♒.

♦ Subtle lighting and brightly coloured high-back chairs add to the modern feel of this Chinese restaurant. Screens separate the tables. Plenty of choice from extensive menu.

XX **Timo** p. 28 **EY c**

343 Kensington High St, W8 6NW, ☎ (020) 7603 3888, *Fax (020) 7603 8111*

▤. 🆗 AE ⓪ VISA JCB

closed Christmas – **Meals** - Italian - 10.00/25.00 ♒.

♦ Modern restaurant with unadorned lime green walls and comfortable seating in brown suede banquettes. Italian menus of contemporary dishes and daily changing specials.

XX **The Ark** p. 36 **AZ r**

122 Palace Gardens Terr, W8 4RT, ☎ (020) 7229 4024, *Fax (020) 7792 8787*

🏠 – ▤. 🆗 AE VISA

closed Sunday dinner, Monday lunch and Bank Holidays – **Meals** - Italian - a la carte 25.50/31.00 ♒.

♦ The hut-like external appearance belies the contemporary interior of this Italian restaurant. Comfortable, bright feel with bar and lounge. Smoothly run, rustic cooking.

XX **Phoenicia** p. 28 **EY** n

11-13 Abingdon Rd, W8 6AH, ℰ (020) 7937 0120, *Fax (020) 7937 7668*

📧. **M⊘** **AE** **①** **VISA** **JCB**

closed 24-25 December – **Meals** - Lebanese - 11.95/30.95 and a la carte 20.05/27.55.

◆ Able and helpful staff make this long-standing Lebanese restaurant a popular local. Carefully prepared food with a wide-ranging lunch time buffet.

X **Kensington Place** p. 36 **AZ** z

201 Kensington Church St, W8 7LX, ℰ (020) 7727 3184, *kpr@placerestaurants. co.uk, Fax (020) 7229 2025*

📧. **M⊘** **AE** **①** **VISA**

closed 25-27 December and 1 January – **Meals** (booking essential) 16.50/ 18.00 (lunch) and a la carte 28.00/39.00 ⵚ.

◆ A cosmopolitan crowd still head for this establishment that set the trend for large, bustling and informal restaurants. Professionally run with skilled modern cooking.

X **Cibo** p. 28 **EY** o

3 Russell Gdns, W14 8EZ, ℰ (020) 7371 6271, *Fax (020) 7602 1371*

M⊘ **AE** **①** **VISA** **JCB**

closed 24 December-2 January, Saturday lunch, Sunday dinner and Bank holidays – **Meals** - Italian - a la carte 23.00/39.90.

◆ Smoothly run Italian restaurant that combines style with the atmosphere of a neighbourhood favourite. Unaffected service with robust and tasty food.

X **Malabar** p. 36 **AZ** e

27 Uxbridge St, W8 7TQ, ℰ (020) 7727 8800, *feedback@malabar-restaurant. co.uk*

M⊘ **VISA**

Meals - Indian - (booking essential) (buffet lunch Sunday) a la carte 18.55/ 25.40 **s.**

◆ Indian restaurant in a residential street. Three rooms with individual personalities and informal service. Extensive range of good value dishes, particularly vegetarian.

X **Wódka** p. 34 **AR** c

12 St Albans Grove, W8 5PN, ℰ (020) 7937 6513, *john@wodka.demon.co.uk, Fax (020) 7937 0021*

M⊘ **AE** **①** **VISA**

closed 1 week Christmas, lunch Saturday and Sunday – **Meals** - Polish - 11.50/13.50 (lunch) and dinner a la carte 16.40/26.50.

◆ Unpretentious Polish restaurant with rustic, authentic menu. Assorted blinis and flavoured vodkas a speciality. Simply decorated, with wooden tables and paper napkins.

North Kensington – ✉ *W2/W10/W11*.

🏨 **Westbourne** p. 36 **AZ** s

165 Westbourne Grove, W11 2RS, ℰ (020) 7243 6008, *info@aliashotels.com, Fax (020) 7229 7201*

without rest. – ⨯⊱ 📧 **TV** ☎. **M⊘** **AE** **VISA** **JCB**. ⅏ – ⚏ 16.50 **20 rm** 175.00/ 225.00.

◆ Immaculately creamwashed converted Georgian townhouse near Portobello Road. Wood-floored lounge with quality soft furnishings. Breakfast terrace. 1950s retro style rooms.

Pembridge Court
p. 36 AZ **n**

34 Pembridge Gdns, W2 4DX, ✆ (020) 7229 9977, *reservations@pemct.co.uk, Fax (020) 7727 4982*
without rest. – |‡| 🖭 📺 ✆. ⓂⓈ 🄰🄴 ⓄⒾ 𝗩𝗜𝗦𝗔
20 rm ⌖ 130.00/200.00.
♦ Privately owned 19C town house with comfortable sitting room and cosy basement bar. Walls dotted with a collection of framed antique clothing. Rooms vary in shape and size.

Abbey Court
p. 36 AZ **u**

20 Pembridge Gdns, W2 4DU, ✆ (020) 7221 7518, *info@abbeycourthotel. co.uk, Fax (020) 7792 0858*
without rest. – ⇆ 📺. ⓂⓈ 🄰🄴 ⓄⒾ 𝗩𝗜𝗦𝗔. ⌗
22 rm 99.00/135.00.
♦ Five-storey Victorian town house with individually decorated bedrooms, with many thoughtful touches. Breakfast served in a pleasant conservatory. Friendly service.

Portobello
p. 28 EV **n**

22 Stanley Gdns, W11 2NG, ✆ (020) 7727 2777, *info@portobello-hotel.co.uk, Fax (020) 7792 9641*
|‡| 📺 ✆. ⓂⓈ 🄰🄴 𝗩𝗜𝗦𝗔
closed 23 December-2 January – **Meals** a la carte approx. 21.00 – ⌖ 8.50 –
24 rm 140.00/320.00.
♦ An attractive Victorian town house in an elegant terrace. Original and theatrical décor. Circular beds, half-testers, Victorian baths: no two bedrooms are the same. Basement restaurant and bar.

Chez Moi
p. 28 EX **n**

1 Addison Ave, Holland Park, W11 4QS, ✆ (020) 7603 8267, *chezmoi_rest@hot mail.com, Fax (020) 7603 3898*
🗏. ⓂⓈ 🄰🄴 ⓄⒾ 𝗩𝗜𝗦𝗔
closed Sunday, Saturday and Monday lunch and Bank Holidays – **Meals** - French - 15.00 (lunch) and a la carte 22.75/34.50.
♦ Long-standing neighbourhood French restaurant known for its warmth and friendliness. Rich red hued walls with imitation wildlife fabrics. Mostly traditional menu.

Pharmacy
p. 36 AZ **a**

150 Notting Hill Gate, W11 3QG, ✆ (020) 7221 2442, *mail@pharmacylondon. com, Fax (020) 7243 2345*
🗏. ⓂⓈ 🄰🄴 ⓄⒾ 𝗩𝗜𝗦𝗔
closed 24-26 December – **Meals** 12.50 (lunch) and a la carte 24.75/40.75 ⌗.
♦ Highly original and known for its Damien Hirst art. Ground floor bar with medicinal-themed décor; dining room upstairs offers a modern menu with European influences.

Notting Hill Brasserie
p. 28 EV **a**

92 Kensington Park Rd, W11 2PN, ✆ (020) 7229 4481, *nottinghill@firmdale. com, Fax (020) 7221 1246*
🗏. ⓂⓈ 🄰🄴 𝗩𝗜𝗦𝗔
closed 25 December and Sunday dinner – **Meals** 14.50/19.50 (lunch) and a la carte 22.00/36.00 ⌗.
♦ Modern, comfortable restaurant with quiet, formal atmosphere set over four small rooms. Authentic African artwork on walls. Contemporary dishes with European influence.

XX **Il Posto** p. 28 EX a
6 Clarendon Rd, W11 3AA, ℰ (020) 7727 3330, *Fax (020) 722 99007*
▤. **⬢⬡** **AE** **VISA** **JCB**
closed 24 December-6 January, Saturday lunch and Sunday dinner – **Meals** -
Italian - (dinner only and Saturday lunch) a la carte 20.00/28.20.
♦ Intimate restaurant with genuine neighbourhood feel. Understated décor
has a snug, modern feel. Appealing, frequently changing menus feature
accomplished rustic dishes.

X **Manor** p. 24 EU s
6-8 All Saints Rd, W11 1HH, ℰ (020) 7243 6363, *mail@manorw11.com,*
Fax (020) 7243 6360
▤. **⬢⬡** **AE** **VISA**
(closed Sunday dinner) – **Meals** (dinner only and lunch Saturday and Sunday)
a la carte 21.00/30.00.
♦ Bustling, vibrant restaurant in the heart of Notting Hill. Wood-floored with
banquette seating. Good sized menus: the cuisine is modern with Spanish
influences.

X **Alastair Little Lancaster Road** p. 24 EU e
136a Lancaster Rd, W11 1QU, ℰ (020) 7243 2220
▤. **⬢⬡** **AE** **◉** **VISA** **JCB**
closed Sunday dinner and Bank Holidays – **Meals** (booking essential) 18.00
(lunch) and a la carte 24.00/29.50 ♇.
♦ Cosy and less formal sister restaurant to the Soho branch. Relaxed and
unfussy service in understated surroundings. Mediterranean-influenced
menu.

X **Notting Grill** p. 24 EV z
123A Clarendon Rd, W11 4JG, ℰ (020) 7229 1500, *notting.grill@virgin.net,*
Fax (020) 7229 8889
▱ – **⬢⬡** **AE** **VISA** **JCB**
closed 25-26 December – **Meals** - Steak specialities - (dinner only and lunch
Saturday and Sunday) a la carte 26.50/39.00 ♇.
♦ Converted pub that retains a rustic feel, with bare brick walls and wooden
tables. Specialises in well sourced, quality meats.

X **Livebait** p. 36 AZ x
175 Westbourne Grove, W11 2SB, ℰ (020) 7727 4321, *gcq-lb-nottinghim@*
groupcchczgcrard.co.uk, Fax (020) 7792 3655
▤. **⬢⬡** **AE** **◉** **VISA**
closed 24-26 December, Monday and Bank Holidays – **Meals** - Seafood - 11.95
(lunch) and a la carte 19.95/32.00 ♇.
♦ Be it simply cooked fish or more inventive seafood you're after, the
extensive menu has something for all palates. Relaxed and buzzy atmosphere. Seafood platters to share.

South Kensington *Gtr London* – ✉ *SW5/SW7/W8*.

▲▲ **Millennium Gloucester** p. 34 BS r
4-18 Harrington Gdns, SW7 4LH, ℰ (020) 7373 6030, *gloucester@mill-cop.com,*
Fax (020) 7373 0409
ℹ – ▤, ✕ rm, ▤ **TV** ☏ ♿ **P** – ⚒ 650. **⬢⬡** **AE** **◉** **VISA** **JCB**
SW7 : **Meals** - Italian - *(closed Sunday)* (dinner only) 15.95 and a la carte
19.95/29.85 ♇
Bugis Street : **Meals** - Singaporean - 7.95/19.50 and a la carte 21.00/36.45 ♇ –
⬚ 15.00 – **604 rm** 250.00, 6 suites.
♦ A large international group hotel. Busy marbled lobby and vast conference
facilities. Smart and well-equipped bedrooms are generously sized, especially
the 'Club' rooms. SW7 has smart ambience. Bugis Street is informal and
compact.

The Pelham p. 34 CS z

15 Cromwell Pl, SW7 2LA, ℘ (020) 7589 8288, *pelham@firmdale.com, Fax (020) 7584 8444*

|🛗|, 🗝 rm, 🖵 📺 📞. 🆖 🆎 *VISA*. 🛇

Kemps : Meals a la carte 24.00/29.25 ♀ – 🖵 17.50 – **48 rm** 176.20/293.70, 3 suites.

♦ Attractive Victorian town house with a discreet and comfortable feel. Wood panelled drawing room and individually decorated bedrooms with marble bathrooms. Detailed service. Warm basement dining room.

 Blakes p. 34 BU n

33 Roland Gdns, SW7 3PF, ℘ (020) 7370 6701, *blakes@easynet.co.uk, Fax (020) 7373 0442*

🍴 – |🛗|, 🍴 rest, 📺 📞. 🆖 🆎 ⓪ *VISA*. 🛇

Meals *(closed 25 December)* 25.00/65.00 – 🖵 23.00 – **44 rm** 199.70/393.60, 5 suites.

♦ Behind the Victorian façade lies one of London's first 'boutique' hotels. Dramatic, bold and eclectic décor, with oriental influences and antiques from around the globe. Dramatic basement restaurant with bamboo and black walls.

 Harrington Hall p. 34 BST n

5-25 Harrington Gdns, SW7 4JW, ℘ (020) 7396 9696, *harringtonsales@compu serve.com, Fax (020) 7396 9090*

🐾, 🛗 – |🛗|, 🗝 rm, 🖵 📺 📞 – 🔥 260. 🆖 🆎 ⓪ *VISA* JCB. 🛇

Wetherby's : Meals *closed lunch Saturday and Sunday* a la carte 24.50/34.00 – 🖵 14.95 – **200 rm** 185.00/245.00.

♦ A series of adjoined terraced houses, with an attractive period façade that belies the size. Tastefully furnished bedrooms, with an extensive array of facilities. Classically decorated dining room.

 Millennium Bailey's p. 34 BS a

140 Gloucester Rd, SW7 4QH, ℘ (020) 7373 6000, *baileys@mill-cop.com, Fax (020) 7370 3760*

|🛗|, 🗝 rm, 🖵 📺 📞 – 🔥 460. 🆖 🆎 ⓪ *VISA*. 🛇

Olives : Meals (bar lunch)/dinner a la carte 23.40/33.95 ♀ – 🖵 15.00 – **211 rm** 135.00/250.00.

♦ Elegant lobby, restored to its origins dating from 1876, with elaborate plasterwork and a striking grand staircase. Victorian feel continues through into the bedrooms. Modern, pastel shaded restaurant.

 Vanderbilt p. 34 BS z

68-86 Cromwell Rd, SW7 5BT, ℘ (020) 7761 9000, *resvand@radisson.com, Fax (020) 7761 9003*

🛗 – |🛗|, 🗝 rm, 🖵 📺 📞 – 🔥 120. 🆖 🆎 ⓪ *VISA* JCB. 🛇

Meals 19.50 and a la carte 23.25/27.25 s. ♀ – 🖵 12.00 – **215 rm** 229.10/298.45.

♦ A Victorian town house, once home to the Vanderbilt family. Retains many original features such as stained glass windows and fireplaces. Now a modern, group hotel. Restaurant has unusual objets d'art and striking cracked glass bar.

 Rembrandt p. 35 DS x

11 Thurloe Pl, SW7 2RS, ℘ (020) 7589 8100, *rembrandt@sarova.co.uk, Fax (020) 7225 3476*

🛗, 🛗, 🗼 – |🛗|, 🗝 rm, 🍴 rest, 📺 – 🔥 200. 🆖 🆎 ⓪ *VISA* JCB. 🛇

Meals (carving lunch) 18.95 and a la carte 14.70/27.40 s. ♀ – **195 rm** 🖵 190.00/240.00.

♦ Built originally as apartments in the 19C, now a well-equipped hotel opposite the V & A museum and a short walk from Harrods. Comfortable lounge, impressive leisure club. Spacious, well-frequented dining room.

Jurys Kensington
p. 34 CT i

109-113 Queen's Gate, SW7 5LR, ℘ (020) 7589 6300, *kensington@jurysdoyle.com, Fax (020) 7581 1492*

🛗, ✂ rm, 🖥 📺 ✆ – 🏋 80. 🆖 A≡ ① *VISA*. ✀

Meals 15.00/20.00 and a la carte – 🍽 20.00 – **173 rm** 210.00/235.00.

♦ A row of 18C town houses that were converted into a hotel in the 1920s. Quiet and restful reading room contrasts with the busy basement Irish pub. Functional bedrooms. Conservatively dining room with relaxing cocktail bar.

Regency
p. 34 CT e

100 Queen's Gate, SW7 5AG, ℘ (020) 7373 7878, *info@regency-london.co.uk, Fax (020) 7370 5555*

I₅, ⊆s – 🛗, ✂ rm, 🖥 📺 ✆ – 🏋 100. 🆖 A≡ ① *VISA* JCB. ✀

Meals *(closed lunch Saturday and Sunday)* (carvery lunch)/dinner 25.00/32.00 **s.** ♀ – 🍽 15.00 – **192 rm** 152.75, 6 suites.

♦ Impressive Regency house in an elegant tree lined street and close to the museums. Bedrooms vary from rather compact singles to spacious duplex suites. Basement restaurant with cocktail bar.

Gore
p. 34 BR n

189 Queen's Gate, SW7 5EX, ℘ (020) 7584 6601, *sales@gorehotel.co.uk, Fax (020) 7589 8127*

🛗, ✂ rm, 📺 ✆. 🆖 A≡ ① *VISA* JCB. ✀

closed 24-25 December

Bistrot 190 : **Meals** (booking essential) a la carte 21.45/28.50 ♀ – (see also **The Restaurant at One Ninety** below) – 🍽 9.50 – **53 rm** 147.00/278.00.

♦ Opened its doors in 1892 and has retained its individual charm. Richly decorated with antiques, rugs, four-poster beds and over 4,000 pictures that cover every inch of wall. Bistro boasts French-influenced décor.

John Howard
p. 34 BQ i

4 Queen's Gate, SW7 5EH, ℘ (020) 7808 8400, *info@johnhowardhotel.co.uk, Fax (020) 7808 8402*

🛗 🖥 📺 ✆. 🆖 A≡ ① *VISA* JCB. ✀

Meals *(closed Sunday)* (dinner only) 15.00 and a la carte 15.25/20.00 **s.** – 🍽 12.50 – **45 rm** 109.00/139.00, 7 suites.

♦ Occupies the site of three mid-19C houses, just a short walk from Kensington Palace. Some rooms with floor to ceiling windows and balconies, others look onto a quiet mews. Candlelit basement dining room.

The Cranley
p. 34 BT c

10-12 Bina Gdns, SW5 0LA, ℘ (020) 7373 0123, *info@thecranley.com, Fax (020) 7373 9497*

🛗 🖥 📺 ✆. 🆖 A≡ ① *VISA* JCB. ✀

Meals (room service only) – 🍽 9.95 – **35 rm** 182.10/258.50, 3 suites.

♦ Attractive Regency town house that artfully combines charm and period details with modern comforts and technology. Individually styled bedrooms; some with four-posters.

Number Sixteen
p. 34 CT c

16 Sumner Pl, SW7 3EG, ℘ (020) 7589 5232, *sixteen@firmdale.com, Fax (020) 7584 8615*

without rest., 🚗 – 📺 ✆. 🆖 A≡ *VISA*

🍽 7.50 **39 rm** 99.80/217.30.

♦ Two Victorian town houses in a smart part of town. Discreet entrance, comfortable sitting room and charming breakfast terrace. Bedrooms in English country house style.

The Gallery
p. 34 **CS** r

8-10 Queensberry Pl, SW7 2EA, ℘ (020) 7915 0000, *gallery@eeh.co.uk,* *Fax (020) 7915 4400*

without rest. – 劇 TV ℡ 👁 AE Ⓞ VISA JCB. ⚡

36 rm ⤳ 141.00/258.50.

◆ Heavy drapes and mahogany panelling give the lounge bar of this Victorian house a clubby feel. Sizeable basement breakfast room. Some bedrooms have small terraces.

The Gainsborough
p. 34 **CS** s

7-11 Queensberry Pl, SW7 2DL, ℘ (020) 7957 0000, *gainsborough@eeh.co.uk,* *Fax (020) 7957 0001*

without rest. – 劇 TV. 👁 AE Ⓞ VISA JCB. ⚡

46 rm ⤳ 78.70/258.50, 3 suites.

◆ Sister property to the Gallery hotel across the street. Prints of the celebrated artist's work decorate the bright and welcoming lobby. Breakfast room doubles as a bar.

Five Sumner Place
p. 34 **CT** u

5 Sumner Pl, SW7 3EE, ℘ (020) 7584 7586, *reservations@sumnerplace.com,* *Fax (020) 7823 9962*

without rest. – 劇 ⚡ TV. 👁 AE Ⓞ VISA JCB. ⚡

13 rm ⤳ 99.00/152.00.

◆ Part of a striking white terrace built in 1848 in this fashionable part of town. Breakfast served in the secluded conservatory. Good sized bedrooms.

Aster House
p. 34 **CT** u

3 Sumner Pl, SW7 3EE, ℘ (020) 7581 5888, *asterhouse@btinternet.com,* *Fax (020) 7584 4925*

without rest., 🚗 – ⚡ ▤ TV ℡. 👁 VISA JCB. ⚡

14 rm ⤳ 99.00/180.00.

◆ End of terrace Victorian house with a pretty little rear garden and first floor conservatory. Ground floor rooms available. A wholly non-smoking establishment.

XXX Bombay Brasserie
p. 34 **BS** a

Courtfield Rd, SW7 4QH, ℘ (020) 7370 4040, *bombaybrasserie@aol.com,* *Fax (020) 7835 1669*

▤. 👁 AE Ⓞ VISA JCB

closed 25-28 December – **Meals** - Indian - (buffet lunch) 16.95 and dinner a la carte 26.50/30.75 ⚡.

◆ Something of a London institution: an ever busy Indian restaurant with Raj-style décor. Ask to sit in the brighter plant-filled conservatory. Popular lunchtime buffet.

XX The Restaurant at One Ninety (at Gore H.)
p. 34 **BR** n

190 Queen's Gate, SW7 5EU, ℘ (020) 7581 5666, *Fax (020) 7581 8172*

▤. 👁 AE Ⓞ VISA JCB

closed 24-25 December, Sunday and Monday – **Meals** - Seafood - (booking essential) (dinner only) 18.00/35.00 and a la carte 24.50/32.00 ⚡.

◆ Located in the basement of the Gore hotel. Clubby feel with soft lighting, wood panelling and good size tables. Attentive service; seafood menu with global influences.

XX Lundum's
p. 34 **BT** o

119 Old Brompton Rd, SW7 3RN, ℘ (020) 7373 7774, *Fax (020) 7373 4472*

🏠 – ▤. 👁 AE Ⓞ VISA JCB

closed 23 December-4 January, last 2 weeks August and Sunday dinner – **Meals** - Danish - 15.50/21.50 and dinner a la carte 23.15/33.75.

◆ A family run Danish restaurant offering an authentic, traditional lunch with a more expansive dinner menu. Comfortable room, with large mirrors. Charming service.

XX **Khan's of Kensington**   p. 34   CS   e

3 Harrington Rd, SW7 3ES, ✆ (020) 7584 4114, *Fax (020) 7581 2900*

📧 M© AE ⓪ VISA

Closed 25 December – **Meals** - Indian - 7.95/25.00 and a la carte 14.15/27.45.
♦ Bright room with wood flooring and a large mural depicting scenes from old India. Basement bar in a colonial style. Authentic Indian cooking with attentive service.

XX **Cambio de Tercio**   p. 34   BT   z

163 Old Brompton Rd, SW5 0LJ, ✆ (020) 7244 8970, *restaurant@cambiodetercio.co.uk, Fax (020) 7373 8817*

M© VISA

closed 2 weeks Christmas – **Meals** - Spanish - a la carte 25.40/28.50.
♦ The keen young owners have created a vibrant room with rich red walls decorated with assorted bullfighting accessories. Sophisticated Spanish cooking.

XX **Pasha**   p. 34   BR   i

1 Gloucester Rd, SW7 4PP, ✆ (020) 7589 7969, *Fax (020) 7581 9996*

📧 M© AE ⓪ VISA JCB

closed 24-26 December, 1-2 January and Sunday lunch – **Meals** - Moroccan - a la carte approx. 24.50 ♀.
♦ A marble fountain, lanterns, spice boxes and silk cushions help create a theatrical Moroccan atmosphere. Service is helpful and able: the menu is more extensive at dinner.

XX **Memories of India**   p. 34   BR   s

18 Gloucester Rd, SW7 4RB, ✆ (020) 7589 6450, *Fax (020) 7584 4438*

📧 M© AE ⓪ VISA JCB

closed 25 December – **Meals** - Indian - a la carte 14.60/19.65.
♦ A long-standing local favourite, decorated in traditional style with whicker chairs and pink linen tablecloths. Polite and able service. Authentic Indian cooking.

X **Café Lazeez**   p. 34   CT   a

93-95 Old Brompton Rd, SW7 3LD, ✆ (020) 7581 9993, *southkensington@cafelazeez.com, Fax (020) 7581 8200*

📧 M© AE ⓪ VISA JCB

Meals - North Indian - a la carte 18.45/28.05 ♀.
♦ Glass-topped tables and tiled flooring add an air of modernity to this Indian restaurant; reflected in the North Indian cooking. Willing service. Upstairs room more formal.

X **Star of India**   p. 34   BT   s

154 Old Brompton Rd, SW5 0BE, ✆ (020) 7373 2901, *info@starofindia.co.uk, Fax (020) 7373 5664*

📧 M© AE ⓪ VISA JCB

closed Bank Holidays – **Meals** - Indian - a la carte 22.20/33.90 ♀.
♦ Murals of classical sculptures and pillars with angels painted on the ceiling set this apart from most Indian restaurants. Cooking is also more contemporary in content.

X **Bangkok**   p. 34   CS   v

9 Bute St, SW7 3EY, ✆ (020) 7584 8529

📧 M© VISA

closed Christmas-New Year, Sunday and Bank Holidays – **Meals** - Thai Bistro - a la carte 17.50/27.00.
♦ This simple Thai bistro has been a popular local haunt for many years. Guests can watch the chefs at work, preparing inexpensive dishes from the succinct menu.

A reservation confirmed in writing is always more certain.

KINGSTON UPON THAMES *Ctr London.*

🏌 *Home Park, Hampton Wick* ☎ *(020) 8977 6645,* **BY**.

Chessington *Surrey – ⊠ Surrey.*

🏨 Travel Inn Metro
p. 12 **BZ** **c**

Leatherhead Rd, KT9 2NE, on A 243, ☎ (01372) 744060, *Fax (01372) 720889*
⇔ rm, 📺 ♿ 🅿 ⓦⓔ 🆎 ⓞ *VISA*. ⅏
Meals (grill rest.) – **42 rm** 54.95.

♦ Modern budget accommodation beside 'World of Adventures' theme park. Spacious rooms, many with additional sofa beds. Popular pub adjacent offers a traditional menu.

Kingston *Surrey – ⊠ Surrey.*

🏨 Kingston Lodge
p. 13 **CY** **u**

Kingston Hill, KT2 7NP, ☎ (020) 8541 4481, *heritagehotels-kingston-upon-thames.kingston-lodge@forte-hotels.com, Fax (020) 8547 1013*
🌐 – ⇔ rm, 🍴 rest, 📺 📞 ♿ 🅿 – 🔼 60. ⓦⓔ 🆎 ⓞ *VISA* ⓙⒸⒷ. ⅏
***The Atrium :* Meals** 16.95 and a la carte 22.45/34.20 – ⊑ 13.50 – **62 rm** 150.00/170.00.

♦ Well-appointed corporate hotel close to the University and Royal parks. Cosy and traditional lounge with open fires. Quietest rooms overlook an attractive courtyard. Relaxed conservatory restaurant.

✗ Ayudhya
p. 13 **CY** **z**

14 Kingston Hill, KT2 7NH, ☎ (020) 8549 5984, *Fax (020) 8546 5878*
ⓦⓔ 🆎 ⓞ *VISA*
closed 25 December, 1 January and Monday – **Meals** - Thai - a la carte 13.45/ 22.85.

♦ Elaborate wood carvings, potted plants and authentic Thai statues feature in this cosy and traditional restaurant. Extensive menu of subtly spiced and fragrant dishes.

Surbiton *Surrey – ⊠ Surrey.*

✗ The French Table
p. 13 **CY** **a**

85 Maple Rd, KT6 4AW, ☎ (020) 8399 2365, *Fax (020) 8390 5353*
🍴. ⓦⓔ *VISA*
closed 25-26 December, 1 week January, last 2 weeks in August, Monday, Sunday dinner and lunch Tuesday and Saturday – **Meals** - French-Mediterranean - 15.50 (lunch) and dinner a la carte 23.55/28.25.

♦ The lively atmosphere makes this narrow room with wooden tables and modern art a popular local. Attentive and relaxed service of a concise French-Mediterranean menu.

LAMBETH *Ctr London.*

Clapham Common *Ctr London – ⊠ SW4.*

🏨 Windmill on the Common
p. 17 **DQ** **e**

Clapham Common South Side, SW4 9DE, ☎ (020) 8673 4578, *windmill@youngs.co.uk, Fax (020) 8675 1486*
⇔ rm, 🍴 📺 📞 ♿ 🅿 ⓦⓔ 🆎 *VISA*. ⅏
closed 24-27 December **Meals** a la carte 14.15/15.45 ⚲ – **29 rm** ⊑ 96.00/ 130.00.

♦ A former Victorian pub that has been sympathetically extended over the years. Pleasant spot on the Common. Well-kept and comfortable rooms of assorted sizes. Dining room and adjacent log-fired bar.

XX **Thyme** p. 17 **DQ** **v**

14 Clapham Park Rd, SW4 7BB, ℘ (020) 7627 2468, *Fax (020) 7627 2424*
MO AE O VISA

closed 2 weeks August and Christmas – **Meals** (dinner only) a la carte 27.50/
30.50 ♈.

◆ Distinct neighbourhood feel with bustling ambience. Interesting concept:
starter size portions, in order to experience wide range of flavours.

X **Tsunami** p. 17 **DQ** **a**

Unit 3, 1-7 Voltaire Rd, SW4 6DQ, ℘ (020) 7978 1610, *Fax (020) 7978 1591*
MO AE O VISA JCB

closed 23 December-3 January and Sunday – **Meals** - Japanese - (dinner only
and Saturday lunch) 30.00/35.00 and a la carte 25.00/35.00 **s**.

◆ Trendy, mininalist-style restaurant. Interesting Japanese menu with many
dishes designed for sharing and plenty of original options. Good Sushi and
Sashimi selection.

Herne Hill *Gtr London* – ✉ *SE24*.

XX **3 Monkeys** p. 14 **FX** **r**

136-140 Herne Hill, SE24 9QH, ℘ (020) 7738 5500, *jan@3monkeysrestaurant.
com, Fax (020) 7738 5505*
✢= ☰. MO AE O VISA JCB

closed 25-26 December – **Meals** - Indian - (dinner only) a la carte 19.85/
23.70 ♈.

◆ 'New wave' Indian restaurant in a converted bank. Dining room in bright
white reached via a bridge over the bar and kitchen. Menu uses influences
from all over India.

Kennington *Gtr London* – ✉ *SE11*.

XX **Kennington Lane** p. 30 **MZ** **s**

205-209 Kennington Lane, SE11 5QS, ℘ (020) 7793 8313, *Fax (020) 7793 8323*
☏ – ☰. MO AE O VISA

Meals 13.75 (lunch) and a la carte 23.90/26.00 ♈.

◆ Green-hued entrance with large awning leads into the contemporary interior. Bare wooden tables and fresh white walls. Purposeful staff, modern
menu with European influences.

X **Lobster Pot** p. 31 **NZ** **e**

3 Kennington Lane, SE11 4RG, ℘ (020) 7582 5556
☰. MO AE O VISA JCB

closed 24 December-first week January, Sunday and Monday – **Meals** - French
Seafood - 13.50/39.50 and a la carte 26.30/45.50.

◆ A nautical theme so bold you'll need your sea legs: fishing nets, shells,
aquariums, portholes, even the sound of seagulls. Classic French seafood
menu is more restrained.

Lambeth *Gtr London* – ✉ *SE1*.

🏨 **Novotel London Waterloo** p. 30 **LMY** **a**

113 Lambeth Rd, SE1 7LS, ℘ (020) 7793 1010, *h1785@accor-hotels.com,
Fax (020) 7793 0202*
Ⅰᵩ, ☎ – ☝, ✢= rm, ☰ 📺 📞 & ⇔ – 🏛 40. MO AE O VISA. ✻

Meals (bar lunch Saturday and Sunday) 19.95 and a la carte 19.40/29.15 **s**. ♈ –
☐ 12.95 – **185 rm** 145.00/165.00, 2 suites.

◆ Modern, group owned purpose-built hotel, convenient for the station.
Uniformly decorated bedrooms, with a good level of extras. Secure basement
parking. Bright all-day brasserie.

Waterloo *Gtr London* – ✉ *SE1.*

Channel Tunnel : Eurostar information and reservations ✆ (08705) 186186.

London Marriott H. County Hall   p. 30   LY   a

SE1 7PB, ✆ (020) 7928 5200, *salesadmin.countyhall@marriotthotels.co.uk,*
Fax (020) 7928 5300

≤, ᵇ₆, ⊜ₛ, 🔲 – 🔢, ⅞= rm, ▤ 📺 ✆ ⅙ – 🔥 70. ⬛⊚ ᴬᴱ ⓞ 𝗩𝗜𝗦𝗔 𝗝𝗖𝗕.
🐾

County Hall : **Meals** 24.50 (lunch) and a la carte 27.00/41.00 ⌸ – 🍵 18.95 –
195 rm 287.80, 5 suites.

◆ Occupying the historic County Hall building. Many of the spacious and
comfortable bedrooms enjoy river and Parliament outlook. Impressive leisure
facilities. Famously impressive views from restaurant.

London County Hall Travel Inn Capital   p. 30   MX   u

Belvedere Rd, SE1 7PB, ✆ (020) 7902 1600, *Fax (020) 7902 1619*
🔢 ⅞=, ▤ rest, 📺 ⅙. ⬛⊚ ᴬᴱ ⓞ 𝗩𝗜𝗦𝗔. 🐾
Meals (grill rest.) (dinner only) – **313 rm** 79.95.

◆ Adjacent to the London Eye and within the County Hall building. Budget
accommodation in a central London location that is the envy of many, more
expensive, hotels.

Days Inn   p. 30   MY   x

54 Kennington Rd, SE1 7BJ, ✆ (020) 7922 1331, Reservations (Free-
phone) 0800 0280400, *waterloo@daysinn.co.uk, Fax (020) 7922 1441*
without rest. – 🔢 ⅞= 📺 ✆ ♿ ⅙. ⬛⊚ ᴬᴱ ⓞ 𝗩𝗜𝗦𝗔. 🐾
162 rm 82.00.

◆ Useful lodge accommodation, opposite the Imperial War Museum. Identical bedrooms are well-equipped and decorated in warm colours. Competitively priced.

When looking for a quiet hotel
use the maps in the introduction
or look for establishments with the sign 🐾*.*

LONDON HEATHROW AIRPORT – *see Hillingdon, London p. 61.*

MERTON *Gtr London.*

Colliers Wood *Gtr London* – ✉ *SW19.*

Express by Holiday Inn   p. 14   EY   a

200 High St, SW19 2BH, on A 24, ✆ (020) 8545 7300, *Fax (020) 8545 7301*
without rest. – 🔢 ⅞= 📺 ✆ ♿ ⅙ 🚗 – 🔥 50. ⬛⊚ ᴬᴱ ⓞ 𝗩𝗜𝗦𝗔
83 rm 89.00.

◆ Modern, corporate budget hotel. Spacious and well-equipped bedrooms;
power showers in en suite bathrooms. Ideal for the business traveller. Continental breakfast included.

Morden *Gtr London* – ✉ *Morden.*

Travelodge   p. 13   DY   c

Epsom Rd, SM4 5PH, Southwest : on A 24, ✆ (08700) 850950,
Fax (020) 8640 8227
without rest. – ⅞= 📺 ⅙ 🅿. ⬛⊚ ᴬᴱ ⓞ 𝗩𝗜𝗦𝗔 𝗝𝗖𝗕. 🐾
32 rm 69.95.

◆ Suitable for both corporate travellers and families alike. Spacious, carefully
designed, bright and modern ensuite bedrooms.

Wimbledon *Ctr London –* ✉ *SW19.*

Cannizaro House
p. 13 **DXY** x

West Side, Wimbledon Common, SW19 4UE, ☎ (0870) 333 9124, *cannizaro house@thistle.co.uk, Fax (0870) 3339224*

🐾, ≤, 🌭, 🏛 – |$|, ⭐ rm, 📺 ☎ 🅿 – 🚹 60. 🆖 AE ⓪ VISA JCB. ⚡

Meals 23.75/26.75 and a la carte 28.75/47.45 � – ⊑ 14.50 – **43 rm** 228.00, 2 suites.

♦ Part Georgian mansion in a charming spot on the Common. Appealing drawing room popular for afternoon tea. Rooms in original house are antique furnished, some with balconies. Refined restaurant overlooks splendid formal garden.

✕ Light House
p. 13 **DY** n

75-77 Ridgway, SW19 4ST, ☎ (020) 8944 6338, *lightrest@aol.com, Fax (020) 8946 4440*

🆖 AE VISA JCB

closed Easter, 25-26 December, Sunday dinner and Monday lunch – **Meals** - Italian influences - a la carte 19.00/32.40 �.

♦ Bright and modern neighbourhood restaurant with open plan kitchen. Informal service of a weekly changing and diverse menu of progressive Italian/fusion dishes.

The Fire Stables
p. 16 **AR** a

27-29 Church Rd, SW19 5DQ, ☎ (020) 8946 3197, *thefirestables@punchgroup. co.uk, Fax (020) 8946 1101*

▤. 🆖 AE VISA JCB

closed 25 December – **Meals** a la carte 19.00/26.50 �.

♦ Modern "gastropub" in village centre. Open-plan kitchen. Polished wood tables and banquettes. Varied modern British dishes. Expect fishcakes, duck confit salad or risotto.

Send us your comments on the restaurants we recommend and your opinion on the specialities and local wines they offer.

REDBRIDGE *Ctr London.*

🛈 *Central Library Ilford Essex* ☎ *(020) 0700 2420.*

Ilford *Essex –* ✉ *Essex.*

🏌 *Wanstead Park Rd* ☎ *(020) 8554 2930,* **HU** – 🏌18, 🏌9 *Fairlop Waters, Forest Rd, Barkingside* ☎ *(020) 8500 9911* **JT**.

Travelodge
p. 11 **HU** e

Beehive Lane, IG4 5DR, ☎ (08700) 850950, *Fax (020) 8550 4248*

⭐ rm, 📺 ♿ 🅿. 🆖 AE ⓪ VISA JCB. ⚡

Meals (grill rest.) – **32 rm** 59.95.

♦ Just off the main A12, a standard lodge-style hotel with well-maintained and spacious bedrooms. Harvester pub alongside provides a menu specialising in grilled dishes.

Travel Inn Metro
p.11 **HU** i

Redbridge Lane East, IG4 5BG, ☎ (020) 8550 7909, *Fax (020) 8550 6214*

|$|, ⭐ rm, ▤ rest, 📺 ♿ 🅿 – 🚹 40. 🆖 AE ⓪ VISA. ⚡

Meals (grill rest.) – **44 rm** 54.95.

♦ Convenient for the M11, well-kept lodge accommodation with standard sized bedrooms, all with extra sofa beds. Beefeater adjacent provides a grill-based menu.

South Woodford *Essex –* ✉ *Essex.*

 Ho-Ho   p. 11   **HU**   **c**

20 High Rd, E18 2QL, ☏ (020) 8989 1041

📖. 🆖 AE ⓪ VISA

closed 25-27 December and Saturday lunch – **Meals** - Chinese (Peking, Sze-chuan) - 16.50/27.50 and a la carte 27.30/44.80 **s.**

◆ Large room with tiled floor and Chinese decoration. Attentive service from smart team. Menu specialises in Peking and Szechuan dishes, with extensive vegetarian choice.

Woodford *Essex –* ✉ *Essex.*

 2 Sunset Ave, Woodford Green ☏ *(020) 8504 0553.*

London 13 – Brentwood 16 – Harlow 16.

 County H. Epping Forest   p. 11   **HT**   **c**

30 Oak Hill, Woodford Green, IG8 9NY, ☏ (020) 8787 9988, *countyepping@corushotels.com, Fax (020) 8506 0941*

📶 ↩, 🍴 rest, TV P – 🛗 150. 🆖 AE ⓪ VISA. ❄

Meals *(closed Saturday lunch)* 19.00 (dinner) and a la carte 16.40/25.40 – ☕ 10.95 – **99 rm** 100.00/130.00.

◆ Purpose-built redbrick hotel on the edge of the historic Forest. Standard sized bedrooms, decorated with pine furniture. Extensive conference facilities. Informal dining room and adjacent bar.

The rates shown may be revised if the cost of living changes to any great extent. Before making your reservations, confirm with the hotelier the exact price that will be charged.

RICHMOND-UPON-THAMES *Gtr London.*

Barnes *Gtr London –* ✉ *SW13.*

 Sonny's   p. 13   **CX**   **x**

94 Church Rd, SW13 0DQ, ☏ (020) 8748 0393, *barnes@sonnys.co.uk, Fax (020) 8748 2698*

📖. 🆖 AE VISA

closed Sunday dinner – **Meals** 13.00/18.50 (lunch) and a la carte 22.50/34.00 ☕.

◆ Dine in the bright, modern and informal restaurant or the equally relaxed café-bar. Attentive service of imaginative Mediterranean influenced dishes.

MVH   p. 13   **CX**   **e**

5 White Hart Lane, SW13 0PX, ☏ (020) 8392 1111, *mvhmm@aol.com, Fax (0208) 878 1919*

🆖 AE ⓪ VISA JCB

Meals 29.00/45.00 ☕.

◆ Restaurant exuding individuality, Bohemian-style bar area and a dining room that mixes a Louis XIV style and modern elements. Unique food in keeping with the mood.

Riva   p. 13   **CX**   **a**

169 Church Rd, SW13 9HR, ☏ (020) 8748 0434, *Fax (020) 8748 0434*

🆖 AE VISA

closed last 2 weeks August, 1 week Christmas-New Year, 4 days Easter, Saturday lunch and Bank Holidays – **Meals** - Italian - a la carte 26.00/34.50 ☕.

◆ The eponymous owner manages the polite service in this unassuming restaurant. Rustic and robust cooking uses some of Italy's finest produce. Extensive all-Italian wine list.

East Sheen *Gtr London* – ⊠ *SW14.*

XX **Redmond's** p. 13 **CX** v
170 Upper Richmond Road West, SW14 8AW, ℘ (020) 8878 1922, *pippahay ward@btconnect.com, Fax (020) 8878 1133*
▤. 🆘 Æ 𝗩𝗜𝗦𝗔
closed 3 days Christmas, first week January, lunch in August Saturday lunch, Sunday dinner and Bank Holidays except Good Friday – **Meals** 21.00/28.50.
♦ Bright, spacious and relaxed restaurant. Friendly and approachable service of modern British cooking, prepared with care.

XX **Crowther's** p. 13 **CX** n
481 Upper Richmond Rd West, SW14 7PU, ℘ (020) 8876 6372, *Pacrowther@aol.com, Fax (020) 8876 6372*
▤. 🆘 𝗩𝗜𝗦𝗔 𝗝𝗖𝗕
closed 2 weeks August, 25-31 December, Sunday and Monday – **Meals** (booking essential) (lunch by arrangement)/dinner 26.50.
♦ This traditional and homely restaurant continues to attract a loyal and local clientele. Concise Anglo-French menu cooked and served by the welcoming owners.

Hampton Court *Surrey* – ⊠ *Surrey.*

🏛 **Carlton Mitre** p. 12 **BY** v
Hampton Court Rd, KT8 9BN, ℘ (020) 8979 9988, *reesmitre@carltonhotels.co. uk, Fax (020) 8979 9777*
≤, 🍴 – 🛗 ⇖ 📺 🅟 – 🔼 25. 🆘 Æ ⓞ 𝗩𝗜𝗦𝗔. ✼
closed 1 January
Rivers Edge : Meals *(closed dinner Sunday and Bank holidays to non-residents and Saturday lunch)* 18.95 (lunch) and a la carte 29.00/37.50 – ⊑ 11.50 – **35 rm** 175.00, 1 suite.
♦ Built in 1665 to accommodate guests of the royal household. Attractive hotel in unrivalled position. Some of the comfy and well-appointed rooms have river or Palace views. Restaurant with superb views along river.

Hampton Hill *Middx* – ⊠ *Middx.*

XX **Monsieur Max** p. 12 **BY** a
❀ 133 High St, TW12 1NJ, ℘ (020) 8979 5546, *monsmax@aol.com, Fax (020) 8979 3747*
▤. 🆘 Æ ⓞ 𝗩𝗜𝗦𝗔
closed Saturday lunch – **Meals** - French - 25.00/37.50 ⊑.
♦ An appealing neighbourhood restaurant. Relaxed and attentive service of robust yet refined French bourgeois cooking. Guests can bring their own wine, if they prefer.
Spec. Grilled quail with boudin of parsley and guinea fowl. Slow-roasted Barbary duck with steamed pak choy and ginger. Strawberry soufflé.

Hampton Wick *Surrey* – ⊠ *Surrey.*

 Chase Lodge p. 12 **BY** e
10 Park Rd, KT1 4AS, ℘ (020) 8943 1862, *info@chaselodgehotel.com, Fax (020) 8943 9363*
📺. 🆘 Æ ⓞ 𝗩𝗜𝗦𝗔 𝗝𝗖𝗕
Meals (lunch by arrangement) a la carte 14.13/23.87 **s.** – **13 rm** ⊑ 65.00/150.00.
♦ Mid-terrace Victorian property in attractive residential road within an area of outstanding architectural and historical interest. Individually furnished, comfortable rooms. Bright, airy conservatory restaurant.

Kew *Surrey –* ⊠ *Surrey.*

XX **The Glasshouse**   p. 13   CX   Z

❁ 14 Station Par, TW9 3PZ, ℘ *(020) 8940 6777, Fax (020) 8940 3833*
🍽. ⓪⑤ AE VISA
closed 4 days at Christmas – **Meals** *19.50/30.00* ℤ.
◆ Light pours in through the glass façade of this forever busy and
contemporary restaurant. Assured service of original modern British cooking.
Spec. Salad of wood pigeon and truffled egg. Fillet of beef with mashed
potato, ceps and shallots. Chocolate fondant, cherry ice cream.

Richmond *Surrey –* ⊠ *Surrey.*

🏌, 🏌 *Richmond Park, Roehampton Gate* ℘ *(020) 8876 3205* CX – 🏌 *Sudbrook
Park* ℘ *(020) 8940 1463* CX.

🛈 *Old Town Hall, Whittaker Ave* ℘ *(020) 8940 9125.*

🏛 **Petersham**   p. 13   CX   C

Nightingale Lane, TW10 6UZ, ℘ *(020) 8940 7471, enq@petershamhotel.co.uk,
Fax (020) 8939 1002*
≤, 🚗 – ⇕ TV P – 🏖 50. ⓪⑤ AE ① VISA. ✻
Meals *– (see **Restaurant** below) –* **60 rm** ☲ *135.00/170.00, 1 suite.*
◆ Extended over the years, a fine example of Victorian Gothic architecture.
Impressive Portland stone, self-supporting staircase. Most comfortable
rooms overlook the Thames.

🏛 **Richmond Gate**   p. 13   CX   C

158 Richmond Hill, TW10 6RP, ℘ *(020) 8940 0061, richmondgate@corushotel
s.com, Fax (020) 8332 0354*
🏋, ⛲, 🔲, 🚗 – ⇥✕ TV 📞 P – 🏖 45. ⓪⑤ AE ① VISA JCB. ✻
Gates On The Park : **Meals** *(closed lunch Saturday) 19.75/31.00* and dinner a la carte – **67 rm** ☲ *150.00/178.00, 1 suite.*
◆ Originally four elegant Georgian town houses and now a very comfortable corporate hotel. Cosy lounges have a period charm. Well-appointed
rooms have thoughtful extras. Small, comfortable, Georgian style
restaurant.

🏨 **Richmond Hill**   p. 13   CX   C

Richmond Hill, TW10 6RW, ℘ *(020) 8940 2247, richmondhill@corushotels.com,
Fax (020) 8940 5424*
🏋, ⛲, 🔲 – ⇕, ⇥✕ rm, ▤ rest, TV 📞 P – 🏖 200. ⓪⑤ AE ① VISA
JCB
Pembrokes : **Meals** *(dancing Saturday evening) (carving lunch Sunday)
16.00/25.00 and a la carte 22.70/34.70 –* **133 rm** ☲ *160.00, 5 suites.*
◆ A modern corporate hotel hides behind the Georgian façade. In an
elevated position, some of the bedrooms have pleasing views of the Thames.
Spacious singles have 4ft beds. Conservatory styled restaurant.

⌂ **Doughty Cottage**   p. 13   CX   C

142A Richmond Hill, TW10 6RN, ℘ *(020) 8332 9434, deniseoneill425@aol.
co.uk, Fax (020) 8948 3716*
without rest., 🚗 – ⇥✕ TV P. ⓪⑤ VISA. ✻
closed 25 December – **3 rm** ☲ *80.00/120.00.*
◆ Positioned high above the river, this attractive 18C Regency house is
discreetly set behind a picturesque walled garden. Thoughtfully equipped
rooms, two with patio gardens.

XXX **Restaurant** (at Petersham H.)   p. 13   **CX**   **C**
Nightingale Lane, TW10 6UZ, ℰ (020) 8939 1084, *Fax (020) 8939 1002*
≼, 🚗 – 🅿, ⓜ⓪ 🄰🄴 ⓞ 𝘝𝘐𝘚𝘈
closed 25-26 December – Meals (residents only Sunday dinner) 20.00/25.00
and a la carte 30.50/37.00 **s.**
♦ Tables by the window have spectacular views across royal parkland and the
winding Thames. Formal surroundings in which to enjoy classic and modern
cooking. See the cellars.

Twickenham *Middx –* ✉ *Middx.*

XX **McClements**   p. 12   **BX**   **a**
2 Whitton Rd, TW1 1BJ, ℰ (020) 8744 9610, *johnmac21@aol.com,*
Fax (020) 8744 9598
▤, ⓜ⓪ 🄰🄴 𝘝𝘐𝘚𝘈
Meals 24.00/34.00 ♀.
♦ An attractive and intimate neighbourhood restaurant. The eponymous
owner offers an elaborate selection of traditional and modern dishes.
'Degustation' menu includes wines.

X **Brula**   p. 12   **BX**   **v**
43 Crown Rd, St Margarets, TW1 3EJ, ℰ (020) 8892 0602, *Fax (020) 8892 7727*
ⓜ⓪ 𝘝𝘐𝘚𝘈
closed 1 week Christmas, Sunday and Bank Holidays – Meals (booking essential) 11.00 (lunch) and a la carte 23.50/28.00.
♦ Behind the stained glass windows and the rose arched entrance, you'll find
an intimate and cosy bistro. Friendly and relaxed service of a weekly
changing, rustic menu.

The Guide changes, so renew your Guide every year.

SOUTHWARK *Gtr London.*

🅩 *London Bridge, 6 Tooley St* ℰ *(020) 7403 8299.*

Bermondsey *Gtr London –* ✉ *SE1.*

🏨 **London Bridge**   p. 31   **PX**   **a**
8-18 London Bridge St, SE1 9SG, ℰ (020) 7855 2200, *sales@london-bridge-hot*
cl.co.uk, Fax (020) 7855 2233
ℐ₆ – 🛗, ⇆ rm, ▤ 📺 📞 ᵬ – ⚖ 100. ⓜ⓪ 🄰🄴 ⓞ 𝘝𝘐𝘚𝘈 🄹🄲🄱. ⚘
Meals – (see *Simply Nico* below) – ⌨ 13.95 – **138 rm** 190.00/225.00, 3 suites.
♦ In one of the oldest parts of London, independently owned with an ornate
façade dating from 1915. Modern interior with classically decorated bedrooms and an impressive gym.

🏨 **London Tower Bridge Travel Inn Capital**   p. 31   **PY**   **a**
159 Tower Bridge Rd, SE1 3LP, ℰ (020) 7940 3700, *Fax (020) 7940 3719*
🛗, ⇆ rest, 📺 ᵬ 🅿, ⓜ⓪ 🄰🄴 ⓞ 𝘝𝘐𝘚𝘈. ⚘
Meals (grill rest.) (dinner only) – **195 rm** 74.95.
♦ Ideal for tourists by being next to a tube station and the famous bridge.
Clean and spacious budget accommodation, with uniform-sized bedrooms.

XXX **Le Pont de la Tour**   p. 31   **PX**   **C**
36d Shad Thames, Butlers Wharf, SE1 2YE, ℰ (020) 7403 8403,
Fax (020) 7403 0267
≼, 🚗 – ⓜ⓪ 🄰🄴 ⓞ 𝘝𝘐𝘚𝘈
closed Saturday lunch – Meals 28.50 (lunch) and dinner a la carte 50.00/60.00
♀.
♦ Elegant and stylish room commanding spectacular views of the Thames
and Tower Bridge. Formal and detailed service. Modern menu with an additional crustacea bar.

XX **Bengal Clipper** p. 31 **PX** e
Cardamom Building, Shad Thames, Butlers Wharf, SE1 2YR, *℘ (020) 7357 9001, clipper@bengalrestaurants.co.uk, Fax (020) 7357 9002*
▤. **MO** **AE** **①** **VISA** **JCB**
Meals - Indian - a la carte 12.00/24.85.
◆ Housed in a Thames-side converted warehouse, a smart Indian restaurant with original brickwork and steel supports. Menu features Bengali and Goan dishes. Evening pianist.

XX **Tentazioni** p. 14 **GV** x
2 Mill St, Lloyds Wharf, SE1 2BD, *℘ (020) 7237 1100, tentazioni@aol.com, Fax (020) 7237 1100*
MO **AE** **VISA** **JCB**
closed 25-26 December, Sunday, lunch Saturday and Monday – **Meals** - Italian - 19.00 (lunch) and a la carte 26.00/34.00 ⌇.
◆ Former warehouse provides a bright and lively environment. Open staircase between the two floors. Keenly run, with a menu offering simple, carefully prepared Italian food.

XX **Simply Nico** (at London Bridge H.) p. 31 **PX** a
8-18 London Bridge St, SE1 9SG, *℘ (020) 7407 4536, simplynico@trpplc.com, Fax (020) 7407 4554*
▤. **MO** **AE** **①** **VISA** **JCB**
closed Christmas-New Year, lunch Saturday and Sunday and Bank Holidays – **Meals** 14.50 and a la carte 20.50/31.50.
◆ Within the hotel, but with its own access from the street. Part of a small chain, providing a modern interpretation of classic French cooking.

X **Blue Print Café** p. 31 **PX** u
Design Museum, Shad Thames, Butlers Wharf, SE1 2YD, *℘ (020) 7378 7031, Fax (020) 7357 8810*
≼ Tower Bridge – **MO** **AE** **①** **VISA**
Meals 22.50 (lunch) and dinner a la carte 28.50/42.00.
◆ Above the Design Museum, with impressive views of the river and bridge: handy binoculars on tables. Eager and energetic service, modern British menus: robust and rustic..

X **Cantina Del Ponte** p. 31 **PX** c
36c Shad Thames, Butlers Wharf, SE1 2YE, *℘ (020) 7403 5403, Fax (020) 7403 4432*
≼, 🍴 – **MO** **AE** **①** **VISA**
closed Sunday dinner – **Meals** - Italian - 12.50 (lunch) and a la carte 20.00/28.00 ⌇.
◆ Quayside setting with a large canopied terrace. Terracotta flooring; modern rustic style décor, simple and unfussy. Tasty, refreshing Mediterranean-influenced cooking.

X **Butlers Wharf Chop House** p. 31 **PX** n
36e Shad Thames, Butlers Wharf, SE1 2YE, *℘ (020) 7403 3403, Fax (020) 7403 3414*
≼ Tower Bridge, 🍴 – **MO** **AE** **①** **VISA**
closed Sunday dinner – **Meals** 23.75 (lunch) and dinner a la carte 30.00/40.00 ⌇.
◆ Book the terrace in summer and dine in the shadow of Tower Bridge. Rustic feel to the interior, with obliging service. Menu focuses on traditional English dishes.

Dulwich *Gtr London* – ✉ *SE19.*

XX **Belair House** p. 14 **FX** e
Gallery Rd, Dulwich Village, SE21 7AB, ℘ (020) 8299 9788, *belairhouse@aol. com, Fax (020) 8299 6793*

closed Sunday dinner and Monday
Meals 27.00/32.00 ♀.
◆ A striking Georgian summer house, floodlit at night, and surrounded by manicured lawns. By contrast, interior is bright and modern with summery colours. Eclectic menu.

Rotherhithe *Gtr London* – ✉ *SE16.*

🏰 **Hilton London Nelson Dock** p. 14 **GV** r
265 Rotherhithe St, Nelson Dock, SE16 5HW, ℘ (020) 7231 1001, *Fax (020) 7231 0599*

closed 22-29 December
Three Crowns : **Meals** (dinner only) a la carte 27.95/33.75 ♀
Columbia's : **Meals** - Chinese - *(closed Sunday)* (dinner only) a la carte approx. 16.95 ♀ – ☒ 15.00
364 rm 125.00, 4 suites.
◆ Redbrick group hotel with glass façade. Guests can catch the river-taxi from the hotel's own pier. Extensive leisure facilities. Standard size rooms with all the mod cons. Three Crowns boasts pleasant views of the dock. Columbia's specialises in stir-fry

Southwark *Gtr London* – ✉ *SE1.*

🏨 **Mercure** p. 31 **ox** r
71-79 Southwark St, SE1 0JA, ℘ (020) 7902 0800, *h2814@accor-hotels.com, Fax (020) 7902 0810*
𝑓ₐ – |‡| ✸× TV 📞 ⅙ – ᴁ 35. ⓝ◎ ᴀᴇ ⓞ VISA
The Loft : **Meals** 12.50 (lunch) and a la carte approx. 26.00 ♀. ☒ 12.95 –
144 rm 140.00/160.00.
◆ Newly converted office block, providing bright and spacious accommodation. Modern, open-plan lobby leads to well-equipped and comfortable bedrooms. Split-level dining room with tiled flooring.

🏛 **Premier Lodge** p. 31 **ox** a
Anchor, Bankside, 34 Park St, SE1 9EF, ℘ (0870) 7001456, *Fax (0870) 7001457*
|‡| ✸× rm, TV 📞 ⅙. ⓝ◎ ᴀᴇ ⓞ VISA. ✸
Meals (grill rest.) a la carte 9.90/19.70
56 rm 69.95.
◆ A good value lodge with modern, well-equipped bedrooms which include a spacious desk area, ideal for the corporate and leisure traveller.

🏛 **Express by Holiday Inn** p. 31 **ox** e
103-109 Southwark St, SE1 0JQ, ℘ (020) 7401 2525, *stay@expresssouthwark. co.uk, Fax (020) 7401 3322*
without rest. – |‡| ✸× TV 📞 ⅙ ℙ. ⓝ◎ ᴀᴇ ⓞ VISA. ✸
88 rm 95.00.
◆ Useful location, just ten minutes from Waterloo. Purpose-built hotel with modern bedrooms in warm pastel shades. Fully equipped business centre.

XXX **Oxo Tower** p. 31 NX a
(8th floor), Oxo Tower Wharf, Barge House St, SE1 9PH, ℰ (020) 7803 3888,
oxo.reservations@harveynichols.co.uk, Fax (020) 7803 3838
London skyline and River Thames, – . **◍◉ AE ◍ VISA**
JCB
closed 25-26 December – **Meals** 28.50 (lunch) and dinner a la carte 27.50/
43.00 – (see also *Oxo Tower Brasserie* below).
♦ Top of a converted factory, providing stunning views of the Thames and
beyond. Stylish, minimalist interior with huge windows. Smooth service, with
modern British cooking.

XX **Baltic** p. 31 NX e
74 Blackfriars Rd, SE1 8HA, ℰ (020) 7928 1111, *info@balticrestaurant.co.uk,
Fax (020) 7928 8487*
◍◉ AE VISA
closed 25 December and Saturday lunch – **Meals** - East European with Baltic
influences - a la carte 18.40/30.65 .
♦ Set in a Grade II listed 18C former coach house. Enjoy authentic and hearty
east European and Baltic influenced food. Interesting vodka selection and live
jazz on Sundays.

X **Oxo Tower Brasserie** p. 31 NX a
(8th floor), Oxo Tower Wharf, Barge House St, SE1 9PH, ℰ (020) 7803 3888,
Fax (020) 7803 3838
London skyline and River Thames, – . **◍◉ AE ◍ VISA**
JCB
closed 25-26 December – **Meals** 23.50 (lunch) and a la carte 21.50/
31.50 .
♦ Same views but less formal than the restaurant. Open-plan kitchen,
relaxed service and the modern menu is slightly lighter. In summer, try to
secure a table on the terrace.

X **Cantina Vinopolis** p. 31 OX z
No 1 Bank End, SE1 9BU, ℰ (020) 7940 8333, *cantina@vinopolis.co.uk,
Fax (020) 7940 8334*
. **◍◉ AE ◍ VISA JCB**
closed Christmas, New Year and Bank Holidays – **Meals** 15.75 (lunch)
and a la carte 27.50/32.50 .
♦ Large, solid brick vaulted room under Victorian railway arches, with an
adjacent wine museum. Modern menu with a huge selection of wines by the
glass.

X **Livebait** p. 31 NX c
43 The Cut, SE1 8LF, ℰ (020) 7928 7211, *Fax (020) 7928 2279*
◍◉ AE ◍ VISA JCB
closed 25 December, 1 January, Sunday and Bank Holidays – **Meals** - Seafood -
15.50 (lunch) and a la carte 21.15/30.50 .
♦ Slight Victorian feel with wall tiles and booths. Lively atmosphere is dis-
tinctly modern. Helpful and obliging service. Comprehensive seafood menu
from the on-view kitchen.

X **Tate Cafe (7th Floor)** p. 31 OX s
Tate Modern, Bankside, SE1 9TE, ℰ (020) 7401 5020, *Fax (020) 7401 5171*
London skyline and River Thames – . **◍◉ AE ◍ VISA**
closed 24-26 December – **Meals** (lunch only and dinner Friday-Saturday)
a la carte 16.00/28.00 .
♦ Modernity to match the museum, with vast murals and huge windows
affording stunning views. Canteen-style menu at a sensible price with obliging service.

Fish!
p. 31 **PX** s

Cathedral St, Borough Market, SE1 9AL, ✆ (020) 7407 3803, *info@fish.plc.uk,*
Fax (020) 7407 3804

🍴 – ▤ 🆖 AE ⓪ *VISA*

closed 25 December – **Meals** - Seafood - a la carte 20.00/25.00.

◆ Under railway arches, an unusual structure made entirely of glass and
metal. Seafood menu where diners choose the fish as well as the accompany-
ing sauce.

SUTTON *Gtr London.*

Carshalton *Surrey* – ✉ *Surrey.*

La Veranda
p. 13 **EZ** c

18-19 Beynon Rd, SM5 3RL, ✆ (020) 8647 4370

▤. 🆖 AE ⓪ *VISA*

closed Sunday and Bank Holidays – **Meals** - Italian - a la carte approx. 21.30.

◆ The rather unassuming façade belies the friendly atmosphere inside. The
regular clientele enjoy selecting their food from the extensive buffet. Traditional Italian cooking.

Sutton *Surrey* – ✉ *Surrey.*

🏌, 🏌 *Oak Sports Centre, Woodmansterne Rd, Carshalton* ✆ *(020) 8643 8363.*

Holiday Inn
p. 13 **DZ** a

Gibson Rd, SM1 2RF, ✆ (020) 8770 1311, *Fax (020) 8770 1539*
f₆, ≋s, 🔲 – 🛗, ✳ rm, ▤ 📺 ✆ & 🅿 – 🔏 180. 🆖 AE ⓪ *VISA* JCB.
✳

Meals 15.00 and a la carte approx 19.40 – ⊇ 14.95 – **115 rm** 165.00, 1 suite.

◆ Centrally located and modern. Offers comprehensive conference facilities.
Spacious and well-equipped bedrooms. An ideal base for both corporate and
leisure guests. Bright, modern, relaxed bar and restaurant.

Thatched House
p. 13 **DZ** e

135-141 Cheam Rd, SM1 2BN, ✆ (020) 8642 3131, *Fax (020) 8770 0684*
🚗 – ✳ rest, 📺 🅿 – 🔏 50. 🆖 ⓪ *VISA* JCB. ✳

Meals *(closed Sunday dinner, Monday lunch and Bank Holidays)* (bar lunch)/
dinner a la carte 12.75/25.00 – **32 rm** ⊇ 50.00/95.00.

◆ Part thatched and gabled private hotel on busy main road just out of the
town centre. Most comfortable and quietest rooms overlook the pretty
gardens. Rustic-styled dining room.

Michelin does not issue wall plaques to the hotels and restaurants
that it lists.

TOWER HAMLETS *Gtr London.*

Blackwall *Gtr London* – ✉ *E14.*

Ibis
p. 15 **HV** c

1 Baffin Way, E14 9PE, ✆ (020) 7517 1100, *h2177@accor-hotels.com,*
Fax (020) 7987 5916
without rest. – 🛗, ✳ rm, ▤ 📺 ✆ &. 🆖 AE ⓪ *VISA*

87 rm 71.95.

◆ Useful and sensibly priced accommodation, convenient for those visiting
Canary Wharf. Bedrooms are all identically shaped, simply decorated and
well-equipped.

Canary Wharf *Gtr London* – ✉ *E14.*

🏨 **Four Seasons** p. 10 **GV** v
Westferry Circus, E14 8RS, ☎ (020) 7510 1999, *caw.reservations@fourseasons.com, Fax (020) 7510 1998*
≤, 🍴, *Là*, ⓔs, 🖼 – 🛗, ⇼ rm, ▤ 🆃🆅 📞 ♿ 🚗 – 🏖 200. ⓶ AE ⑩ 𝗩𝗜𝗦𝗔 JCB ⚅

***Quadrato* : Meals** - Italian - 25.00/28.00 and a la carte 26.00/36.00 **s.** –
⊡ 18.50 – **128 rm** 329.00/411.25, 14 suites.
♦ Stylish new hotel opened in 2000, with striking river and city views. Atrium lobby leading to modern bedrooms boasting every conceivable extra. Detailed service. Sleek, stylish dining room with open-plan kitchen.

🏨 **Circus Apartments** p. 14 **GV** a
39 Westferry Circus, E14 8RW, ☎ (020) 7719 7000, *res@circusapartments.co.uk, Fax (020) 7719 7001*
without rest., *Là*, ⓔs, 🖼 – 🛗 ⇼ ▤ 🆃🆅 📞 🚗. ⓶ AE ⑩ 𝗩𝗜𝗦𝗔. ⚅
49 suites 240.00/290.00.
♦ Smart, contemporary, fully serviced appartment block close to Canary Wharf: rooms, comfortable and spacious, can be taken from one day to one year.

🍴🍴 **Ubon by Nobu** p. 14 **GV** a
34 Westferry Circus, E14 8RR, ☎ (020) 7719 7800, *ubon@noburestaurants.com, Fax (020) 7719 7801*
≤ River Thames and city skyline – 🛗 ▤ 🅿. ⓶ AE ⑩ 𝗩𝗜𝗦𝗔 JCB
closed Christmas-New Year, Bank Holidays, Sunday and Saturday lunch –
Meals - Japanese - 19.50/70.00 and a la carte approx. 45.00 ℧.
♦ Light, airy, open-plan restaurant, with floor to ceiling glass and great Thames views. Informal atmosphere. Large menu with wide selection of modern Japanese dishes.

🍴 **Fish!** p. 10 **GV** v
Hanover House, 33 West Circus, E14 8RR, ☎ (020) 7519 6020, *info@fish.plc.uk, Fax (020) 7519 6038*
🍴 – ▤. ⓶ AE ⑩ 𝗩𝗜𝗦𝗔
closed 25 December
Meals - Seafood - a la carte 20.00/25.00.
♦ Thames-side setting, beneath a large apartment block. Open-plan kitchen with a menu based around simply cooked seafood. Bright, informal room with obliging service.

East India Docks *Gtr London* – ✉ *E14.*

🏨 **Travelodge** p. 14 **GV** s
A 13 Coriander Ave, off East India Dock Rd, E14 2AA, off East India Dock Rd, ☎ (08700) 850950, *Fax (020) 7515 9178*
≤ – 🛗, ⇼ rm, ▤ rest, 🆃🆅 ♿ 🅿. ⓶ AE ⑩ 𝗩𝗜𝗦𝗔. ⚅
Meals (grill rest.)
232 rm 69.95.
♦ Overlooking the Millennium Dome, a larger than average lodge-style hotel with uniform sized bedrooms. Acres of parking and an informal café-bar on the ground floor.

St Katherine's Dock *Gtr London –* ✉ *E 1.*

XX **The Aquarium**   p. 14 **GV** **i**
Ivory House, E1W 1AT, ℰ (020) 7480 6116, *info@theaquarium.co.uk,*
Fax (020) 7480 5973
≼, 🕌 – ▤. 🐼 AE ⓪ VISA
closed 24-25 December, 1 January, Monday dinner, Sunday and Bank Holidays
– **Meals** *-* Seafood - 17.50/20.50 a la carte 23.00/82.00 ♀.
♦ Seafood restaurant in a pleasant marina setting with views of the boats
from some tables. Simple, smart modern décor. Menu of market-fresh, sea-
food dishes.

Spitalfields *Gtr London –* ✉ *E1.*

XX **Bengal Trader**   p. 27 **PU** **x**
44 Artillery Lane, E1 7NA, ℰ (020) 7375 0072, *trader@bengalrestaurant.com,*
Fax (020) 7247 1002
▤. 🐼 AE ⓪ VISA
Meals - Indian - a la carte 9.90/18.90.
♦ Contemporary Indian paintings feature in this stylish basement room be-
neath a ground floor bar. Menu provides ample choice of Indian dishes.

Whitechapel *Gtr London –* ✉ *E1.*

XX **Cafe Spice Namaste**   p. 14 **GV** **z**
16 Prescot St, E1 8AZ, ℰ (020) 7488 9242, *info@cafespice.co.uk,*
Fax (020) 7481 0508
▤. 🐼 AE ⓪ VISA JCB
closed 1 week Christmas, Sunday, Saturday lunch and Bank Holidays – **Meals** -
Indian - 20.00/40.00 and a la carte 14.50/19.25 ♀.
♦ A riot of colour from the brightly painted walls to the flowing drapes.
Sweet-natured service adds to the engaging feel. Fragrant and competitively
priced Indian cooking.

Wapping *Gtr London –* ✉ *E1.*

X **Wapping Food**   p. 14 **GV** **n**
Wapping Wall, E1W 3ST, ℰ (020) 7680 2080, *wappingfood@wapping-wpt.
com, Fax (020) 7680 2081*
🕌 – P. 🐼 AE ⓪ VISA
closed Christmas and New year and Sunday dinner **Meals** a la carte 25.25/
30.00 ♀.
♦ Something a little unusual; a combination of restaurant and gallery in a
converted hydraulic power station. Enjoy the modern menu surrounded by
turbines and TV screens.

WANDSWORTH *Gtr London.*

Battersea *Gtr London –* ✉ *SW8/SW11.*

🏨 **Express by Holiday Inn**   p. 16 **BQ** **a**
Smugglers Way, SW18 1EG, ℰ (020) 8877 5950, *wandsworth@oreil-leisure.co.
uk, Fax (020) 8877 0631*
without rest. – 🛗 ⤨ ▤ 📺 ☎ ⅙ P – 🔬 35. 🐼 AE ⓪ VISA, ⚇
148 rm 89.00.
♦ Modern, purpose-built hotel on major roundabout, very much designed
for the cost-conscious business guest or traveller. Adjacent steak house.
Sizeable, well-kept bedrooms.

Travelodge
p. 17   CQ   c

200 York Rd, SW11 3SA, ✆ (08700) 850950, *Fax (020) 7978 5898* without rest. – |≣| ⤨ TV & P, ✆ AE ⓪ VISA JCB. ✗

87 rm 69.95.

♦ Budget hotel in a converted office block. Good sized bedrooms, with large work desks and sofa beds. Clean, good value accommodation, close to the river.

Chada
p. 17   CQ   x

208-210 Battersea Park Rd, SW11 4ND, ✆ (020) 7622 2209, *Fax (020) 7924 2178*

▤ , ✆ AE ⓪ VISA JCB

closed Sunday and Bank Holidays – **Meals** - Thai - (dinner only) a la carte 13.30/27.75 ℃.

♦ Weather notwithstanding, the Thai ornaments and charming staff in traditional silk costumes transport you to Bangkok. Carefully prepared and authentic dishes.

The Stepping Stone
p. 17   DQ   c

123 Queenstown Rd, SW8 3RH, ✆ (020) 7622 0555, *thesteppingstone@aol. com, Fax (020) 7622 4230*

▤ . ✆ VISA

closed 5 days Christmas, Saturday lunch, Sunday and Bank Holidays – **Meals** a la carte 18.00/30.00.

♦ Big bold colours and thoughtful service make this pleasant contemporary restaurant a local favourite. Eclectic, modern menu. Small bar to the rear.

Ransome's Dock
p. 29   HZ   c

35-37 Parkgate Rd, SW11 4NP, ✆ (020) 7223 1611, *chef@ransomesdock.co.uk, Fax (020) 7924 2614*

⛱ – ✆ AE ⓪ VISA JCB

closed Christmas, August Bank Holiday and Sunday dinner – **Meals** a la carte 21.00/37.25 ℃.

♦ Secreted in a warehouse development, with a dock-side terrace in summer. Vivid blue interior, crowded with pictures. Chef patron produces reliable brasserie-style cuisine.

Duke of Cambridge
p. 17   CQ   a

228 Battersea Bridge Rd, SW11 3AA, ✆ (020) 7223 5662, *Fax (020) 7801 9684*

⛱ – ✆ VISA

Meals a la carte 15.85/22.85 ℃.

♦ Friendly neighbourhood pub, given a rustic makeover, with bookshelves and wooden flooring. Short menu, with blackboard specials, provides pub food with a modern twist.

Putney – ✉ SW15.

Putney Bridge
p. 16   AQ   u

Lower Richmond Rd, SW15 1LB, ✆ (020) 8780 1811, *Fax (020) 8780 1211*

⇐ – ▤ . ✆ AE ⓪ VISA JCB

closed 2 weeks Christmas-New Year, Sunday dinner and Monday – **Meals** 22.50/48.50 and a la carte 33.00/46.00 ℃.

♦ Winner of architectural awards, this striking glass and steel structure enjoys a charming riverside location. Exacting service; accomplished and detailed modern cooking.

Spec. Slow-roasted lobster, cream with Asian flavours. Roast squab with warm spiced bulgar, squash with argan oil. Chocolate moelleux, barley milk ice cream.

XX **Enoteca Turi** p. 16 AQ n

28 Putney High St, SW15 1SQ, ☏ (020) 8785 4449, *Fax (020) 8785 4449*
📧, 🅼🅾 🆎 ⑩ 𝗩𝗜𝗦𝗔

closed 25-26 December, 1 January, Sunday and Bank Holidays – **Meals** *-* Italian *- a la carte 22.50/30.75* ♎.

♦ A friendly neighbourhood Italian restaurant, overseen by the owner. Rustic cooking, with daily changing specials. Good selection of wine by the glass.

X **The Phoenix** p. 16 AQ s

Pentlow St, SW15 1LY, ☏ (020) 8780 3131, *phoenix@sonny's.co.uk, Fax (020) 8780 1114*
🍽 – 📧, 🅼🅾 🆎 𝗩𝗜𝗦𝗔

closed 25-26 December, 1 January and Bank Holidays – **Meals** *-* Italian influences *- 15.00/18.50 (lunch) and a la carte 22.25/32.70* ♎.

♦ Light and bright interior with French windows leading out on to a spacious terrace. Unfussy and considerate service. An eclectic element to the modern Mediterranean menu.

📠 **Coat and Badge** p. 16 AQ r

8 Lacy Rd, SW15 1NL, ☏ (020) 8788 4900, *Fax (020) 8780 5733*
🍽 – 🅼🅾 𝗩𝗜𝗦𝗔

Meals (bookings not accepted) a la carte approx 16.50 ♎.

♦ Edwardian pub with a modern facelift. Warm pastel colours, bookshelves and a large bar. Sit anywhere to eat from the blackboard menu, offering simple, tasty dishes.

Southfields *Gtr London –* ✉ *SW18.*

XX **Sarkhel's** p. 16 BR e

199 Replingham Rd, SW18 5LY, ☏ (020) 8870 1483, *veronica@sarkhels.co.uk, Fax (020) 8874 6603*
📧, 🅼🅾 🆎 ⑩ 𝗩𝗜𝗦𝗔

closed 25-26 December and Monday – **Meals** *-* Indian *- 10.00 (lunch) and a la carte 12.70/25.35* ♎.

♦ Recently expanded Indian restaurant with a large local following. Authentic, carefully prepared and well-priced dishes from many different Indian regions. Obliging service.

Tooting *Gtr London –* ✉ *SW17.*

X **Kastoori** p. 17 CR v

188 Upper Tooting Rd, SW17 7EJ, ☏ (020) 8767 7027
📧, 🅼🅾 𝗩𝗜𝗦𝗔

closed 25-26 December and lunch Monday and Tuesday – **Meals** *-* Indian Vegetarian *- a la carte 12.65/15.75.*

♦ Specialising in Indian vegetarian cooking with a subtle East African influence. Family-run for many years, a warm and welcoming establishment with helpful service.

X **Oh Boy** p. 17 CR c

843 Garratt Lane, SW17 0PG, ☏ (020) 8947 9760, *Fax (020) 8879 7867*
📧, 🅼🅾 🆎 ⑩ 𝗩𝗜𝗦𝗔 🅹🅲🅱

closed 25-26 December and Monday – **Meals** *-* Thai *- (dinner only) a la carte 12.90/15.95.*

♦ Long-standing neighbourhood Thai restaurant. Extensive menu offers authentic and carefully prepared dishes, in simple but friendly surroundings.

Wandsworth *Gtr London –* ✉ *SW12/SW17/SW18.*

※※ **Chez Bruce** (Poole)   p. 17   **CR**   e
❀   2 Bellevue Rd, SW17 7EG, ✆ (020) 8672 0114, *Fax (020) 8767 6648*
📧, 🆖 AE ⓪ VISA
Meals (booking essential) 23.00/30.00 ♀.
◆ An ever-popular restaurant, overlooking the Common. Simple yet considered modern British cooking. Convivial and informal, with enthusiastic service.
Spec. Risotto nero, red mullet and grilled squid. Pot-au-feu. Apricot and almond tart, amaretto ice cream.

※ **Bombay Bicycle Club**   p. 17   **DR**   o
95 Nightingale Lane, SW12 8NX, ✆ (020) 8673 6217, *Fax (020) 8673 9100*
🆖 AE ⓪ VISA
closed Christmas and Sunday – **Meals** - Indian - (dinner only) a la carte 23.50/28.00.
◆ Nestling in a residential area and decorated with plants and murals. Relaxed atmosphere with helpful service. Sound Indian cooking.

※ **Ditto**   p. 16   **BQ**   n
55-57 East Hill, SW18 2QE, ✆ (020) 8877 0110, *christian-gilles@ditto1.fsnet.co.uk, Fax (020) 8875 0110*
🆖 VISA JCB
closed 25-26 December, Saturday lunch and Sunday dinner – **Meals** 18.50 and a la carte 22.50/28.45 ♀.
◆ Relaxed bar on one side, informal restaurant on the other. Bright walls with modern pictures and a contemporary menu. Personally run by the young owners.

Prices
For notes on the prices quoted in this Guide,
see the explanatory pages.

WESTMINSTER (City of) *Gtr London.*

Bayswater and Maida Vale *Gtr London –* ✉ *W2/W9.*

🏨 **Royal Lancaster**   p. 37   **DZ**   e
Lancaster Terr., W2 2TY, ✆ (020) 7262 6737, *sales@royallancaster.com, Fax (020) 7724 3191*
⇐ – 🛗, ⇄ rm, 🗐 TV 📞 ⅙ P – 🎿 1400. 🆖 AE ⓪ VISA JCB. ⅏
The Pavement : Meals *(Sunday, Saturday)* a la carte 19.40/27.80 **s.** ♀ – (see also **Nipa** below) – ⌣ 15.00 – **394 rm** 290.00/378.00, 22 suites.
◆ Imposing purpose-built hotel overlooking Hyde Park. Some of London's most extensive conference facilities. Well-equipped bedrooms are decorated in an Asian style. Park overlooks charming Italian Gardens. Pavement is a relaxed brasserie.

🏨 **Hilton London Metropole**   p. 25   **GU**   c
Edgware Rd, W2 1JU, ✆ (020) 7402 4141, *Fax (020) 7724 8866*
⇐, ⅙, ⇌ , 🔲 – 🛗, ⇄ rm, 🗐 TV 📞 P – 🎿 2000. 🆖 AE ⓪ VISA JCB. ⅏
Meals a la carte 24.00/28.50 ♀ – ⌣ 17.00 – **1033 rm** 346.60, 25 suites.
◆ One of London's most popular convention venues by virtue of both its size and transport links. Well-appointed and modern rooms have state-of-the-art facilities. Vibrant restaurant and bar.

Hilton London Paddington
p. 37 **DZ a**

146 Praed St, W2 1EE, ℘ (020) 7850 0500, *rm_paddington@hilton.com, Fax (020) 7850 0600*

𝕀𝕓 – ⌂, ⇔ rm, ▤ TV 🕿 ⅙ – 🛁 400. ⓐ AE ⓞ VISA JCB. ✗

The Brasserie : Meals 20.00/30.00 ♀ – ⌑ 18.50 – **335 rm** 205.60, 20 suites.

♦ Early Victorian railway hotel, sympathetically restored in contemporary style with Art Deco details. Co-ordinated bedrooms with high tech facilities continue the modern style. Contemporarily styled brasserie offering a modern menu.

Marriott
p. 24 **FS c**

Plaza Parade, NW6 5RP, ℘ (020) 7543 6000, *marriottmaidavale@btinternet. com, Fax (020) 7543 2100*

𝕀𝕓, ⇌s, ▨ – ⌂, ⇔ rm, ▤ TV 🕿 ⅙ ⇔ – 🛁 200. ⓐ AE ⓞ VISA. ✗

Fratelli : Meals - Italian - (dinner only) a la carte 26.00/32.90 **s.** ♀ – ⌑ 13.95 – **207 rm** 116.30/139.80, 16 suites.

♦ A capacious hotel, a short walk from Marble Arch and Oxford Street. Well-equipped with both business and leisure facilities including 12m pool. Suites have small kitchens. Informal restaurant and brasserie.

The Hempel
p. 36 **CZ a**

31-35 Craven Hill Gdns, W2 3EA, ℘ (020) 7298 9000, *hotel@the-hempel.co.uk, Fax (020) 7402 4666*

✎, ↫ – ⌂ ▤ TV 🕿 ⅙. ⓐ AE ⓞ VISA JCB. ✗

I-Thai : Meals - Thai-Italian -(closed Sunday) 25.00/30.00 (lunch) and dinner a la carte 42.00/50.00 ♀ – ⌑ 17.50 – **40 rm** 323.10, 6 suites.

♦ A striking example of minimalist design. Individually appointed bedrooms are understated yet very comfortable. Relaxed ambience. Modern basement restaurant.

Thistle Hyde Park
p. 36 **CZ v**

Bayswater Rd, 90-92 Lancaster Gate, W2 3NR, ℘ (020) 7262 2711, *Fax (020) 7262 2147*

⌂ ⇔ ▤ TV 🕿 P – 🛁 30. ⓐ AE ⓞ VISA JCB. ✗

Meals *(closed Sunday)* (bar lunch Saturday) 19.50 (lunch) and a la carte 23.00/ 32.00 **s.** – ⌑ 16.95 – **52 rm** 204.45/233.80, 2 suites.

♦ Behind the ornate pillared façade sits an attractively restored hotel. Appealing to the corporate and leisure traveller, the generally spacious rooms retain a period feel. Aperitifs in relaxed conservatory before formal dining.

Hilton London Hyde Park
p. 36 **BZ c**

129 Bayswater Rd, W2 4RJ, ℘ (020) 7221 2217, *reservations@hydepark.stakis. co.uk, Fax (020) 7229 0557*

⌂ ⇔, ▤ rest, TV 🕿 – 🛁 100. ⓐ AE ⓞ VISA JCB. ✗

Meals (bar lunch)/dinner a la carte approx. 24.50 ♀ – ⌑ 12.95 – **128 rm** 158.60, 1 suite.

♦ Classical Victorian hotel on busy main road. Well-appointed bedrooms enjoy up to date facilities. Rooms to front have Park views. Intimate dining room or relaxed bar for meals.

Ramada Jarvis Hyde Park
p. 36 **BZ o**

150 Bayswater Rd, W2 4RT, ℘ (020) 7229 1212, *gm.hydepark@ramadajarvis.co .uk, Fax (020) 7229 2623*

⌂, ⇔ rm, TV 🕿 P – 🛁 100. ⓐ AE ⓞ VISA JCB

Meals a la carte 18.50/20.85 **s.** ♀ – ⌑ 10.95 – **212 rm** 150.00/170.00, 1 suite.

♦ Suitable for both business travellers and families alike. Spacious, carefully designed, bright and modern bedrooms. Studio rooms have extra workspace. Informal, open-plan bar and grill.

Mornington
p. 37   DZ s

12 Lancaster Gate, W2 3LG, ℰ (020) 7262 7361, *london@mornington.co.uk,*
Fax (020) 7706 1028
without rest. – |⬧| ⤙ TV. ⓜⓞ AE ⓞ VISA JCB
closed 23-27 December – **66 rm** ⌷ 125.00/170.00.
♦ The classic portico façade belies the cool and modern Scandinavian influ-
enced interior. Modern bedrooms are well-equipped and generally spacious.
Duplex rooms available.

Colonnade Town House
p. 24   FU e

2 Warrington Cres, W9 1ER, ℰ (020) 7286 1052, *res_colonnade@etontown*
house.com, Fax (020) 7286 1057
without rest. – |⬧| ⤙ 🖹 TV. ✆. ⓜⓞ AE ⓞ VISA JCB. ⅍
⌷ 12.50 – **40 rm** 148.00/210.00, 3 suites.
♦ Two Victorian townhouses and birthplace of code-breaker Alan Turing.
Stylish and comfortable bedrooms with heavy drapes and many extra
touches. Basement breakfast room.

Commodore
p. 36   CZ r

50 Lancaster Gate, W2 3NA, ℰ (020) 7402 5291, *reservations@commodore-ho*
tel.com, Fax (020) 7262 1088
|⬧|, ⤙ rm, TV. ✆. ⓜⓞ AE ⓞ VISA JCB. ⅍
Meals (dinner only) a la carte 14.00/26.50 – ⌷ 12.50 – **76 rm** 135.00/175.00,
3 suites.
♦ Three converted Georgian town houses in a leafy residential area. Bedrooms vary considerably in size and style. Largest rooms decorated with a
Victorian theme. Relaxed, casual bistro.

Miller's
p. 36   AZ a

111A Westbourne Grove, W2 4UW, ℰ (020) 7243 1024, *enquiries@millersuk.*
com, Fax (020) 7243 1064
without rest. – TV. ✆. ⓜⓞ AE ⓞ VISA. ⅍
8 rm 188.00/264.00.
♦ Victorian house brimming with antiques and knick-knacks. Charming sitting room provides the setting for a relaxed breakfast. Individual, theatrical
rooms named after poets.

Byron
p. 36   CZ z

36-38 Queensborough Terr, W2 3SH, ℰ (020) 7243 0987, *byron@capricornhot*
els.co.uk, Fax (020) 7792 1957
without rest. – |⬧| 🖹 TV. ⓜⓞ AE ⓞ VISA JCB. ⅍
44 rm ⌷ 78.00/120.00, 1 suite.
♦ Centrally located and refurbished in the late 1990's - an ideal base for
tourists. Bright and modern bedrooms are generally spacious and all have
showers ensuite.

Delmere
p. 37   DZ v

130 Sussex Gdns, W2 1UB, ℰ (020) 7706 3344, *delmerehotel@compuserve.*
com, Fax (020) 7262 1863
|⬧|, ⤙ rm, TV. ✆. ⓜⓞ AE ⓞ VISA JCB. ⅍
Meals *(closed Sunday)* (dinner only) 19.00 – ⌷ 6.00 – **36 rm** 86.00/
107.00.
♦ Attractive stucco fronted and porticoed Victorian property. Now a friendly
private hotel. Compact bedrooms are both well-equipped and kept. Modest
prices. Bright, relaxed restaurant and adjacent bar.

Comfort Inn p. 36 CZ e
18-19 Craven Hill Gdns, W2 3EE, ℘ (020) 7262 6644, *comfortinn_hydepark@compuserve.com, Fax (020) 7262 0673*
without rest. – 📶 ✉ 📺 📞, 🆖 AE ① *VISA*, 🚭
🛏 4.50 – **67 rm** 84.00/104.00.
♦ Situated in a fairly quiet and attractive residential area. Functional, clean and well-kept budget accommodation appeals to the tourist.

Nipa (at Royal Lancaster H.) p. 37 DZ e
Lancaster Terr, W2 2TY, ℘ (020) 7262 6737, *Fax (020) 7724 3191*
🍽 **P**, 🆖 AE ① *VISA* JCB
closed Saturday lunch, Sunday and Bank Holidays – **Meals** - Thai - 14.90/28.00 and a la carte 30.30/42.30 **s**.
♦ On the 1st floor and overlooking Hyde Park. Authentic and ornately decorated restaurant offers subtly spiced Thai cuisine. Keen to please staff in traditional silk costumes.

Al San Vincenzo p. 37 EZ o
30 Connaught St, W2 2AF, ℘ (020) 7262 9623
🆖 *VISA* JCB
closed Saturday lunch and Sunday – **Meals** - Italian - (booking essential) 28.50/34.50 🍷.
♦ A traditional Italian restaurant that continues to attract a loyal clientele. Rustic, authentic cooking and a wholly Italian wine list. Attentive service overseen by owner.

Jason's p. 24 FU c
Blomfield Rd, Little Venice, W9 2PA, ℘ (020) 7286 6752, *enquiries@jasons.co.uk, Fax (020) 7266 2656*
🍽 – 🆖 AE *VISA*
closed 25 December 1 January and Sunday dinner – **Meals** - Seafood - 18.95 and a la carte 21.75/28.90.
♦ Hidden behind a wall, one finds this charming spot beside Regent's Canal. Seafood can be enjoyed in the bright dining room or on the busy terrace beside the boats for hire.

Green Olive p. 24 FU a
5 Warwick Pl, W9 2PX, ℘ (020) 7289 2469, *Fax (020) 7266 5522*
🍽. 🆖 AE *VISA*
Meals - Italian - (booking essential) 14.50/24.00.
♦ Attractive neighbourhood restaurant in a smart residential area. Modern Italian food served in the bright street level room or the more intimate basement.

Assaggi p. 36 AZ c
39 Chepstow Pl, (above Chepstow pub), W2 4TS, ℘ (020) 7792 5501, *nipi@assaggi1.demon.co.uk*
🍽. 🆖 ① *VISA* JCB
closed 2 weeks Christmas, Sunday and Bank Holidays – **Meals** - Italian - a la carte 29.85/36.40.
♦ Polished wood flooring, tall windows and modern artwork provide the bright surroundings for this forever busy restaurant. Concise menu of robust Italian dishes.

The Vale p. 24 ET z
99 Chippenham Rd, W9 2AB, ℘ (020) 7266 0990, *Fax (020) 7286 7224*
🍽. 🆖 ① *VISA* JCB
closed Christmas Sunday dinner and lunch Monday and Saturday – **Meals** 12.00/15.00 and a la carte 21.00/25.00 🍷.
♦ Dine in either the light and spacious conservatory, or in the original bar of this converted pub. Modern British food with Mediterranean influences. Destination bar below.

✗ Ginger
p. 36 **AZ** **v**

115 Westbourne Grove, W2 4UP, ☎ (020) 7908 1990, *info@gingerrestaurant. co.uk, Fax (020) 7908 1991*

▤ **M⊙** **AE** **VISA** **JCB**

closed 25 December – **Meals** - Bangladeshi - a la carte approx. 22.45 ♈.
◆ Bengali specialities served in contemporary styled dining room. True to its name, ginger is a key flavouring; dishes range from mild to spicy and are graded accordingly.

✗ L'Accento
p. 36 **BZ** **a**

16 Garway Rd, W2 4NH, ☎ (020) 7243 2201, *laccentorest@aol.com, Fax (020) 7243 2201*

☂ – **M⊙** **AE** **VISA** **JCB**

closed Sunday and Bank holidays – **Meals** - Italian - 17.00 and a la carte 22.00/ 26.50.
◆ Rustic surroundings and provincial, well priced, Italian cooking. Menu specialises in tasty pasta, made on the premises, and shellfish. Rear conservatory with removable roof.

✗ Formosa Dining Room (at Prince Alfred)
pg. 24 **FU** **n**

5A Formosa St, W9 1EE, ☎ (020) 7286 3287, *theprincealfred@thespiritgroup. com, Fax (020) 7286 3383*

▤ **M⊙** **AE** **VISA** **JCB**

closed 25 December – **Meals** a la carte 20.00/29.00 ♈.
◆ Traditional pub appearance and a relaxed dining experience on offer behind the elegant main bar. Contemporary style of cooking.

⛾ The Waterway
p. 24 **FU** **o**

54 Formosa St, W9 2JU, ☎ (020) 7266 3557, *info@thewaterway.co.uk, Fax (020) 7266 3547*

☂ – ▤. **M⊙** **VISA**

closed Christmas – **Meals** a la carte 17.40/28.00 ♈.
◆ Pub with a thoroughly modern, metropolitan ambience. Spacious bar and large decked terrace overlooking canal. Concise, well-balanced menu served in open plan dining room.

⛾ The Chepstow
p. 36 **AZ** **c**

39 Chepstow Pl, W2 4TS, ☎ (020) 7229 0323, *thechepstow@dial.pipex.com, Fax (020) 7288 1502*

▤. **M⊙** **VISA**

Meals a la carte 25.25/31.45.
◆ Dine in the bar with the regulars or the small restaurant behind. Modern and busy "gastropub" provides a daily changing menu of contemporary British dishes.

Belgravia *Gtr London* – ✉ *SW1.*

🏨 The Lanesborough
p. 29 **IY** **a**

Hyde Park Corner, SW1X 7TA, ☎ (020) 7259 5599, *info@lanesborough.com, Fax (020) 7259 5606*

🖬 – 🛗, ⇌ rm, ▤ 📺 ☏ & 🅿 – 🔬 90. **M⊙** **AE** **①** **VISA** **JCB**. ✑
The Conservatory : **Meals** 15.00/32.00 and a la carte approx. 46.00 **s.** ♈ – ⌁ 22.50 – **86 rm** 323.00/558.00, 9 suites.
◆ Converted from St. George's hospital in the 1990s, a grand and traditional atmosphere prevails. Butler service offered. Regency-era decorated, lavishly appointed rooms . Ornate, glass-roofed dining room with palm trees and fountains.

The Berkeley p. 35 FQ e
Wilton Pl, SW1X 7RL, ☏ (020) 7235 6000, info@the-berkeley.co.uk,
Fax (020) 7235 4330

🛁, ⇌s, ▭ – 🛗, ⟵✕⟶ rm, ▤ TV ☎ 🚗 – 🔥 220. ⦿⦿ AE ⦿ VISA JCB. ⦸

Meals – (see **Vong** below) – ☕ 21.50 – **186 rm** 376.00/493.00, 28 suites.
♦ A gracious and discreet hotel. Relax in the ornately gilded and panelled
Lutyens lounge or enjoy a swim in the roof-top pool with its retracting roof.
Opulent bedrooms.

 The Halkin p. 36 AV a
5 Halkin St, SW1X 7DJ, ☏ (020) 7333 1000, res@halkin.co.uk,
Fax (020) 7333 1100

🛗 ⟵✕⟶ ▤ TV ☎. ⦿⦿ AE ⦿ VISA JCB. ⦸

Meals – (see **Nahm** below) – ☕ 18.00 – **37 rm** 346.00/528.00, 4 suites.
♦ One of London's first minimalist hotels. The cool, marbled reception and
bar have an understated charm. Spacious rooms have every conceivable
facility.

 Sheraton Belgravia p. 35 FR u
20 Chesham Pl, SW1X 8HQ, ☏ (020) 7235 6040, reservations_central_london@
sheraton.com, Fax (020) 7201 1926

🛗, ⟵✕⟶ rm, ▤ TV ☎ & P – 🔥 25. ⦿⦿ AE ⦿ VISA JCB. ⦸

The Mulberry : Meals 17.00/22.00 and a la carte 25.00/32.75 ♀ – ☕ 17.50 –
82 rm 276.00/329.00, 7 suites.
♦ Modern corporate hotel overlooking Chesham Place. Comfortable and
well-equipped for the tourist and business traveller alike. A few minutes' walk
from Harrods.

 The Lowndes p. 35 FR i
21 Lowndes St, SW1X 9ES, ☏ (020) 7823 1234, contact@lowndeshotel.com,
Fax (020) 7235 1154

🍽 – 🛗, ⟵✕⟶ rm, ▤ TV ☎ P – 🔥 25. ⦿⦿ AE ⦿ VISA JCB. ⦸
closed 25 December
Brasserie 21 : Meals 18.50 and a la carte 26.50/35.25 ♀ – ☕ 16.00 – **77 rm**
293.75/299.60, 1 suite.
♦ Compact yet friendly modern corporate hotel within this exclusive residential area. Good levels of personal service offered. Close to the famous
shops of Knightsbridge. Modern restaurant opens onto street terrace.

🏠 **Diplomat** p. 35 FR a
2 Chesham St, SW1X 8DT, ☏ (020) 7235 1544, diplomat.hotel@btinternet.
co.uk, Fax (020) 7259 6153

without rest. – 🛗 TV ☎. ⦿⦿ AE ⦿ VISA JCB. ⦸
26 rm ☕ 98.00/175.00.
♦ Imposing Victorian corner house built in 1882 by Thomas Cubitt. Attractive
glass-domed stairwell and sweeping staircase. Spacious and well-appointed
bedrooms.

XX **Zafferano** p. 35 FR i
❀ 15 Lowndes St, SW1X 9EY, ☏ (020) 7235 5800, Fax (020) 7235 1971
▤. ⦿⦿ AE ⦿ VISA
closed 1 week Christmas-New Year and Bank Holidays – **Meals** - Italian -
24.50/37.50 ♀.
♦ Forever busy and relaxed. No frills, robust and gutsy Italian cooking, where
the quality of the produce shines through. Wholly Italian wine list has some
hidden treasures.
Spec. Pan-fried scallops with saffron vinaigrette. Linguine with lobster and
tomato. Veal cutlet with garlic.

XX **Nahm** (at The Halkin H.)   p. 36   AV a

5 Halkin St, SW1X 7DJ, ℰ (020) 7333 1234, *Fax (020) 7333 1100*
▤. 🆖 🅰🅴 🅾 *VISA* 🄹🄲🄱
closed lunch Saturday and Sunday – **Meals** - Thai - (booking essential) 25.00/
47.00 **s.** ⚎.
♦ Wood floored restaurant with uncovered tables and understated decor.
Menu offers the best of Thai cooking with some modern interpretation and
original use of ingredients.
Spec. Yam bpuu sot (lobster with mint). Geng krua hoi (red clam curry with
aubergine). Yam pla kem (deep-fried turbot with cashews and chillies).

XX **Vong** (at The Berkeley H.)   p. 35   FQ e

Wilton Pl, SW1X 7RL, ℰ (020) 7235 1010, *Fax (020) 7235 1011*
▤. 🆖 🅰🅴 *VISA* 🄹🄲🄱
closed Sunday Lunch – **Meals** - French-Thai - (booking essential) 20.00
(lunch) and a la carte 33.00/62.00 ⚎.
♦ Bright and cool modern restaurant. Original approach combines classical
French cooking with Thai ingredients and fragrant Asian flavours. Approachable and helpful service.

XX **Mango Tree**   p. 36   AX a

46 Grosvenor Pl, SW1X 7EQ, ℰ (020) 7823 1888, *mangotree@mangotree.org.
uk, Fax (020) 7838 9275*
▤. 🆖 🅰🅴 *VISA*
closed 25-26 December and Saturday lunch – **Meals** - Thai - 12.50/38.50
and a la carte 22.00/27.75 ⚎.
♦ Thai staff in regional dress in contemporarily styled dining room of refined
yet minimalist furnishings sums up the cuisine: authentic Thai dishes with
modern presentation.

XX **Noura Brasserie**   p. 36   AX n

16 Hobart Pl, SW1W 0HH, ℰ (020) 7235 9444, *Fax (020) 7235 9244*
▤. 🆖 🅰🅴 🅾 *VISA*
Meals - Lebanese - 14.50/28.50 and a la carte 20.50/28.25.
♦ Dine in either the bright bar or the comfortable, contemporary restaurant.
Authentic, modern Lebanese cooking specialises in char-grilled meats and
mezzes.

Hyde Park and Knightsbridge *Gtr London* – ✉ *SW1/SW7.*

🏨🏨 **Mandarin Oriental Hyde Park**   p. 35   FQ x

66 Knightsbridge, SW1X 7LA, ℰ (020) 7235 2000, *reserve-molon-info@mogh.
com, Fax (020) 7235 2001*
≼, 🛁, ⇌🅂 – 🛗, ✹ rm, ▤ 📺 ☏ 🔧 – 🛎 220. 🆖 🅰🅴 🅾 *VISA* 🄹🄲🄱.
✹
The Park : Meals 21.50 (lunch) and a la carte 25.00/42.00 ⚎ – (see also
Foliage below) – ⚌ 19.00 – **173 rm** 299.00/640.00, 25 suites.
♦ Built in 1889 this classic hotel, with striking façade, remains one of
London's grandest. Many of the luxurious bedrooms enjoy Park views.
Immaculate and detailed service. Relaxed, elegant dining room.

🏠 **Knightsbridge Green**   p. 35   EQ z

159 Knightsbridge, SW1X 7PD, ℰ (020) 7584 6274, *thekghotel@aol.com,
Fax (020) 7225 1635*
without rest. – 🛗 ✹ ▤ 📺 ☏. 🆖 🅰🅴 🅾 *VISA*. ✹ – ⚌ 10.50 – **16 rm**
110.00/145.00, 12 suites 170.00.
♦ Privately owned hotel, boasting peaceful sitting room with writing desk.
Breakfast - sausage and bacon from Harrods. - served in the generously
proportioned bedrooms.

Foliage (at Mandarin Oriental Hyde Park H.)   p. 35   FQ   **x**
66 Knightsbridge, SW1X 7LA, ℰ (020) 7201 3723, *Fax (020) 7235 4552*
■. **⑩** AE ⑪ VISA JCB.
Meals 25.00/50.00 ℤ.
♦ Reached via a glass-enclosed walkway that houses the cellar. Hyde Park outside the window reflected in the foliage-themed décor. Gracious service, skilled modern cooking.
Spec. Mosaic of salmon, red mullet and foie gras with bacon and herb salad. Roast sea bass, red wine risotto and cinnamon cream. Raspberry soufflé with panna cotta.

Isola   p. 35   EQ   **a**
(basement) 145 Knightsbridge, SW1X 7PA, ℰ (020) 7838 1044, *isola@gruppo. co.uk, Fax (020) 7838 1099*
■. **⑩** AE ⑪ VISA
closed Sunday – **Meals** - Italian - 16.50 (lunch) and a la carte 20.50/40.50 ℤ.
♦ In a contemporary basement, the main restaurant offers clean Italian cooking and prime ingredients. Large selection of wines by the glass.

Zuma   p. 35   EQ   **c**
5 Raphael St, SW7 1DL, ℰ (020) 7584 1010, *info@zumarestaurant.com, Fax (020) 7584 5005*
■. **⑩** AE ⑪ VISA JCB
closed 25-26 December and 1 January – **Meals** - Japanese - a la carte 17.00/38.50 ℤ.
♦ Strong modern feel with exposed pipes, modern lighting and granite flooring. A theatrical atmosphere around the Sushi bar and a varied and interesting modern Japanese menu.

Mr Chow   p. 35   EQ   **a**
151 Knightsbridge, SW1X 7PA, ℰ (020) 7589 7347, *Fax (020) 7584 5780*
■. **⑩** AE ⑪ VISA JCB
closed 24-26 December, 1 January and Easter Monday – **Meals** - Chinese - 18.00 (lunch) and a la carte 36.50/41.50 ℤ.
♦ Cosmopolitan Chinese restaurant with branches in New York and L.A. Well established ambience. Walls covered with mirrors and modern art. House specialities worth opting for.

Mayfair *Gtr London* – ✉ *W1*.

Dorchester   p. 32   BN   **a**
Park Lane, W1A 2HJ, ℰ (020) 7629 8888, *reservations@dorchesterhotel.com, Fax (020) 7409 0114*
ℹ₆, ℇ₅ – ▯, ℀ rm, ■ TV ☎ ₺ ⟺ – ⛛ 550. **⑩** AE ⑪ VISA JCB. ✂
Meals – (see *The Oriental* and *Grill Room* below) – ☐ 24.50 – **201 rm** 346.00/452.30, 49 suites 587.50/2,496.80.
♦ A sumptuously decorated, luxury hotel offering every possible facility. Impressive marbled and pillared promenade. Rooms quintessentially English in style. Faultless service.

Claridge's   p. 32   BL   **c**
Brook St, W1A 2JQ, ℰ (020) 7629 8860, *info@claridges.co.uk, Fax (020) 7499 2210*
ℹ₆ – ▯, ℀ rm, ■ TV ☎ ₺ – ⛛ 200. **⑩** AE ⑪ VISA JCB. ✂
Meals 29.50 a la carte 30.50/67.00 ℤ – (see also *Gordon Ramsay at Claridge's* below) – ☐ 22.00 – **143 rm** 370.00/493.50, 60 suites.
♦ The epitome of English grandeur, celebrated for its Art Deco. Exceptionally well-appointed and sumptuous bedrooms, all with butler service. Magnificently restored foyer.

Le Meridien Grosvenor House

p. 32 **AM** a

Park Lane, W1K 7TN, ℰ (020) 7499 6363, *grosvenor.reservations@forte-hotels .com, Fax (020) 7493 3341*

↓₆, ⇔s , ◩ – ⊪, ↤ rm, ▤ ▣ ✆ ↆ, ⇔ – ▲ 2000. ⫴ ⚎ ⓞ VISA JCB. ⌦

La Terrazza : Meals - Italian influences - *(closed Saturday lunch)* a la carte 31.25/39.25 ℤ – ⊂ 18.50 – **378 rm** 470.00/517.00, 74 suites.
♦ Over 70 years old and occupying an enviable position by the Park. Edwardian style décor. The Great Room, an ice rink in the 1920s, is Europe's largest banqueting room. Bright, relaxing dining room with contemporary feel.

Four Seasons

p. 32 **BP** a

Hamilton Pl, Park Lane, W1A 1AZ, ℰ (020) 7499 0888, *fsh.london@fourseason s.com, Fax (020) 7493 1895*

↓₆ – ⊪, ↤ rm, ▤ ▣ ✆ ↆ, ⇔ – ▲ 500. ⫴ ⚎ ⓞ VISA. ⌦
Lanes : Meals 37.00/35.00 and a la carte 35.50/47.75 s. ℤ – ⊂ 21.00 – **185 rm** 346.00/423.00, 35 suites.
♦ Set back from Park Lane so shielded from the traffic. Large, marbled lobby; its lounge a popular spot for light meals. Spacious rooms, some with their own conservatory. Restaurant's vivid blue and stained glass give modern, yet relaxing, feel.

Le Meridien Piccadilly

p. 33 **EM** a

21 Piccadilly, W1J OBH, ℰ (020) 7734 8000, *lmpiccres@lemeridien-hotels.com, Fax (020) 7437 3574*

↓₆, ⇔s , ◩, squash – ⊪, ↤ rm, ▤ ▣ ✆ ↆ, – ▲ 250. ⫴ ⚎ ⓞ VISA JCB

Meals – (see ***Terrace*** below) – ⊂ 21.50 – **248 rm** 330.00/395.00, 18 suites.
♦ Comfortable international hotel, in a central location. Boasts one of the finest leisure clubs in London. Individually decorated bedrooms, with first class facilities.

London Hilton

p. 32 **BP** e

22 Park Lane, W1K 4BE, ℰ (020) 7493 8000, *reservations@hilton.com, Fax (020) 7208 4146*

≼ London, ↓₆, ⇔s – ⊪, ↤ rm, ▤ ▣ ✆ ↆ, – ▲ 1000. ⫴ ⚎ ⓞ VISA JCB. ⌦

Trader Vics (ℰ (020) 7208 4113) : Meals *(closed Saturday, Sunday and lunch Bank Holidays)* 17.00 and a la carte 32.50/47.50 ℤ
Park Brasserie : Meals 23.50/26.50 and a la carte 33.50/43.50 ℤ – (see also ***Windows*** below) – ⊂ 21.00 – **396 rm** 411.25, 65 suites.
♦ This 28 storey tower is one of the city's tallest hotels, providing impressive views from the upper floors. Club floor bedrooms are particularly comfortable. Exotic Trader Vics with bamboo and plants. A harpist adds to the relaxed feel of Park Brasserie.

Connaught

p. 32 **BM** e

Carlos Pl, W1K 2AL, ℰ (020) 7499 7070, *info@the-connaught.co.uk, Fax (020) 7495 3262*

↓₆ – ⊪ ▤ ▣ ✆. ⫴ ⚎ ⓞ VISA JCB. ⌦
Menu : Meals - Italian influences - (booking essential) 21.00/38.00 ℤ
Grill Room : Meals (booking essential) 21.00/38.00 ℤ – ⊂ 26.50 – **68 rm** 352.50/499.00, 23 suites.
♦ 19C quintessentially English hotel, with the ambience of a country house. The grand mahogany staircase leads up to antique furnished bedrooms. Menu offers contemporary Italian inspired cuisine. Grill Room takes pride in classically based cooking.

Raffles Brown's
p. 33 **DM** e

Albemarle St, W1S 4BP, ☎ (020) 7493 6020, *emailus.browns@raffles.com,*
Fax (020) 7493 9381

☒ – 📶 ▤ 📺 ☎ – ☁ 70. 🆗 🅰🅴 ⓪ *VISA* ᴊᴄʙ. ⌘

Meals – (see *1837* below) – ☕ 22.50 – **112 rm** 340.00/376.00, 6 suites.

♦ Opened in 1837, a classic English hotel, celebrated for its afternoon tea.
Past guests include Alexander Graham Bell who made his successful telephone call from here.

Inter-Continental
p. 32 **BP** o

1 Hamilton Pl, Hyde Park Corner, W1J 7QY, ☎ (020) 7409 3131, *london@interc*
onti.com, Fax (020) 7493 3476

≼, ☒, ⓢ – 📶, ⌘ rm, ▤ 📺 ☎ ⅙ ☁ – ☁ 1000. 🆗 🅰🅴 ⓪ *VISA* ᴊᴄʙ.
⌘

Meals 28.00/34.00 and a la carte 28.00/48.50 ♀

Le Souffle : **Meals** *(closed Saturday lunch, Sunday dinner, Monday and Bank*
Holidays) 31.50/42.00 and a la carte 37.00/56.50 ♀ – ☕ 22.50 – **418 rm**
320.00/370.00, 40 suites.

♦ A large, purpose-built, international group hotel that dominates Hyde
Park Corner. Spacious marbled lobby and lounge. Well-equipped bedrooms,
many of which have Park views. Informal cafe style dining or more intimate
Souffle.

Park Lane
p. 32 **CP** X

Piccadilly, W1Y 8BX, ☎ (020) 7499 6321, *central.london.reservations@sherato*
n.com, Fax (020) 7499 1965

☒ – 📶, ⌘ rm, ▤ 📺 ☎ ⅙ ☁ – ☁ 500. 🆗 🅰🅴 ⓪ *VISA* ᴊᴄʙ.
⌘

Citrus (*☎ (020) 7290 7364*) : **Meals** 15.00/22.00 and a la carte 25.00/35.00 **s.** ♀
– ☕ 19.95 – **287 rm** 317.00/340.00, 20 suites.

♦ The history of the hotel is reflected in the elegant 'Palm Court' lounge
and ballroom, both restored to their Art Deco origins. Bedrooms vary
in shape and size. Summer pavement tables in restaurant opposite
Hyde Park.

Westbury
p. 33 **DM** a

Bond St, W1S 2YF, ☎ (020) 7629 7755, *sales@westburymayfair.com,*
Fax (020) 7495 1163

☒ – 📶, ⌘ rm, ▤ 📺 ☎ ⅙ – ☁ 120. 🆗 🅰🅴 ⓪ *VISA* ᴊᴄʙ. ⌘

closed 25-26 December – **Meals** *(closed lunch Saturday and Sunday)* 14.00/
21.50 and a la carte 27.00/43.00 **s.** ♀ – ☕ 16.75 – **233 rm** 282.00/340.75,
21 suites.

♦ Surrounded by London's most fashionable shops; the renowned Polo bar
and lounge provide soothing sanctuary. Some suites have their own terrace.
Bright, fresh restaurant enhanced by modern art.

The Metropolitan
p. 32 **BP** c

Old Park Lane, W1Y 4LB, ☎ (020) 7447 1000, *res@metropolitan.co.uk,*
Fax (020) 7447 1100

≼, ☒ – 📶, ⌘ rm, ▤ 📺 ☎ ☁. 🆗 🅰🅴 ⓪ *VISA* ᴊᴄʙ. ⌘

Meals – (see *Nobu* below) – ☕ 18.00 – **152 rm** 293.00, 3 suites.

♦ Minimalist interior and a voguish reputation make this the favoured hotel
of pop stars and celebrities. Innovative design and fashionably attired staff set
it apart.

Athenaeum
p. 32 **CP** s

116 Piccadilly, W15 7BS, ✆ (020) 7499 3464, *info@athenaeumhotel.com, Fax (020) 7493 1860*

ƒ₄, ⇆s – |‡|, ⇆ rm, ▤ ⭐ ✆ – ♨ 55. 🅜 🅐🅔 🅞 *VISA* JCB. ✘

Bulloch's at 116 : Meals *(closed lunch Saturday and Sunday)* 14.50/30.00 (lunch) and a la carte approx. 32.90 ⬮ – ⤳ 22.50 – **124 rm** 311.00/334.00, 33 suites.

◆ Built in 1925 as a luxury apartment block. Comfortable bedrooms with video and CD players. Individually designed suites are in an adjacent Edwardian townhouse. Conservatory roofed dining room renowned for its mosaics and malt whiskies.

London Marriott Grosvenor Square
p. 32 **BL** a

Duke St, Grosvenor Sq, W1K 6JP, ✆ (020) 7493 1232, *reservations@londonmarriott.co.uk, Fax (020) 7491 3201*

ƒ₄ – |‡|, ⇆ rm, ▤ ⭐ ✆ ዿ – ♨ 600. 🅜 🅐🅔 🅞 *VISA* JCB. ✘

Diplomat : Meals *(closed lunch Saturday and Bank Holidays)* 19.50/23.00 (lunch) and a la carte 23.10/41.90 ⬮ – ⤳ 15.95 – **209 rm** 233.00/282.00, 12 suites.

◆ A well-appointed international group hotel that benefits from an excellent location. Many of the bedrooms specifically equipped for the business traveller. Formal dining room with its own cocktail bar.

Washington Mayfair
p. 32 **CN** s

5-7 Curzon St, W1J 5HE, ✆ (020) 7499 7000, *sales@washington-mayfair.co.uk, Fax (020) 7495 6172*

ƒ₄ – |‡|, ⇆ rm, ▤ ⭐ ✆ – ♨ 90. 🅜 🅐🅔 🅞 *VISA* JCB. ✘

Meals 17.95 and a la carte 20.85/33.85 ⬮ – ⤳ 16.95 – **166 rm** 235.00, 5 suites.

◆ Successfully blends a classical style with modern amenities. Relaxing lounge with traditional English furniture and bedrooms with polished, burred oak. Piano bar annex to formal dining room.

Chesterfield
p. 32 **CN** c

35 Charles St, W1J 5EB, ✆ (020) 7491 2622, *bookch@chmail.com, Fax (020) 7491 4793*

|‡|, ⇆ rm, ▤ ⭐ ✆ – ♨ 110. 🅜 🅐🅔 🅞 *VISA* JCB

Meals *(closed Saturday lunch)* 16.50 (lunch) and a la carte 30.00/42.50 ⬮ – ⤳ 16.50 – **106 rm** 246.75/293.75, 4 suites.

◆ An assuredly English feel to this Georgian house. Discreet lobby leads to a clubby bar and wood panelled library. Individually decorated bedrooms, with some antique pieces. Classically decorated restaurant.

Flemings
p. 32 **CN** z

Half Moon St, W1J 7BH, ✆ (020) 7499 2964, *sales@flemings-mayfair.co.uk, Fax (020) 7629 4063*

|‡|, ⇆ rm, ▤ ⭐ ✆ – ♨ 55. 🅜 🅐🅔 🅞 *VISA* JCB. ✘

Meals 15.00/26.50 and a la carte 22.50/31.50 s. ⬮ – ⤳ 18.00 – **120 rm** 199.25/233.80, 10 suites.

◆ A Georgian town house where the oil paintings and English furniture add to the charm. Apartments located in adjoining house, once home to noted polymath Henry Wagner. Candlelit basement restaurant with oil paintings.

No 5 Maddox St
p. 33 **DK** a

5 Maddox St, W1S 2QD, ✆ (020) 7647 0200, *no5maddoxst@living-rooms.co.uk, Fax (020) 7647 0300*

without rest. – ▤ ⭐ ✆. 🅜 🅐🅔 🅞 *VISA* JCB. ✘

⤳ 16.50, **12 suites** 270.00/675.00.

◆ No grand entrance or large foyer, just a discreet door bell and brass plaque. All rooms are stylish and contemporary suites, with kitchenettes and every conceivable mod con.

🏨 Hilton London Green Park
p. 32   CN   a

Half Moon St, W1J 7BN, ℘ (020) 7629 7522, *greenparkhotel@btinternet.com*, *Fax (020) 7491 8971*

🛗 ✋ 📺 – 🏋 130. 🅿️ 🆎 ⓿ *VISA* JCB, ⌦

Meals 12.50/18.50 and a la carte 15.45/29.95 ♈ – ⌷ 16.50 – **161 rm** 151.50/175.00.

♦ A row of sympathetically adjoined townhouses, dating from the 1730s. Discreet marble lobby. Bedrooms share the same décor but vary in size and shape. Monet prints decorate light, airy dining room.

🏨 Hilton London Mews
p. 32   BP   u

2 Stanhope Row, W1J 7BS, ℘ (020) 7493 7222, *lonmwtw@hilton.com*, *Fax (020) 7629 9423*

🛗 ✋ ▤ 📺 – 🏋 50. 🅿️ 🆎 ⓿ *VISA* JCB, ⌦

Meals (dinner only) a la carte 17.95/27.50 ♈ – ⌷ 16.50 – **71 rm** 149.00/169.00.

♦ Tucked away in a discreet corner of Mayfair. This modern, group hotel manages to retain a cosy and intimate feel. Well-equipped bedrooms to meet corporate needs. Meals in cosy dining room or lounge.

Le Gavroche (Roux)
p. 32   AM   c

43 Upper Brook St, W1K 7QR, ℘ (020) 7408 0881, *bookings@le-gavroche.com*, *Fax (020) 7491 4387*

▤. 🅿️ 🆎 ⓿ *VISA* JCB

closed Christmas-New Year, Sunday, Saturday lunch and Bank Holidays – **Meals** – French - (booking essential) 42.00 (lunch) and a la carte 56.40/94.40.

♦ Long standing basement restaurant with a clubby, formal atmosphere. Accomplished classical French cuisine, served by smartly attired and well-drilled staff.

Spec. Foie gras chaud et pastilla de canard à la cannelle. Râble de lapin et galette au parmesan. Le palet au chocolat amer et praline croustillant.

The Oriental (at Dorchester H.)
p. 32   BN   a

Park Lane, W1A 2HJ, ℘ (020) 7317 6328, *Fax (020) 7317 6464*

▤. 🅿️ 🆎 ⓿ *VISA* JCB

closed August, Christmas-New Year, Saturday lunch, Sunday and Bank Holidays – **Meals** – Chinese (Canton) - 17.00/48.00 and a la carte 42.00/64.00 **s**. ♈.

♦ London's grandest Chinese restaurant, decorated with sculptures, antique silks and gilded mirrors. Asian themed private dining rooms. A variety of menus available.

Grill Room (at Dorchester H.)
p. 32   BN   a

Park Lane, W1A 2HJ, ℘ (020) 7317 6336, *Fax (020) 7317 6464*

▤. 🅿️ 🆎 ⓿ *VISA* JCB

Meals - English - 22.00/39.50 and a la carte 39.00/56.00 **s**. ♈.

♦ Ornate Spanish influenced, baroque decoration with gilded ceiling, tapestries and highly polished oak tables. Formal and immaculate service. Traditional English cooking.

1837 (at Brown's H.)
p. 33   DM   e

Albemarle St, W1S 4BP, ℘ (020) 7408 1837, *brownshotel@ukbusiness.com*, *Fax (020) 7493 9381*

▤. 🅿️ 🆎 ⓿ *VISA* JCB

closed Saturday lunch and Sunday – **Meals** 31.00/48.00 and a la carte 26.00/60.00 ♈.

♦ The name refers to the date the hotel opened. An elegant and comfortable wood panelled room that evokes a bygone age. By contrast, the kitchen provides contemporary cooking.

XXXX **Windows** (at London Hilton H.)   p. 32   **BP**   **e**
22 Park Lane, W1Y 4BE,   (020) 7208 4021, *wow@hilton.com, Fax (020) 7208 4147*
☀ London – ▤. **MC** **AE** **①** **VISA** **JCB**
closed Saturday lunch and Sunday dinner – **Meals** 42.50 (lunch) and dinner a la carte 41.00/59.50 ☂.
♦ Enjoys some of the city's best views. The lunchtime buffet provides a popular alternative to the international menu. Formal service and a busy adjoining piano bar.

XXX **Gordon Ramsay at Claridge's**   p. 32   **BL**   **C**
✿ Brook St, W1A 2JQ,   (020) 7499 0099, *Fax (020) 7499 3099*
▤. **MC** **AE** **VISA**
Meals (booking essential) 25.00/60.00 ☂.
♦ A thoroughly comfortable dining room with a charming and gracious atmosphere. Serves classically inspired food executed with a high degree of finesse.
Spec. Fricassée of calves sweetbreads, truffle cream. Canon of lamb, confit of shoulder, white bean purée. Tarte Tatin, vanilla ice cream.

XXX **The Square** (Howard)   p. 32   **CM**   **V**
✿✿ 6-10 Bruton St, W1J 6PU,   (020) 7495 7100, *info@squarerestaurant.com, Fax (020) 7495 7150*
▤. **MC** **AE** **①** **VISA**
closed 24-26 December, 1 January and lunch Saturday, Sunday and Bank Holidays – **Meals** 25.00/55.00 ☂.
♦ Marble flooring and bold abstract canvasses add an air of modernity. Extensive menus showcase French influenced cooking of the highest order. Prompt and efficient service.
Spec. Lasagne of crab with langoustine and basil cappuccino. Tournedos Rossini. Soufflé of raisins and sherry.

XXX **Mirabelle**   p. 32   **CN**   **X**
✿ 56 Curzon St, W1J 8PA,   (020) 7499 4636, *sales@whitestarline.org.uk, Fax (020) 7499 5449*
🌿 – ▤. **MC** **AE** **①** **VISA**
Meals 19.95 (lunch) and a la carte 30.95/53.50 ☂.
♦ As celebrated now as it was in the 1950s. Stylish bar with screens and mirrors, leather banquettes and rows of windows. Modern interpretation of some classic dishes.
Spec. Ballottine of salmon with herbs. Parfait of foie gras with truffles en gelée. Roast venison au poivre, grand veneur sauce.

XXX **Greenhouse**   p. 32   **BN**   **e**
✿ 27a Hay's Mews, W1X 7RJ,   (020) 7499 3331, *reservations@greenhouserestaurant.co.uk, Fax (020) 7499 5368*
▤. **MC** **AE** **①** **VISA** **JCB**
closed Saturday lunch and Bank Holidays – **Meals** 21.00 (lunch) and a la carte 31.00/49.50 ☂.
♦ A canopied walkway leads into this well established mews restaurant. Modern British cooking to be enjoyed along with some inventive touches.
Spec. Smoked chicken ravioli with bacon and tarragon. Breast of guinea fowl with smoked sausage pie. Chocolate fondant, peanut butter ice cream.

XXX **La Rascasse** (at Café Grand Prix)   p. 33 DN n
50A Berkeley St, W1J 8HA, ℘ (020) 7409 4712, *reservations@cafegrandprix.com*, *Fax (020) 7629 8884*
▤. **MO** **AE** **VISA**
closed Saturday lunch, Sunday and Bank Holidays – **Meals** 15.00 (lunch) and a la carte approx 29.00 ☲.
♦ A basement restaurant with an interior of striking, stark elegance. Sit in sumptuous banquettes or armchairs at tables clad in crisp linen. Modern menus.

XXX **Embassy**   p. 33 DM u
29 Old Burlington St, W1X 3AN, ℘ (020) 7437 9933, *Fax (020) 7734 3224*
🍽 – ▤. **MO** **AE** **VISA**
closed Saturday lunch Sunday and Bank Holidays – **Meals** 19.95 (lunch) and a la carte 31.00/45.00.
♦ Marble floors, ornate cornicing and a long bar create a characterful, moody dining room. Tables are smartly laid and menus offer accomplished, classic dishes.

XXX **Terrace** (at Le Meridien Piccadilly H.)   p. 33 EM a
21 Piccadilly, W1V 0BH, ℘ (020) 7851 3085, *Fax (020) 7851 3090*
🍽 – ▤. **MO** **AE** **①** **VISA** **JCB**
Meals a la carte 27.00/34.00 ☲.
♦ On the second floor of the hotel, a bright and airy room. Large conservatory style glass ceiling and seating area by the balcony. Modern cooking with a subtle French bias.

XXX **Cecconi's**   p. 33 DM c
5a Burlington Gdns, W1X 1LE, ℘ (020) 7434 1500, *Fax (020) 7494 2440*
▤. **MO** **AE** **VISA**
closed 25 December and 1 January – **Meals** - Italian - a la carte 26.50/50.00 ☲.
♦ While the décor is modern - fine leather banquettes and high-back armchairs, wooden floors - the menus call on the Italian classics with unusual touches: grass pea ravioli.

XXX **Tamarind**   p. 32 CN e
❀ 20 Queen St, W1J 5PR, ℘ (020) 7629 3561, *tamarind.restaurant@virgin.net*, *Fax (020) 7499 5034*
▤. **MO** **AE** **①** **VISA** **JCB**
closed 25-26 December, 1 January lunch Saturday and Bank Holidays – **Meals** - Indian - 16.50 (lunch) and a la carte 25.50/48.00 ☲.
♦ Gold coloured pillars add to the opulence of this basement room. Windows allow diners the chance to watch the kitchen prepare original and accomplished Indian dishes.
Spec. Kekda salad (crabmeat with ginger and mustard). Seafood Moilee (squid, scallops and kingfish in coconut sauce). Rogan Josh (classic Kashmiri lamb curry).

XXX **Sartoria**   p. 33 DL c
20 Savile Row, W1X 1AE, ℘ (020) 7534 7000, *sartoriareservations@conran-restaurants.co.uk*, *Fax (020) 7534 7070*
▤. **MO** **AE** **①** **VISA**
closed Sunday lunch – **Meals** - Italian - 17.50/21.50 (lunch) and a la carte 30.00/45.00 ☲.
♦ In the street renowned for English tailoring, a coolly sophisticated restaurant to suit those looking for modern Italian cooking. Eagerly efficient service.

XXX **Scotts**   p. 32 **BM** **a**
20 Mount St, W1K 2HE, ✆ (020) 7629 5248, *bc@scottsrestaurant.co.uk, Fax (020) 7499 8246*
🍴. **MO** **AE** **①** **VISA** **JCB**
Meals - English - 25.00 (lunch) and a la carte 25.00/59.00 ♀.
◆ Established in 1851 and a favoured haunt of Winston Churchill. Now a stylish and contemporary restaurant specialising in seafood. Pianist in the smart downstairs bar.

XXX **Kaspia**   p. 32 **CM** **i**
18-18A Bruton Pl, W1X 7AA, ✆ (020) 7493 2612, *Fax (020) 7408 1627*
🍴. **MO** **AE** **①** **VISA** **JCB**
closed Sunday and Bank Holidays – **Meals** - Caviar specialities - 22.00/43.00 and a la carte 33.50/125.50 ♀.
◆ A restaurant within a caviar shop, in a quiet mews. Small, comfortable room decorated with porcelain and crockery. Modern cooking, with an extensive caviar menu.

XXX **Kai**   p. 32 **BM** **c**
65 South Audley St, W1K 2QV, ✆ (020) 7493 8988, *kai@kaimayfair.com, Fax (020) 7493 1456*
🍴. **MO** **AE** **①** **VISA** **JCB**
closed 25-26 December and 1 January – **Meals** - Chinese - a la carte 24.00/57.50 ♀.
◆ Marble flooring and mirrors add to the opulent feel of this smoothly run Chinese restaurant. Extensive menu offers dishes ranging from the luxury to the more familiar.

XX **Deca**   p. 33 **DL** **X**
23 Conduit St, W1S 2XS, ✆ (020) 7493 7070, *Fax (020) 7493 7090*
🍴. **MO** **AE** **①** **VISA**
closed 10 days Christmas, 4 days Easter, Sunday and Bank Holidays – **Meals** a la carte 29.00/48.00 ♀.
◆ Modern styling in a restaurant split over two floors, the upper being lighter and more private. Menu offers an appealing mix of modern French and traditional English dishes.

XX **Noble Rot**   p. 33 **DL** **r**
3-5 Mill St, W1R 9TF, ✆ (020) 7629 8877, *noble@noblerot.com, Fax (020) 7629 8878*
🍴. **MO** **AE** **①** **VISA**
closed 25-26 December, 1 January, Saturday lunch Sunday and Bank Holidays – **Meals** 15.95/19.50 (lunch) and a la carte 31.25/44.45 ♀.
◆ A modern room with framed photographs, tiled flooring and venetian blinds. Ambient lighting and music. Modern cooking with some French regional specialities.

XX **Alloro**   p. 33 **DM** **r**
19-20 Dover St, W1S 4LU, ✆ (020) 7495 4768, *Fax (020) 7629 5348*
🍴. **MO** **AE** **①** **VISA**
closed 25 and 31 December Saturday lunch and Sunday – **Meals** - Italian - 23.50/35.00 ♀.
◆ One of the new breed of stylish Italian restaurants, with contemporary art and leather seating. A separate, bustling bar. Smoothly run, with modern cooking.

XX **Nobu** (at The Metropolitan H.)   p. 32 BP **c**
❀ 19 Old Park Lane, W1Y 4LB, ℘ (020) 7447 4747, *confirmations@noburestauran
ts.com, Fax (020) 7447 4749*
⇐ – 🍽. **MC** **AE** **①** **VISA** **JCB**
*closed 25-26 and 31 December, 1 January, lunch Saturday-Sunday and Bank
Holidays* – **Meals** - Japanese with South American influences - (booking
essential) 24.50 (lunch) and a la carte 55.00/85.00 ♈.
◆ Its celebrity clientele has made this one of the most glamorous spots. Staff
are fully conversant in the unique menu that adds South American influences
to Japanese cooking.
Spec. Yellowtail sashimi. Black cod with miso. Chocolate bento box, green tea
ice cream.

XX **Sumosan**   p.33 DM **i**
26 Albemarle St, W1S 4HY, ℘ (020) 7495 5999, *info@sumosan.co.uk,
Fax (020) 7355 1247*
🍽. **MC** **AE** **①** **VISA**
closed lunch Saturday, Sunday and Bank holidays – **Meals** - Japanese - 25.00/
65.00 and a la carte 25.50/49.50.
◆ A very smart interior in which diners sit in comfy banquettes and armchairs. Sushi bar to the rear with some semi-private booths. Extensive menus
of Sushi and Sashimi.

XX **Chor Bizarre**   p. 33 DM **s**
16 Albemarle St, W1S 4HW, ℘ (020) 7629 9802, *chorbizarrelondon@oldworldh
osptials.com, Fax (020) 7493 7756*
🍽. **MC** **AE** **①** **VISA** **JCB**
closed 25-26 December and Sunday lunch – **Meals** - Indian - a la carte 32.00/
55.00 ♈.
◆ Translates as 'thieves market' and the décor is equally vibrant; antiques,
curios, carvings and ornaments abound. Cooking uses influences and recipes
from all over India.

XX **Yatra**   p. 33 DM **o**
34 Dover St, W1S 4NF, ℘ (020) 7493 0200, *yatra@lineone.net,
Fax (020) 7493 4228*
🍽. **MC** **AE** **VISA**
closed 25 December, 1 January and Saturday lunch – **Meals** - Indian - 14.50
(lunch) and a la carte 24.75/30.50 ♈.
◆ Behind the large bar, a richly decorated room with a choice of high or low
level seating. Elaborate and ornate table setting. Indian cooking with an
innovative twist

XX **Bentley's**   p. 33 EM **i**
11-15 Swallow St, W1B 4DG, ℘ (020) 7734 4756, *Fax (020) 7287 2972*
🍽. **MC** **AE** **①** **VISA** **JCB**
closed 25-26 December and 1 January – **Meals** - Seafood - a la carte 30.45/
51.50 ♈.
◆ One of London's oldest restaurants. Ground floor oyster bar leads to the
upstairs dining room. Booth seating and walls adorned with oil paintings.
Specialises in seafood.

XX **Langan's Brasserie**   p.33 DN **e**
Stratton St, W1J 8LB, ℘ (020) 7491 8822, *admin@langansrestaurants.co.uk,
Fax (020) 7493 8309*
🍽. **MC** **AE** **①** **VISA** **JCB**
closed Sunday, Saturday lunch and Bank Holidays – **Meals** a la carte 30.75/
38.25.
◆ A veritable institution and one of London's original brasseries. Large paintings of previous owners hang on one wall. Extensive menu with traditional
dishes. Forever busy.

XX **Teca** p. 32 CL a
54 Brooks Mews, W1Y 2NY, ℘ (020) 7495 4774, *Fax (020) 7491 3545*
CO **AE** **VISA**
closed 1 week Christmas, Easter, Sunday, Saturday lunch and Bank Holidays –
Meals - Italian - 19.50/36.00 ⌐.
• A glass-enclosed cellar is one of the features of this modern, slick Italian restaurant. Set price menu, with the emphasis on fresh, seasonal produce.

XX **Hush** p. 32 CL v
8 Lancashire Court, Brook St, W1S 1EY, ℘ (020) 7659 1500, *steamroller@hush. co.uk, Fax (020) 7659 1501*
$ **▤**. **CO** **AE** **①** **VISA** **JCB**
closed Sunday and 25 December
hush down 🍴 *:* **Meals** a la carte 27.00/44.00 ⌐
hush up *:* **Meals** *(closed Sunday)* (booking essential) 26.50 (lunch) and dinner a la carte 29.00/51.00 ⌐.
• Tucked away down a side street: spacious, informal hush down brasserie with a secluded courtyard terrace. Serves tasty modern classics. Join the fashionable set in the busy bar or settle down on the banquettes at hush up. Serves robust, satisfying dishes.

XX **Shogun** (at Millennium Mayfair H.) p. 32 BM x
Adams Row, W1Y 5DF, ℘ (020) 7493 1255, *britannia.res@mill_cop, Fax (020) 7493 1255*
▤. **CO** **AE** **①** **VISA** **JCB**
closed Monday – **Meals** - Japanese - (dinner only) 42.00.
• An attractively decorated basement room with a separate small sushi bar. Attentive staff overseen by the owner. Range of menus, offering authentic Japanese food.

XX **Momo** p. 33 EM n
25 Heddon St, W1B 4BH, ℘ (020) 7434 4040, *momoresto@aol.com, Fax (020) 7287 0404*
▤. **CO** **AE** **①** **VISA** **JCB**
closed 24-26 and 31 December – **Meals** - Moroccan - 17.00 (lunch) and dinner a la carte 21.75/36.50.
• Elaborate adornment of rugs, drapes and ornaments mixed with Arabic music lend an authentic feel to this busy Moroccan restaurant. Helpful service. Popular basement bar.

XX **Nicole's** (at Nicole Farhi) p. 33 DM n
158 New Bond St, W1Y 9PA, ℘ (020) 7499 8408, *Fax (020) 7409 0381*
▤. **CO** **AE** **①** **VISA** **JCB**
closed 25 December, Saturday dinner, Sunday and Bank Holidays – **Meals** (booking essential) a la carte 33.85/36.95 ⌐.
• A basement room as stylish as the shop above and popular at lunch times. Bright, cool surroundings and a Mediterranean influenced menu. Snacks and drinks also available.

X **Veeraswamy** p. 33 EM c
Victory House, 99 Regent St, W1B 4RS, entrance on Swallow St, ℘ (020) 7734 1401, *Fax (020) 7439 8434*
▤. **CO** **AE** **①** **VISA** **JCB**
Meals - Indian - 15.00 (lunch) and a la carte 22.00/31.25 ⌐.
• The country's oldest Indian restaurant boasts a new look with vivid coloured walls and glass screens. The menu also combines the familiar with some modern twists.

✗ **The Cafe** (at Sotheby's) p. 33 DL e
34-35 New Bond St, W1A 2AA, ℘ (020) 7293 5077, *Fax (020) 7293 5920*
⇥✗. **MO AE � VISA**
closed 24 December-2 January, last 2 weeks August, Saturday, Sunday and Bank Holidays – **Meals** (booking essential) (lunch only) a la carte 21.50/29.50 **s. ⚥.**
♦ A velvet rope separates this simple room from the main lobby of this famous auction house. Pleasant service from staff in aprons. Menu is short but well-chosen and light.

✗ **Zinc Bar & Grill** p. 33 EM x
21 Heddon St, W1R 7LF, ℘ (020) 7255 8899, *Fax (020) 7255 8888*
MO AE ⓘ VISA
closed Sunday – **Meals** 14.00 (lunch) and a la carte 21.00/30.00 ⚥.
♦ The eponymous bar takes up half the room and is a popular after-work meeting place. Parquet flooring and laminated tabletops. Offers a wide selection of modern cooking.

✗ **Truc Vert** p. 32 AL a
42 North Audley St, W1K 6ZR, ℘ (020) 7491 9988, *trucvert@madasafish, Fax (020) 7491 7717*
⇥✗ ▤. **MO AE VISA JCB**
closed 3 days Christmas, Saturday and Sunday dinner and Bank Holidays – **Meals** (booking essential) a la carte 19.40/28.25 ⚥.
♦ The dining room with its blond wooden Shaker-style furniture is filled with elegantly packaged produce that appears on the plate and is on sale in the shop. Modern cuisine.

Regent's Park and Marylebone *Gtr London* – ✉ *NW1/NW6/NW8/W1.*

 Landmark London p. 25 HU a
222 Marylebone Rd, NW1 6JQ, ℘ (020) 7631 8000, *reservations@thelandmark.co.uk, Fax (020) 7631 0000*
Iₒ, ⇌s, ▨ – |≣|, ⇥✗ rm, ▤ TV ☏ & ⇦ – ⚤ 350. **MO AE ⓘ VISA JCB**. ⚡
Winter Garden · **Meals** 24.50 and a la carte 31.00/42.00 s. ⚥ – (see also *John Burton-Race* below) – ⚌ 20.00 – **290 rm** 387.75/417.00, 9 suites.
♦ Imposing Victorian Gothic building with a vast glass enclosed atrium, overlooked by many of the modern, well-equipped bedrooms. Winter Garden popular for afternoon tea.

 Langham Hilton p. 25 JU e
1c Portland Pl, Regent St, W1B 1JA, ℘ (020) 7636 1000, *langham@hilton.com, Fax (020) 7323 2340*
Iₒ, ⇌s, ▨ – |≣|, ⇥✗ rm, ▤ TV ☏ & – ⚤ 250. **MO AE ⓘ VISA JCB**. ⚡
Memories : **Meals** 15.00/45.00 and a la carte 34.00/59.00 ⚥
Tsar's : **Meals** *(closed Sunday)* a la carte 24.00/31.00 – ⚌ 21.50 – **409 rm** 276.10, 20 suites.
♦ Opposite the BBC, with Colonial inspired décor. Polo themed bar and barrel vaulted Palm Court. Concierge Club rooms offer superior comfort and butler service. Memories is bright, elegant dining room. Russian influenced Tsar's: hundreds of vodkas available

Churchill Inter-Continental
p. 32   AJ   X

30 Portman Sq., W1A 4ZX, ☎ (020) 7486 5800, *churchill@interconti.com*, *Fax (020) 7486 1255*

⮐, ⟨⟩, ✕ – ⬧, ✚ rm, 📺 📺 ☎ ⬥ – 🏋 300. 🅌 🄰🄴 ⓪ 𝐕𝐈𝐒𝐀. ✕

Terrace on Portman Square : **Meals** a la carte 24.25/40.50 **s.** ⬤ – ⬜ 20.75 – **405 rm** 376.00, 40 suites.

◆ Modern property overlooking attractive square. Elegant marbled lobby. Cigar bar open until 2am for members. Well-appointed rooms have the international traveller in mind. Restaurant provides popular Sunday brunch entertainment.

Selfridge Thistle
p. 32   AK   e

Orchard St., W1H 6JS, ☎ (020) 7408 2080, *selfridge@thistle.co.uk*, *Fax (020) 7409 2295*

⬧, ✚ rm, 📺 📺 ☎ – 🏋 250. 🅌 🄰🄴 ⓪ 𝐕𝐈𝐒𝐀 🄹🄲🄱. ✕

Terrace : **Meals** (buffet lunch)/dinner and a la carte 17.00/25.00 **s.** – ⬜ 16.50 – **290 rm** 208.00/244.00, 4 suites.

◆ A traditional atmosphere prevails at this centrally located hotel opposite the flagship Marks & Spencer store. Spacious bedrooms have plenty of thoughtful touches.

Charlotte Street
p. 26   KU   V

15 Charlotte St, W1T 1RJ, ☎ (020) 7806 2000, *charlotte@firmdale.com*, *Fax (020) 7806 2002*

⮐ – ⬧ 📺 📺 ☎ ⬥ – 🏋 65. 🅌 🄰🄴 𝐕𝐈𝐒𝐀. ✕

Meals – (see ***Oscar*** below) – ⬜ 17.50 – **44 rm** 217.30/346.60, 8 suites.

◆ Interior designed with a charming and understated English feel. Welcoming lobby laden with floral displays. Individually decorated rooms with CDs and mobile phones.

Sanderson
p.33   EJ   C

50 Berners St, W1P 3NG, ☎ (020) 7300 1400, *sanderson@ianschragerhotels. com*, *Fax (020) 7300 1401*

🌣, ⮐ – ⬧, ✚ rm, 📺 📺 ☎. 🅌 🄰🄴 ⓪ 𝐕𝐈𝐒𝐀. ✕

Spoon + : **Meals** 25.00 (lunch) and a la carte 37.00/59.00 ⬤ – ⬜ 20.00 – **150 rm** 311.30/340.75.

◆ Designed by Philipe Starck: the height of contemporary design. Bar is the place to see and be seen. Bedrooms with minimalistic white décor have DVDs and striking bathrooms. Stylish Spoon + allows diners to construct own dishes.

The Leonard
p. 32   AK   n

15 Seymour St, W1H 7JW, ☎ (020) 7935 2010, *theleonard@dial.pipex.com*, *Fax (020) 7935 6700*

⮐ – ⬧ ✚ 📺 📺 ☎. 🅌 🄰🄴 ⓪ 𝐕𝐈𝐒𝐀 🄹🄲🄱. ✕

Meals (room service only) – ⬜ 18.50 – **21 rm** 152.00/258.00, **20 suites** 329.00/646.00.

◆ Around the corner from Selfridges, an attractive Georgian townhouse: antiques and oil paintings abound. Informal, stylish café bar offers light snacks. Well-appointed rooms.

Radisson SAS Portman
p. 32   AJ   O

22 Portman Sq, W1H 7BG, ☎ (020) 7208 6000, *sales.london@raddissonsas. com*, *Fax (020) 7208 6001*

⮐, ⟨⟩, ✕ – ⬧, ✚ rm, 📺 📺 ☎ – 🏋 650. 🅌 🄰🄴 ⓪ 𝐕𝐈𝐒𝐀. ✕

Talavera : **Meals** (buffet lunch)/dinner a la carte 24.50/31.50 **s.** – ⬜ 18.50 – **265 rm** 229.10/293.75, 7 suites.

◆ This modern, corporate hotel offers check-in for both British Midland and SAS airlines. Rooms in attached towers decorated in Scandinavian, Chinese and Italian styles. Restaurant renowned for its elaborate buffet lunch.

Montcalm p. 37 EZ x
Great Cumberland Pl, W1H 7TW, ✆ (020) 7402 4288, *montcalm@montcalm.co.uk*, *Fax (020) 7724 9180*
rm, – 80. MC AE VISA JCB.
Meals – (see ***The Crescent*** below) – 17.95 – **110 rm** 270.00/352.00, 10 suites.
◆ Named after the 18C French general, the Marquis de Montcalm. In a charming crescent a short walk from Hyde Park. Spacious bedrooms with a subtle oriental feel.

Ramada Plaza p. 25 GT v
18 Lodge Rd, NW8 7JT, ✆ (020) 7722 7722, *regentspark@jarvis.co.uk*, *Fax (020) 7483 2408*
rm, – 150. MC AE VISA JCB.
Minsky's : **Meals** *closed Saturday lunch* 19.50/20.95 and a la carte 19.50/30.50
Kashinoki : **Meals** - Japanese - *(closed Monday)* a la carte 15.30/22.00 – 15.50 – **376 rm** 199.00, 1 suite.
◆ Modern hotel offers extensive conference facilities. Some of the functional bedrooms either overlook Regent's Park or Lord's cricket ground. Minsky's is designed on a New York deli theme. Kashinoki has Oriental ambience.

Berners p. 33 EJ r
10 Berners St, W1A 3BE, ✆ (020) 7666 2000, *berners@berners.co.uk*, *Fax (020) 7666 2001*
rm, rest, – 160. MC AE VISA JCB.
Meals *closed Saturday lunch* (carving lunch) 16.95 (lunch) and a la carte 19.90/30.90 – 15.95 – **213 rm** 190.00/215.00, 3 suites.
◆ Series of five converted Georgian houses. Impressive lobby with ornately carved plasterwork ceiling. The floor of club rooms have their own lounge and compact gym. Art Deco themed restaurant..

Jurys Clifton Ford p. 32 BH a
47 Welbeck St, W1M 8DN, ✆ (020) 7486 6600, *clifton@jurysdoyle.com*, *Fax (020) 7486 7492*
– rm, – 230. MC AE VISA.
Meals *(closed lunch Saturday and Sunday)* 25.00/35.00 **s.** and a la carte – 20.00 – **253 rm** 220.00/250.00, 2 suites.
◆ A fairly quiet spot, despite being a short stroll away from the Oxford Street shops. Modern, corporate hotel benefits from an extensive leisure club. Spacious modern rooms. Subtly Irish influence to menu.

Holiday Inn Regent's Park p. 25 JU i
Carburton St, W1W 5EE, ✆ (0870) 400 9111, *reservations-londonregentspark@6c.com*, *Fax (020) 7387 2806*
rm, – 350. MC AE VISA JCB.
Junction : **Meals** a la carte 19.65/28.85 **s.** – 14.95 – **333 rm** 179.00.
◆ Modern corporate hotel and a forever busy conference destination. 1st floor lounges are particularly spacious. Bright bedrooms have a certain Scandinavian feel. International menus.

London Marriott Marble Arch p. 37 EZ i
134 George St, W1H 5DN, ✆ (0870) 400 7255, *salesadmin.marblearch@marriott.co.uk*, *Fax (020) 7402 0666*
– rm, – 150. MC AE VISA JCB.
Mediterrano : **Meals** *(closed lunch Saturday and Sunday)* a la carte 18.40/29.35 – 16.45 – **240 rm** 198.50.
◆ Centrally located and modern. Offers comprehensive conference facilities. Leisure centre underground. An ideal base for both corporate and leisure guests. Mediterranean-influenced cooking.

Berkshire p. 32 BK n

350 Oxford St, W1N 0BY, *ℰ* (020) 7629 7474, *resberk@radisson.com,* *Fax (020) 7629 8156*

|$|, ⇆ rm, ▤ 🖵 ☎ – 🎄 40. 🆗 AE ⓞ VISA JCB. ⅀

Ascots : **Meals** (dinner only) 25.00 **s.** – ⬡ 15.00 – **145 rm** 290.20/334.80, 2 suites.

♦ Above the shops of Oxford St. Reception areas have a pleasant traditional charm. Comfortably appointed bedrooms have plenty of thoughtful touches. Personable staff. Stylish, relaxed dining room.

 Durrants p. 32 AH e

26-32 George St, W1H 5BJ, *ℰ* (020) 7935 8131, *enquiries@durrantshotel.co.uk,* *Fax (020) 7487 3510*

|$|, ▤ rest, 🖵 ☎ – 🎄 55. 🆗 AE VISA. ⅀

Meals 19.50 and a la carte 28.00/44.00 – ⬡ 13.50 – **88 rm** 92.50/165.00, 4 suites.

♦ First opened in 1790 and family owned since 1921. Traditionally English feel with the charm of a bygone era. Cosy wood panelled bar. Attractive rooms vary somewhat in size. Semi-private booths in quintessentially British dining room.

 Dorset Square p. 25 HU s

39-40 Dorset Sq, NW1 6QN, *ℰ* (020) 7723 7874, *dorset@firmdale.com,* *Fax (020) 7724 3328*

🚗 – |$| ▤ 🖵 ☎. 🆗 AE VISA. ⅀

The Potting Shed : **Meals** *(closed Saturday lunch and Sunday dinner)* (booking essential) (live music Tuesday and Saturday dinner) and a la carte 23.90/29.90 ⅀ – ⬡ 14.00 – **38 rm** 115.15/282.00.

♦ Converted Regency townhouses in a charming square and the site of the original Lord's cricket ground. A relaxed country house in the city. Individually decorated rooms. The Potting Shed features live entertainment.

 Sherlock Holmes p. 25 HU c

108 Baker St, W1U 6LJ, *ℰ* (020) 7486 6161, *info@shh-w1.com,* *Fax (020) 7486 0884*

f♣, ⊜ – ⇆ ▤ 🖵 ☎ – 🎄 45. 🆗 AE ⓞ VISA JCB

Meals 16.50 (lunch) and a la carte 21.50/45.00 ⅀ – ⬡ 12.50 – **116 rm** 258.50/323.10.

♦ A stylish building with a relaxed contemporary feel. Comfortable guests' lounge with Holmes pictures on the walls. Bedrooms welcoming and smart, some with wood floors. Brasserie style dining.

10 Manchester Street p. 32 AH c

10 Manchester St, W1U 4DG, *ℰ* (020) 7486 6669, *stay@10manchesterstreet.fsnet.co.uk, Fax (020) 7224 0348*

without rest. – |$| 🖵. 🆗 AE VISA. ⅀ – ⬡ 5.00 – **37 rm** 120.00/150.00, 9 suites.

♦ Redbrick hotel built in 1919; speciality shops and Wallace Collection are on the doorstep. Thoughtful extras such as mineral water, chocolates complement comfortable rooms.

Hart House p. 32 AH a

51 Gloucester Pl, W1U 8JF, *ℰ* (020) 7935 2288, *reservations@harthouse.co.uk,* *Fax (020) 7935 8516*

without rest. – ⇆ 🖵. 🆗 AE ⓞ VISA JCB. ⅀

15 rm ⬡ 70.00/105.00.

♦ Once home to French nobility escaping the 1789 Revolution. Now an attractive Georgian, mid-terraced private hotel. Warm and welcoming service. Well kept bedrooms.

St George p. 32 AH i
49 Gloucester Pl, W1U 8JE, ☎ (020) 7486 8586, *reservations@stgeorge-hotel.net, Fax (020) 7486 6567*
without rest. – TV. MC AE D VISA JCB.
19 rm 85.00/125.00.
◆ Terraced house on a busy street, usefully located within walking distance of many attractions. Offers a warm welcome and comfortable bedrooms which are spotlessly maintained.

John Burton-Race (at Landmark London H.) p. 25 HU a
222 Marylebone Rd, NW1 6JQ, ☎ (020) 7723 7800, *jbrthelandmark@btconnect.com, Fax (020) 7723 4700*
MC AE D VISA
closed first week January, Saturday lunch, Sunday and Bank Holidays – **Meals** - French - 29.50/65.00 ♀.
◆ A tranquil atmosphere prevails in this impressive and ornately decorated room. Slick and professional service of some of London's finest French cuisine. Notable wine list.
Spec. Roast quail in Sauternes sauce with French beans in truffle oil. Poached lobster, artichoke and truffle salad. Plate of chocolate desserts.

Orrery p. 25 IU a
55 Marylebone High St, W1M 3AE, ☎ (020) 7616 8000, *Fax (020) 7616 8080*
MC AE D VISA JCB
closed 1-3 January and 25 December – **Meals** (booking essential) 23.50 (lunch) and a la carte 31.00/57.00 ♀.
◆ Contemporary elegance: a smoothly run 1st floor restaurant in converted 19C stables, with a Conran shop below. Accomplished modern British cooking.
Spec. Seared scallops, pork belly and cauliflower. Barbary duck with pain d'épices and foie gras Tatin. Palette of chocolate.

Locanda Locatelli p. 32 AJK a
8 Seymour St, W1H 7JZ, ☎ (020) 7935 9088, *info@locandalocatelli.com, Fax (020) 7935 1149*
MC AE VISA
closed Christmas-New year, 2 weeks in August and Sunday – **Meals** - Italian - a la carte 22.00/38.50 ♀.
◆ Very stylishly appointed restaurant with banquettes and cherry wood or glass dividers which contribute to an intimate and relaxing ambience. Accomplished Italian cooking.
Spec. Ox tongue in parsley sauce. Roast rabbit with Parma ham and polenta. White chocolate and yoghurt, pistachio ice cream.

The Crescent (at Montcalm H.) p. 37 EZ x
Great Cumberland Pl, W1H 7TW, ☎ (020) 7402 4288, *reservations@montcalm.co.uk, Fax (020) 7724 9180*
MC AE D VISA JCB
closed lunch Saturday, Sunday and Bank Holidays – **Meals** 25.00 ♀.
◆ Discreetly appointed room favoured by local residents. Best tables overlook a pretty square. Frequently changing fixed price modern menu includes half bottle of house wine.

Oscar (at Charlotte Street H.) p. 26 KU v
15 Charlotte St, W1T 1RJ, ☎ (020) 7907 4005, *charlotte@firmdale.com, Fax (020) 7806 2002*
MC AE VISA
closed Sunday – **Meals** (booking essential) a la carte 31.00/43.50 ♀.
◆ Adjacent to hotel lobby and dominated by a large, vivid mural of contemporary London life. Sophisticated dishes served by attentive staff: oysters, wasabi and soya dressing.

XX **The Providores**   p. 32 **BH** s
109 Marylebone High St, W1U 4RX, ℰ (020) 7935 6175, *anyone@theprovidore
s.co.uk, Fax (020) 7935 6877*
✶✕. ⓂⓈ AE VISA
closed 25-26 December and 1 January – **Meals** a la carte 23.20/34.60 ℉.
◆ Swish, stylish restaurant on first floor; unusual dishes with New World base
and fusion of Asian, Mediterranean influences. Tapas and light meals in downstairs Tapa Room.

XX **La Porte des Indes**   p. 32 **AK** r
32 Bryanston St, W1H 7EG, ℰ (020) 7224 0055, *pilondon@aol.com,
Fax (020) 7224 1144*
▤. ⓂⓈ AE ⓄⒹ VISA JCB
closed 25-26 December, 1 January and Saturday lunch – **Meals** - Indian -
30.00/34.00 and a la carte 27.50/45.20 ℉.
◆ Don't be fooled by the discreet entrance: inside there is a spectacularly
unrestrained display of palm trees, murals and waterfalls. French influenced
Indian cuisine.

XX **Rosmarino**   p. 24 **FS** s
1 Blenheim Terr, NW8 0EH, ℰ (020) 7328 5014, *Fax (020) 7625 2639*
� – ▤. ⓂⓈ AE ⓄⒹ VISA
closed 25 December and 1 January – **Meals** - Italian - 18.00/30.00 ℉.
◆ Modern, understated and relaxed. Friendly and approachable service of
robust and rustic Italian dishes. Set priced menu is carefully balanced.

XX **Ozer**   p. 25 **JU** z
4-5 Langham Pl, Regent St, W1B 3DG, ℰ (020) 7323 0505, *info@sofra.co.uk,
Fax (020) 7323 0111*
▤. ⓂⓈ AE ⓄⒹ VISA JCB
Meals - Turkish - a la carte 14.85/28.25.
◆ Behind the busy and vibrantly decorated bar you'll find a smart modern
restaurant. Lively atmosphere and efficient service of modern, light and
aromatic Turkish cooking.

XX **Rasa Samudra**   p. 26 **KU** r
5 Charlotte St, W1T 1RE, ℰ (020) 7637 0222, *Fax (020) 7637 0224*
✶✕. ⓂⓈ AE ⓄⒹ VISA JCB
closed 1 week Christmas and Sunday lunch – **Meals** - Indian Seafood and
Vegetarian - 10.00/30.00 and a la carte 21.45/27.00.
◆ Comfortably appointed, richly decorated and modern Indian restaurant.
Authentic Keralan (south Indian) cooking with seafood and vegetarian
specialities.

XX **Levant**   p. 32 **BJ** c
Jason Court, 76 Wigmore St, W1H 9DQ, ℰ (020) 7224 1111,
Fax (020) 7486 1216
▤. ⓂⓈ AE ⓄⒹ VISA JCB
Meals - Lebanese - 9.50/39.50 and a la carte 18.20/39.00 ℉.
◆ The somewhat unpromising entrance leads down to a vibrantly decorated
basement. Modern Lebanese cooking featuring subtly spiced dishes.

XX **Caldesi**   p. 32 **BJ** e
15-17 Marylebone Lane, W1V 2NE, ℰ (020) 7935 9226, *Fax (020) 7935 9228*
▤. ⓂⓈ AE ⓄⒹ VISA JCB
closed 25 December, Saturday lunch, Sunday and Bank Holidays – **Meals** -
Italian - a la carte 26.40/28.50.
◆ A traditional Italian restaurant that continues to attract a loyal clientele.
Robust and authentic dishes with Tuscan specialities. Attentive service by
established team.

XX **Bertorelli's**   p. 26   **KU** v
19-23 Charlotte St, W1P 1HP, ✆ (020) 7636 4174, *Fax (020) 7467 8902*
🍽. **MC** **AE** **①** **VISA** **JCB**
closed 25-26 December, Easter and Sunday – **Meals** - Italian - a la carte 16.50/
23.50 ℤ.
◆ Above the informal and busy bar/café. Bright and airy room with vibrant
décor and informal atmosphere. Extensive menu combines traditional and
new wave Italian dishes.

XX **Blandford Street**   p. 32   **BH** e
5-7 Blandford St, W1U 3DB, ✆ (020) 7486 9696, *info@blandford-street.co.uk*,
Fax (020) 7486 5067
🍽. **MC** **AE** **①** **VISA**
closed Christmas and New Year, Saturday lunch, Sunday and Bank Holidays –
Meals 21.50/25.00 (lunch) and a la carte 28.56/37.50 ℤ.
◆ Understated interior with plain walls hung with modern pictures and
subtle spot-lighting. Contemporary menu with a notably European
character.

XX **L'Aventure**   p. 24   **FS** s
3 Blenheim Terr, NW8 0EH, ✆ (020) 7624 6232, *Fax (020) 7625 5548*
☂ – **MC** **AE** **VISA**
closed 1-15 January, Sunday, Saturday lunch and Bank Holidays – **Meals** -
French - 18.50/29.50.
◆ Behind the pretty tree lined entrance you'll find a charming neighbour-
hood restaurant. Relaxed atmosphere and service by personable owner.
Authentic French cuisine.

X **Villandry**   p. 25   **JU** s
170 Great Portland St, W1N 5TB, ✆ (020) 7631 3131, *Fax (020) 7631 3030*
✖ 🍽. **MC** **AE** **①** **VISA**
closed 25 December, 1 January and Sunday dinner – **Meals** a la carte 22.00/
30.00 ℤ.
◆ The senses are heightened by passing through the well-stocked deli to the
dining room behind. Bare walls, wooden tables and a menu offering simple,
tasty dishes.

X **Ibla**   p. 25   **IU** e
89 Marylebone High St, W1U 4QY, ✆ (020) 7224 3799, *ibla@ibla.co.uk*,
Fax (020) 7486 1370
MC **AE** **VISA**
closed 24 December-3 January, Saturday lunch and Sunday – **Meals** 30.00/
45.00 and a la carte ℤ.
◆ Booking is advisable for this forever busy Italian restaurant. Whilst the dark
painted room to the rear offers more privacy, the one at the front has a
livelier atmosphere.

X **Mash**   p. 33   **DJ** a
19-21 Great Portland St, W1N 5DB, ✆ (020) 7637 5555, *Fax (020) 7637 7333*
🍽. **MC** **AE** **①** **VISA**
closed Sunday and Bank Holidays – **Meals** (booking essential) a la carte 20.00/
25.00.
◆ An antidote to tradition, appealing to a younger clientele. A shop, a busy
bar, a micro-brewery and an upstairs restaurant: all decorated in a futuristic
style.

※ **Innecto**   p. 32   AH   n
66 Baker St, W1U 7DH, ℰ (020) 7935 4545, *info@innecto.uk.com,*
Fax (020) 7486 6888
📧. 💳 AE 💳 VISA
closed Christmas, Easter, lunch Saturdays and Sundays – **Meals** 16.50
(lunch) and a la carte 15.00/31.90.
◆ Quite an unusual style in a dining room decorated with strips of walnut and
light-filtering amber panels. Italian tenor to the menu featuring traditional
and modern dishes.

※ **Union Café**   p. 32   BH   c
96 Marylebone Lane, W1M 5FP, ℰ (020) 7486 4860, *unioncafe@winegallery.fs*
net.co.uk, Fax (020) 7486 4860
💳 AE VISA
closed Sunday
Meals 25.00 and a la carte 19.00/28.00.
◆ No standing on ceremony at this bright, relaxed restaurant. The open
kitchen at one end produces modern Mediterranean cuisine. Ideal for visitors
to the Wallace Collection.

※ **The Lane**   p. 32   BH   u
120-122 Marylebone Lane, W1M 5FZ, ℰ (020) 7486 5696
📧. 💳 AE VISA
closed 25 December and Sunday dinner – **Meals** 13.00 and a la carte 21.50/
30.45 s. ⅖.
◆ Bright dining room with huge windows on two sides and spiral staircase to
a lounge bar. Friendly, informal atmosphere and modern menu mixing British
and European styles.

※ **Caffè Caldesi**   p. 32   BH   u
1st Floor, 118 Marylebone Lane, W1U 2QF, ℰ (020) 7935 1144,
Fax (020) 7935 8832
📧. 💳 AE 💳 VISA JCB
closed Sunday and Bank Holidays – **Meals** - Italian - a la carte 19.50/
24.50 ⅖.
◆ Converted pub with a simple modern interior in which to enjoy tasty,
uncomplicated Italian dishes. Downstairs is a lively bar with a deli counter
serving pizzas and pastas.

※ **Chada Chada**   p. 32   BJ   i
16-17 Picton Pl, W1M 5DE, ℰ (020) 7935 8212, *Fax (020) 7924 2178*
📧. 💳 AE 💳 VISA JCB
closed Sunday and Bank Holidays – **Meals** - Thai - a la carte 12.50/
26.95 ⅖.
◆ Authentic and fragrant Thai cooking; the good value menu offers some
interesting departures from the norm. Service is eager to please in the
compact and cosy rooms.

※ **No.6 George St**   p. 32   BH   a
6 George St, W1U 3QX, ℰ (020) 7935 1910, *Fax (020) 7935 6036*
⇖ 📧. 💳 VISA
closed 2 weeks August, 2 weeks Christmas, Saturday and Sunday – **Meals**
(lunch only) a la carte 25.40/30.45.
◆ To the front is a charming delicatessen offering fresh produce and behind
is a simple, well-kept dining room. Daily changing menu with good use of
fresh ingredients.

✗ **Purple Sage**   p. 32   **BJ** **a**
92 Wigmore St, W1U 3RE, ℰ (020) 7486 1912, *Fax (020) 7486 1913*
▤. **MO AE VISA**
Meals - Italian - 14.50 (lunch) and a la carte 19.00/25.50 ℤ.
◆ Simple and unfussy surroundings in which to enjoy modern Italian cooking with a variety of pasta specials. Relaxed service of a monthly changing menu. One of a small group.

✗ **Stanleys**   p. 25   **JU** **a**
6 Little Portland St, W1W 7JE, ℰ (020) 7462 0099, *info@stanleysausages.com, Fax (020) 7462 0088*
▤. **MO AE VISA**
closed 24 December-3 January and Sunday – **Meals** - specialising in sausages - a la carte 15.00/22.00.
◆ A twist on the classic American diner: booth seating, a long bar with a good choice of beers and ciders. Specialises in home-made sausages. A family favourite at weekends.

▯◻ **The Salt House**   p. 24   **FS** **z**
63 Abbey Rd, NW8 0AE, ℰ (020) 7328 6626, *saltrestbar@aol.com, Fax (020) 7625 9168*
🌿 – ▤. **MO AE VISA**
closed 24-26 December and 1 January – **Meals** (booking essential) a la carte 18.65/22.40 ℤ.
◆ Sit in the comfortable lounge or the back-room restaurant. Modern 'gastropub' offers contemporary British cooking in relaxed surroundings. Beatles zebra crossing nearby.

St James's *Gtr London* – ✉ *W1/SW1/WC2.*

🏨 **Ritz**   p. 33   **DN** **a**
150 Piccadilly, W1J 9BR, ℰ (020) 7493 8181, *enquire@theritzlondon.com, Fax (020) 7493 2687*
♨ – ▯, ❄ rm, ▤ TV ☎ – 🛎 50. **MO AE O VISA JCB**. ✗
Meals – (see ***The Restaurant*** below) – ☲ 24.00 – **116 rm** 364.25/511.00, 17 suites.
◆ Opened 1906, a fine example of Louis XVI architecture and decoration. Elegant Palm Court famed for afternoon tea. Many of the lavishly appointed rooms overlook the park.

🏨 **Sofitel St James London**   p. 33   **FN** **a**
6 Waterloo Pl, SW1Y 4AN, ℰ (020) 7747 2200, *h3144@accor-hotels.com, Fax (020) 7747 2210*
♨ – ▯, ❄ rm, ▤ TV ☎ ♿ – 🛎 180. **MO AE O VISA JCB**. ✗
Meals – (see ***Brasserie Roux*** below) – ☲ 21.00 – **179 rm** 323.12/376.00, 7 suites.
◆ Grade II listed building in smart Pall Mall location. Classically English interiors include floral Rose Lounge and club-style St. James bar. Comfortable, well-fitted bedrooms.

🏨 **Dukes**   p. 33   **EP** **x**
35 St James's Pl, SW1A 1NY, ℰ (020) 7491 4840, *bookings@dukeshotel.com, Fax (020) 7493 1264*
🐾, ♨ – ▯, ❄ rest, ▤ TV ☎ – 🛎 50. **MO AE O VISA JCB**. ✗
Meals *(closed Saturday lunch and Bank Holidays)* (residents only) 16.50/19.50 (lunch) and dinner a la carte 30.50/38.50 – ☲ 16.00 – **82 rm** 229.00/305.50, 7 suites.
◆ Privately owned, discreet and quiet hotel. Traditional bar, famous for its martini's and Cognac collection. Well-kept spacious rooms in a country house style.

The Trafalgar
p. 33 **GN** a

2 Spring Gdns, SW1A 2TS, ℘ (020) 7870 2900, *lontshirm@hilton.com*, *Fax (020) 7870 2911*

[symbols] rm, ⊞ 🖵 📞 ♿ – 🅿 50. ⓌⓈ 🅰🅴 ⓄⒹ *VISA* JCB. 🚭

Jago : **Meals** *(closed Saturday)* 17.50 (lunch) and a la carte 28.50/40.00 ♀ – 🍽 18.50 – **127 rm** 234.00, 2 suites.

♦ Enjoys a commanding position on the square of which the deluxe rooms, some split-level, have views. Bedrooms are in pastel shades with leather armchairs or stools; mod cons. Low-lit restaurant with open-plan kitchen.

Stafford
p. 33 **DN** u

16-18 St James's Pl, SW1A 1NJ, ℘ (020) 7493 0111, *info@thestaffordhotel.co.uk*, *Fax (020) 7493 7121*

 – [symbols] ⊞ 🖵 📞 – 🅿 40. ⓌⓈ 🅰🅴 ⓄⒹ *VISA*

Meals *(closed Saturday lunch)* 23.50/27.00 and a la carte 35.50/53.00 **s.** ♀ – 🍽 16.50 – **75 rm** 282.00/364.25, 6 suites.

♦ A genteel atmosphere prevails in this elegant and discreet country house in the city. Do not miss the famed American bar. Well-appointed rooms created from 18C stables. Refined, elegant, intimate dining room.

Cavendish
p. 33 **EN** i

81 Jermyn St, SW1Y 6JF, ℘ (020) 7930 2111, *cavendish.reservations@devere-hotels.com*, *Fax (020) 7839 2125*

[symbols] rm, ⊞ 🖵 📞 🚗 – 🅿 100. ⓌⓈ 🅰🅴 ⓄⒹ *VISA* JCB. 🚭

Meals *(closed lunch Saturday and Sunday)* 24.50 and a la carte 24.20/37.75 ♀ – 🍽 16.95 – **227 rm** 235.00/265.00, 3 suites.

♦ Modern hotel opposite Fortnum & Mason. Contemporary, minimalist style of rooms with prints of London. Top five floors offer far-reaching views over the city.

22 Jermyn Street
p. 33 **FM** e

22 Jermyn St, SW1Y 6HL, ℘ (020) 7734 2353, *office@22jermyn.com*, *Fax (020) 7734 0750*

[symbols] ⊞ 🖵 📞. ⓌⓈ 🅰🅴 ⓄⒹ *VISA* JCB. 🚭

Meals *(room service only)* – 🍽 17.00 – **5 rm** 246.75, **13 suites** 346.60/393.60.

♦ Discreet entrance amid famous shirt-makers' shops leads to this exclusive boutique hotel. Stylishly decorated bedrooms more than compensate for the lack of lounge space.

Thistle Piccadilly
p. 33 **FGM** a

39 Coventry St, W1D 6BZ, ℘ (0870) 3339118, *piccadilly@thistle.co.uk*, *Fax (0870) 3339218*

without rest. – [symbols] ⊞ 🖵 📞. ⓌⓈ 🅰🅴 ⓄⒹ *VISA* JCB. 🚭

🍽 14.50 – **92 rm** 204.45/242.05.

♦ Striking, classic Victorian property on busy main road. Refurbished in 2000, the well-appointed bedrooms are suited to both corporate and tourist travellers.

Thistle Trafalgar Square
p. 33 **GM** r

Whitcomb St, WC2H 7HG, ℘ (020) 7930 4477, *trafalgarsquare@thistle.co.uk*, *Fax (020) 7925 2149*

[symbols] ⊞ rest, 🖵 📞. ⓌⓈ 🅰🅴 ⓄⒹ *VISA* JCB. 🚭

Meals 16.95 – 🍽 14.50 – **116 rm** 152.00/185.00.

♦ Well located between Leicester and Trafalgar Squares, in a fairly quiet location. Spacious rooms in modern colours. Executive rooms on 6th floor have air-conditioning. Up-to-the-minute ground-floor brasserie.

XXXXX **The Restaurant** (at Ritz H.) p. 33 **DN** a
150 Piccadilly, W1V 9DG, ✆ (020) 7493 8181, *Fax (020) 7493 2687*
– ▤. MC AE ① VISA JCB
Meals (dancing Friday and Saturday evenings) 35.00 (lunch) and a la carte 10.50/102.50 **s.** ♀.
◆ The height of opulence: magnificent Louis XVI décor with trompe l'oeil and ornate gilding. Delightful terrace over Green Park. Refined service, classic and modern menu.

XXX ✿ **Pétrus** (Wareing) p. 33 **EN** v
33 St James's St, SW1A 1HD, ✆ (020) 7930 4272, *Fax (020) 7930 9702*
▤. MC AE ① VISA JCB
closed 2 weeks Christmas, Sunday, Saturday lunch and Bank Holidays – **Meals** (booking essential) 26.00/55.00 ♀.
◆ Accomplished cooking and service in discreet, elegant surroundings. Wine list features an extensive collection of one of the world's most renowned clarets.
Spec. Confit of salmon on glazed chicory, sea urchin velouté. Roast breast of Anjou pigeon on a parsnip galette, truffle game jus. Coconut soufflé, dark chocolate sauce, coconut and Malibu ice cream.

XXX ✿ **L'Oranger** p. 33 **EP** a
5 St James's St, SW1A 1EF, ✆ (020) 7839 3774, *Fax (020) 7839 4330*
▤. MC AE ① VISA
closed Christmas-New Year 2 weeks August, Saturday lunch and Sunday – **Meals** 25.00/39.50 ♀.
◆ Behind the period façade lies a stylish, understated and comfortable restaurant. The refined and precise dishes are enjoyed by the regular clientele. Booking recommended.
Spec. Sautéed scallops in a lettuce velouté. Roast Challans duckling with broad beans. Hazelnut soufflé with chocolate sauce and praline ice cream.

XXX **Suntory** p. 33 **EP** z
72-73 St James's St, SW1A 1PH, ✆ (020) 7409 0201, *Fax (020) 7499 0208*
▤. MC AE ① VISA JCB
closed Easter, Christmas-New Year – **Meals** - Japanese - 17.00/53.00 and a la carte 39.00/68.00 **s.**
◆ Long established, renowned Japanese restaurant. Staff in traditional costume provide attentive service of the precise dishes. Prices reflect quality of produce.

XX **Quaglino's** p. 33 **EN** r
16 Bury St, SW1Y 6AL, ✆ (020) 7930 6767, *Fax (020) 7839 2866*
▤. MC AE ① VISA
Meals (booking essential) 16.00 (lunch) and a la carte 30.00/35.00 ♀.
◆ Descend the sweeping staircase into the capacious room where a busy and buzzy atmosphere prevails. Watch the chefs prepare everything from osso bucco to fish and chips.

XX **Criterion Grill Marco Pierre White** p. 33 **FM** c
224 Piccadilly, W1J 9HP, ✆ (020) 7930 0488, *sales@whitestarline.org.uk*, *Fax (020) 7930 8380*
▤. MC AE ① VISA
closed 25-26 December 1 January and Sunday – **Meals** 17.95 (lunch) and a la carte 28.95/32.95 ♀.
◆ A stunning modern brasserie behind the revolving doors. Ornate gilding, columns and mirrors aplenty. Bustling, characterful atmosphere, Pre and post-theatre menus.

Brasserie Roux
XX
p. 33 **FN** **a**

8 Pall Mall, SW1Y 5NG, *(020) 7968 2900, h3144-fb4@accor-hotels.com, Fax (020) 7747 2242*

▤, **MO** **AE** **VISA** **JCB**

Meals - French - a la carte 21.00/27.00 ⅀.

◆ Informal and smart with classic brasserie style and large windows that make the most of the superb location. Large menu of French classics and a comprehensive wine list.

Le Caprice
XXX
p. 33 **DN** **c**

Arlington House, Arlington St, SW1A 1RT, *(020) 7629 2239, Fax (020) 7493 9040*

▤, **MO** **AE** **①** **VISA** **JCB**

closed 25-26 December, 1 January and August Bank Holiday – **Meals** (Sunday brunch) a la carte 25.50/55.00 ⅀.

◆ Still attracting a fashionable clientele and as busy as ever. Dine at the bar or in the smoothly run restaurant. Food combines timeless classics with modern dishes.

Café de Nikolaj
XX
p. 33 **DN** **s**

161 Piccadilly, W1V 9DF, *(020) 7409 0445, jp.esmilaire@talk21.com, Fax (020) 7493 1667*

▤, **MO** **AE** **①** **VISA** **JCB**

closed Sunday and Bank Holidays – **Meals** - Caviar specialities - 22.50 (lunch) and a la carte 31.50/47.00 ⅀.

◆ Walk through the fine delicatessen into this small yet comfortable restaurant overlooking Piccadilly. Impressive linen-clad tables. Caviar and other luxuries.

Che
XX
p. 33 **EN** **O**

23 St James's St, SW1A 1HE, *(020) 7747 9380, chelondon@yahoo.co.uk, Fax (020) 7747 9389*

|$| ▤, **MO** **AE** **①** **VISA**

closed Saturday lunch, Sunday and Bank Holidays – **Meals** 22.95 (lunch) and a la carte 32.50/39.50 ⅀.

◆ Modern international cooking offered in the comfortable 1st floor restaurant of this former bank. More informal dining available in the bar, frequented by cigar aficionados.

The Avenue
XXX
p. 33 **EP** **e**

7-9 St James's St, SW1A 1EE, *(020) 7321 2111, avenue@egami.co.uk, Fax (020) 7321 2500*

▤, **MO** **AE** **①** **VISA**

closed 25-26 December and 1 January – **Meals** 17.50/19.50 (lunch) and dinner a la carte 25.70/30.75 ⅀.

◆ The attractive and stylish bar is a local favourite. Behind is a striking, modern and busy restaurant. Appealing and contemporary food. Pre-theatre menu available.

Matsuri
XX
p. 33 **EN** **r**

15 Bury St, SW1Y 6AL, *(020) 7839 1101, Fax (020) 7930 7010*

▤, **MO** **AE** **①** **VISA** **JCB**

closed Bank Holidays – **Meals** - Japanese (Teppan-Yaki, Sushi) - a la carte 21.00/36.00 ⅀.

◆ Specialising in theatrical and precise teppan-yaki cooking. Separate restaurant offers sushi delicacies. Charming service by traditionally dressed staff.

Al Duca
p.33 EN O

4-5 Duke of York St, SW1Y 6LA, ℰ (020) 7839 3090, *info@alduca-restaurants. co.uk, Fax (020) 7839 4050*

📄 ⓂⓌ ᴬᴱ Ⓓ 𝑉𝐼𝑆𝐴 ᴶᶜᴮ

closed 25-26 December and Sunday – Meals - Italian - 19.50/23.00 ♈.

♦ Relaxed, modern, stylish restaurant. Friendly and approachable service of robust and rustic Italian dishes. Set priced menu is both refreshing and good value.

China House
p. 33 DN i

160 Piccadilly, W1V 9DF, ℰ (020) 7499 6996, *sales@chinahouse.co.uk, Fax (020) 7499 7779*

ⓂⓌ ᴬᴱ 𝑉𝐼𝑆𝐴

closed 25 December, 1 January, Sunday and Bank Holidays – Meals - Chinese - a la carte 16.85/31.45 ♈.

♦ The elaborate, columned period interior of this former bank is a stunning backdrop for this modern and informal Chinese restaurant. Eager service.

Soho *Gtr London* – ✉ *W1/WC2.*

Hampshire
p. 33 GM s

Leicester Sq, WC2H 7LH, ℰ (020) 7839 9399, *reshamp@radisson.com, Fax (020) 7930 8122*

🏠, ⅙ – 📶, ↮ rm, 📄 📺 ☎ – 🔄 100. ⓂⓌ ᴬᴱ Ⓓ 𝑉𝐼𝑆𝐴 ᴶᶜᴮ, ⌗

The Apex : Meals *closed Saturday lunch* 25.00/45.00 s. – ⌧ 16.00 – **119 rm** 386.50/426.50, 5 suites.

♦ The bright lights of the city are literally outside and many rooms overlook the bustling Square. Inside, it is tranquil and comfortable, with well-appointed bedrooms. Formal yet relaxing dining room with immaculately dressed tables.

Hazlitt's
p. 33 FK u

6 Frith St, W1D 3JA, ℰ (020) 7434 1771, *reservations@hazlitts.co.uk, Fax (020) 7439 1524*

without rest. – 📺 ☎. ⓂⓌ ᴬᴱ Ⓓ 𝑉𝐼𝑆𝐴 ᴶᶜᴮ

22 rm 205.60/240.80, 1 suite.

♦ A row of three adjoining early 18c town houses and former home of the eponymous essayist. Individual and charming bedrooms, many with antique furniture and Victorian baths.

L'Escargot
p. 33 GK e

48 Greek St, W1D 5EF, ℰ (020) 7437 2679, *sales@whitestarlin.org.uk, Fax (020) 7437 0790*

📄 ⓂⓌ ᴬᴱ 𝑉𝐼𝑆𝐴

Ground Floor : Meals *(closed 25-26 December, Sunday and lunch Saturday and Bank Holidays)* 17.95 (lunch) and a la carte approx. 26.95 ♈

Picasso Room « Collection of limited edition Picasso art » *:* Meals *(closed 23 December-7 January, August, Sunday, Monday, Saturday lunch and Bank Holidays)* 25.50/42.00 ♈.

♦ Ground Floor is chic, vibrant brasserie with early-evening buzz of theatre-goers. Finely judged modern dishes. Intimate and more formal upstairs Picasso Room famed for its limited edition art.

Spec. Lobster langoustines, fennel bouillon. Squab "en vessie" with root vegetables. Millefeuille of Muscat grapes.

XXX **Quo Vadis** p. 33 **FK** v
26-29 Dean St, W1D 3LL, ☎ (020) 7437 9585, *sales@whitestarline.org.uk,*
Fax (020) 7734 7593
▤, ⓒⓔ ⒶⒺ ⓪ **VISA**
closed 25-26 December, 1 January, Sunday and Saturday lunch – **Meals** -
Italian influences - 19.95 (lunch) and a la carte 21.70/41.50 ♀.
♦ Stained glass windows and a neon sign hint at the smooth modernity of
the interior. Modern artwork abounds. Contemporary cooking and a serious
wine list.

XXX **Red Fort** p. 33 **FK** x
77 Dean St, W1D 3SH, ☎ (020) 7437 2525, *info@redfort.co.uk,*
Fax (020) 7434 0721
▤, ⓒⓔ ⒶⒺ ⓪ **VISA**
closed Sunday lunch – **Meals** - Indian - a la carte 30.50/53.50 ♀.
♦ Smart, stylish restaurant with modern water feature and glass ceiling to
rear. Seasonally changing menus of authentic dishes handed down over
generations.

XX **Richard Corrigan at Lindsay House** p. 33 **GL** i
✿ 21 Romilly St, W1V 5TG, ☎ (020) 7439 0450, *richardcorrigan@lindsayhouse.co.*
uk, Fax (020) 7437 7349
▤, ⓒⓔ ⒶⒺ ⓪ **VISA**
closed 1 week Christmas, Sunday and Saturday lunch – **Meals** 19.50/48.00.
♦ One rings the doorbell before being welcomed into this handsome 18C
town house, retaining many original features. Skilled and individual cooking
with a subtle Irish hint.
Spec. Sardines with shellfish soufflé and marinated tomato. Saddle of rabbit,
black pudding polenta and garlic confit. Rhubarb compote, vanilla ice
cream.

XX **Café Lazeez** p. 33 **FJ** a
21 Dean St, W1V 5AH, ☎ (020) 7434 9393, *soho@cafelazeez.com,*
Fax (020) 7434 0022
▤, ⓒⓔ ⒶⒺ ⓪ **VISA** JCB
closed Sunday and Bank Holidays – **Meals** - North Indian - 15.00 (lunch)
and a la carte 18.85/27.10 ♀.
♦ In the same building as Soho Theatre; the bar hums before shows, restaurant is popular for pre- and post-theatre meals of modern Indian fare. Refined décor; private booths.

XX **Teatro** p. 33 **GL** e
93-107 Shaftesbury Ave, W1D 5DY, ☎ (020) 7494 3040, *info@teatrosoho.*
co.uk, Fax (020) 7494 3050
▤, ⓒⓔ ⒶⒺ ⓪ **VISA** JCB
closed 25 December-2 January, Sunday, Saturday lunch and Bank Holidays –
Meals 20.00 (lunch) and dinner a la carte 26.50/47.00 ♀.
♦ Unassuming entrance leads upstairs to a bright and stylish room, with a
sizeable bar attached. Popular pre- and post-theatre. Menu mixes the familiar
with the modern.

XX **The Sugar Club** p.33 **EL** r
21 Warwick St, W1R 5RB, ☎ (020) 7437 7776, *Fax (020) 7437 7778*
✺⊱ ▤, ⓒⓔ ⒶⒺ ⓪ **VISA** JCB
closed early January – **Meals** a la carte 30.00/40.50 ♀.
♦ Light interior with a glass-fronted bar and additional basement seating.
Asian and Oriental influenced cuisine with good use of diverse ingredients
and combinations.

XX **Circus** p. 33 EL **e**
1 Upper James St, W1F 4DF, *ℰ (020) 7534 4000, circus@egami.co.uk, Fax (020) 7534 4010*
▤ ⬤◉ AE ⓞ *VISA*
closed 24-26 December, 1 January, Sunday and lunch Saturday – **Meals** 19.50 (lunch) and dinner a la carte 21.50/31.80 ₤.
♦ Frosted glass and soft lighting give the establishment a stylish feel. Downstairs, the basement bar is a lively spot. Modern British cooking with international influences..

XX **Mezzo** p. 33 FK **a**
Lower Ground Floor, 100 Wardour St, W1F 0TN, *ℰ (020) 7314 4000, Fax (020) 7314 4040*
▤ ⬤◉ AE ⓞ *VISA*
closed Sunday and lunch Monday, Tuesday and Saturdays – **Meals** 15.50 (lunch) and a la carte 33.00/37.00 ₤.
♦ Through the vast bar and down the sweeping staircase to this enormous and sonorous basement. Well-drilled service. Windows into the kitchen which produces modern cooking.

X **Bertorelli** p. 33 FK **s**
First Floor, 11-13 Frith St, W1D 4RB, *ℰ (020) 7494 3491, Fax (020) 7437 3091*
🏠 – ▤. ⬤◉ AE ⓞ *VISA* JCB
closed 25 December – **Meals** - Italian - a la carte approx. 23.50 ₤.
♦ A haven of tranquilllity from the bustling street below. Discreet and professionally run first floor restaurant with Italian menu. Popular ground floor café.

X **Il Forno** p. 33 FJK **n**
🍽 63-64 Frith St, W1V 5TA, *ℰ (020) 7734 4545, info@ilforno-restaurant.co.uk, Fax (020) 7287 8624*
▤. ⬤◉ AE *VISA* JCB
closed 18-31 August, 25-26 December, lunch Saturday, Monday, Sunday, Bank Holidays and last 2 weeks October – **Meals** - Italian - 12.50 (lunch) and a la carte 18.00/24.25 ₤.
♦ Brightly decorated with large windows looking onto the busy Soho streets. Convivial atmosphere. Well-priced Italian cooking ranging from pizzas to more elaborate dishes.

X **Sri Siam Soho** p. 33 GK **r**
16 Old Compton St, W1V 5PE, *ℰ (020) 7434 3544, Fax (020) 7287 1311*
▤. ⬤◉ AE ⓞ *VISA*
closed 25-26 December, 1 January and Sunday lunch – **Meals** - Thai - (booking essential) 18.95 and a la carte 18.50/29.00 ₤.
♦ Pastel coloured walls, stencilled with scenes depicting tropical Thailand. Extensive Thai menu with authentic cooking. Service is alert and efficient.

X **La Trouvaille** p. 33 EK **a**
12A Newburgh St, W1F 7RR, *ℰ (020) 7287 8488, Fax (020) 7434 4170*
🏠 – ⬤◉ AE *VISA*
closed Sunday – **Meals** - French - 19.75 (lunch) and dinner a la carte 28.95/34.15 ₤.
♦ Atmospheric restaurant located just off Carnaby Street. Hearty, robust French cooking with a rustic character. French wine list with the emphasis on southern regions.

✗ Alastair Little

p. 33   **FK**   **o**

49 Frith St, W1D 5SG, ☎ (020) 7734 5183, *Fax (020) 7734 5206*

🖪. 🝆🄰 🄰🄴 🄾 **VISA**

closed Sunday, Saturday lunch and Bank Holidays – **Meals** (booking essential) 27.00/35.00 ♀.

◆ The eponymous owner was at the vanguard of Soho's culinary renaissance. Tasty, daily changing British based cuisine; the compact room is rustic and simple.

✗ Vasco and Piero's Pavilion

p. 33   **EJK**   **i**

15 Poland St, W1F 8QE, ☎ (020) 7437 8774, *vascosfood@hotmail.com, Fax (020) 7437 0467*

🖪. 🝆🄰 🄰🄴 🄾 **VISA** **JCB**

closed Sunday, Saturday lunch and Bank Holidays – **Meals** - Italian - (lunch booking essential) 22.50 (dinner) and lunch a la carte 28.50/33.00.

◆ A long standing, family run Italian restaurant with a loyal local following. Pleasant service under the owners' guidance. Warm décor and traditional cooking.

✗ itsu

p. 33   **FK**   **c**

103 Wardour St, W1V 3TD, ☎ (020) 7479 4794, *glenn.edwards@itsu.co.uk, Fax (020) 7479 4795*

🖪. 🝆🄰 🄰🄴 **VISA** **JCB**

closed 23 December-2 January – **Meals** - Japanese - (bookings not accepted) a la carte 12.00/18.00.

◆ Japanese dishes of Sushi, Sashimi, handrolls and miso soup turn on a conveyor belt in a pleasingly hypnotic fashion. Hot bowls of chicken and coconut soup also appear.

✗ Aurora

p. 33   **EK**   **e**

49 Lexington St, W1F 9AP, ☎ (020) 7494 0514, *aurora-restaurant@yahoo. co.uk, Fax (020) 7494 4357*

🏡 – 🝆🄰 **VISA**

closed 22 December-4 January and Sunday – **Meals** (booking essential) a la carte 18.40/23.85.

◆ An informal, no-nonsense, bohemian style bistro with a small, but pretty, walled garden terrace. Short but balanced menu; simple fresh food. Pleasant, languid atmosphere.

✗ Soho Spice

p. 33   **FJ**   **e**

124-126 Wardour St, W1V 3LA, ☎ (020) 7434 0808, *info@sohospice.co.uk, Fax (020) 7434 0799*

🖪. 🝆🄰 🄰🄴 🄾 **VISA** **JCB**

Meals - Indian - (bookings not accepted) 14.95/24.95 and a la carte 15.85/21.45 ♀.

◆ Busy, buzzy, café-style Indian restaurant with basement cocktail bar. Vivid colours on the wall matched by the staff uniforms. Indian food with a contemporary twist.

✗ Fung Shing

p. 33   **GL**   **a**

15 Lisle St, WC2H 7BE, ☎ (020) 7437 1539, *Fax (020) 7734 0284*

🖪. 🝆🄰 🄰🄴 🄾 **VISA**

closed 24-26 December and lunch Bank Holidays – **Meals** - Chinese (Canton) - a la carte 20.00/33.95.

◆ A long-standing Chinese restaurant on the edge of Chinatown. Chatty and pleasant service. A mix of authentic, rustic dishes and the more adventurous chef's specials.

Strand and Covent Garden *Gtr London –* ✉ *WC2.*

 Savoy   p. 37 DEY a
Strand, WC2R 0EU, ☎ (020) 7836 4343, *info@the-savoy.co.uk,*
Fax (020) 7240 6040
🛗, ⇌, 🔲 – ♨ , 🌿 rm, 🖥 📺 📞 🚗 – 🔼 500. 🆗 ᴀᴇ Ⓞ 𝗩𝗜𝗦𝗔, ✄
River : Meals (dancing Friday and Saturday dinner) 33.50/43.50 and a la carte
52.50/67.50 ♀
Grill : Meals *(closed August, Sunday, Saturday lunch and Bank Holidays)*
a la carte 37.50/58.50 ♀ – � 24.50 – **236 rm** 340.75/434.75, 27 suites.
◆ Since 1889, famous the world over for epitomising English elegance and
style. Celebrated for its Art Deco features, luxurious bedrooms and the
renowned American Bar. Immaculate service from classical menus at River.
Timelessly grand, wood-panelled Grill.

 Le Meridien Waldorf   p. 37 EX x
Aldwych, WC2B 4DD, ☎ (0870) 400 8484, *reception.waldorf@lemeridien.com,*
Fax (020) 7836 7244
🛗, ⇌, 🔲 – ♨ , 🌿 rm, 🖥 rm, 📺 📞 – 🔼 200. 🆗 ᴀᴇ Ⓞ 𝗩𝗜𝗦𝗔 ᴊᴄʙ. ✄
Palm Court : Meals 13.95 (lunch) and a la carte 23.50/34.50 ♀
Aldwyck Brasserie a la carte 23.50/34.50 ♀ – ⊕ 18.00 – **286 rm** 329.00/
340.75, 6 suites.
◆ Grand Edwardian hotel, ideally placed in theatreland. Sumptuous bedrooms decorated in a traditional English style, blending antique furniture with
modern facilities. Palm Court rekindles the charm of bygone days. Brasserie
offers marble-topped tables and simple dishes.

 Swissôtel London, The Howard   p. 37 EX e
Temple Pl, WC2R 2PR, ☎ (020) 7836 3555, *reservations.london@swissotel.*
com, Fax (020) 7379 4547
≼, 🏡 – ♨ , 🌿 rm, 🖥 📺 📞 🚗 – 🔼 150. 🆗 ᴀᴇ Ⓞ 𝗩𝗜𝗦𝗔 ᴊᴄʙ. ✄
Jaan : Meals *(closed Saturday lunch)* 23.00/29.00 and a la carte 36.00/45.00 ♀
– ⊕ 23.50 – **148 rm** 346.60, 41 suites.
◆ Traditional elegance is the order of the day at this handsomely appointed
hotel. Many of the comfortable rooms enjoy balcony views of the Thames.
Old fashioned hospitality. Modern restaurant with oriental influence.

One Aldwych   p. 37 EX r
`1 Aldwych, WC2B 4RH, ☎ (020) 7300 1000, *reservations@onealdwych.com,*
Fax (020) 7300 1001
🛗, ⇌, 🔲 – ♨ , 🌿 rm, 🖥 📺 📞 🔥 ᴘ – 🔼 50. 🆗 ᴀᴇ Ⓞ 𝗩𝗜𝗦𝗔 ᴊᴄʙ. ✄
Indigo : Meals a la carte 26.75/37.00 ♀ – (see also *Axis* below) – ⊕ 19.25 –
96 rm 346.00/446.50, 9 suites.
◆ Decorative Edwardian building, former home to the Morning Post news-
paper. Now a stylish and contemporary address with modern artwork, a
screening room and hi-tech bedrooms. All-day restaurant looks down on
fashionable bar.

St Martins Lane   p. 37 DY e
45 St Martin's Lane, WC2N 4HX, ☎ (020) 7300 5500, *sml@ianschragerhotels.*
com, Fax (020) 7300 5501
🏡, 🛗 – ♨ , 🌿 rm, 🖥 📺 📞 🚗 – 🔼 40. 🆗 ᴀᴇ Ⓞ 𝗩𝗜𝗦𝗔 ᴊᴄʙ. ✄
Asia de Cuba : Meals - Asian - (closed lunch Saturday and Sunday) a la carte
31.00/70.00
Tuscan : Meals *(closed Sunday dinner)* 16.00/45.00 and a la carte ♀ – ⊕ 20.00
– **200 rm** 276.00/305.50, 4 suites.
◆ The unmistakable hand of Philippe Starck evident at this most contemporary of hotels. Unique and stylish, from the starkly modern lobby to the
state-of-the-art rooms. 350 varieties of rum at fashionable Asia de Cuba.
Famously large meats at Tuscan.

Thistle Charing Cross

p. 37   DY   a

Strand, WC2N 5HX, ℘ (020) 7839 7282, *charingcross@thistle.co.uk,*
Fax (020) 7839 3933

🔋, ⇥ rm, 📺 📺 📞 ⚙ – 🚶 140. 🆀 🆎 ⓪ 𝗩𝗜𝗦𝗔 JCB. ✗

The Strand Terrace : Meals 22.95 and a la carte approx. 32.40 ℤ – ☐ 16.50 –
238 rm 262.00.

◆ Classic Victorian hotel built above the station. In keeping with its origins,
rooms in the Buckingham wing are traditionally styled whilst others have
contemporary décor. Watch the world go by from restaurant's pleasant
vantage point.

Ivy

p. 33   GK   z

1 West St, WC2H 9NQ, ℘ (020) 7836 4751, *Fax (020) 7240 9333*

📖. 🆀 🆎 ⓪ 𝗩𝗜𝗦𝗔 JCB

closed dinner 24-26 and 31 December, 1 January and August Bank Holiday –
Meals a la carte 23.25/61.50 ℤ.

◆ Wood panelling and stained glass combine with an unpretentious menu to
create a veritable institution. A favourite of 'celebrities', so securing a table
can be challenging.

Axis

p. 37   EX   r

1 Aldwych, WC2B 4RH, ℘ (020) 7300 0300, *sales@onealdwych.co.uk,*
Fax (020) 7300 0301

📖. 🆀 🆎 ⓪ 𝗩𝗜𝗦𝗔 JCB

closed Christmas, Saturday Lunch, Sundays and Bank Holidays – **Meals** (live
jazz at dinner Tuesday and Wednesday) 24.75 (lunch) and a la carte 28.75/
34.70 ℤ.

◆ Lower-level room overlooked by gallery bar. Muted tones, black leather
chairs and vast futuristic mural appeal to the fashion cognoscenti. Globally-
influenced menu.

J.Sheekey

p. 37   DX   v

28-32 St Martin's Court, WC2N 4AL, ℘ (020) 7240 2565, *Fax (020) 7240 8114*

📖. 🆀 🆎 ⓪ 𝗩𝗜𝗦𝗔 JCB

closed dinner 24 December-2 January and Bank Holidays – **Meals** - Seafood -
(booking essential) a la carte 25.00/63.00 ℤ.

◆ Walls festooned with photographs of actors and linked to the theatrical
world since opening in 1890. Wood panels and alcove tables add famed
intimacy. Traditional British seafood and desserts.

Rules

p. 37   DX   n

35 Maiden Lane, WC2E 7LB, ℘ (020) 7836 5314, *info@rules.co.uk,*
Fax (020) 7497 1081

⇥ 📖. 🆀 🆎 𝗩𝗜𝗦𝗔

closed 4 days Christmas – **Meals** - English - (booking essential) a la carte
29.70/36.40 ℤ.

◆ London's oldest restaurant boasts a fine collection of antique cartoons,
drawings and paintings. Tradition continues in the menu, specialising in game
from its own estate.

Adam Street

p. 37   DY   c

9 Adam St, WC2N 6AA, ℘ (020) 7379 8000, *info@adamstreet.co.uk,*
Fax (020) 7379 1444

📖. 🆀 🆎 𝗩𝗜𝗦𝗔

closed Christmas-New Year, Saturday, Sunday and Bank Holidays – **Meals**
(lunch only) 17.50 and a la carte 25.00/32.90 ℤ.

◆ Set in the striking vaults of a private members club just off the Strand.
Sumptuous suede banquettes and elegantly laid tables. Well executed classic
and modern English food.

XX **The Admiralty**   p. 37   EY   X
Somerset House, The Strand, WC2R 1LA, ℰ (020) 7845 4646,
Fax (020) 7845 4658
✕. 🆖 AE ⓪ VISA
closed 25-26 December and Sunday dinner
Meals 25.00/33.00 ℤ.
♦ Interconnecting rooms with bold colours and informal service contrast
with its setting within the restored Georgian splendour of Somerset House.
'Cuisine de terroir'.

XX **Weststreet**   p. 33   GK   n
13-15 West St, WC2H 9NE, ℰ (020) 7010 8600, *office@westreet.net,*
Fax (020) 7010 8601
with rm – 🖩 TV ✆ – 🔾 35. 🆖 AE ⓪ VISA
closed 24-26 December and Sunday dinner – **Meals** 17.50 (lunch)
and a la carte 27.00/47.00 ℤ – **3 rm** � 294.00/528.00.
♦ Black granite and dark leather seating in the restaurant approached via a
bridge over the basement bar area. Modern menu with Italian tone. Minimalist bedrooms.

XX **Bank**   p. 37   EX   s
1 Kingsway, Aldwych, WC2B 6XF, ℰ (020) 7379 9797, *aldres@bankrestaurants.*
com, Fax (020) 7379 5070
🖩. 🆖 AE ⓪ VISA
closed 25 December, 1 January and Bank Holidays – **Meals** 15.00
(lunch) and a la carte 25.75/30.80 ℤ.
♦ Ceiling decoration of hanging glass shards creates a high level of interest
in this bustling converted bank. Open-plan kitchen provides an extensive
array of modern dishes.

XX **Le Deuxième**   p. 37   DV   e
65a Long Acre, WC2E 9JH, ℰ (020) 7379 0033, *Fax (020) 7379 0066*
🖩. 🆖 AE ⓪ VISA
closed 24-25 December – **Meals** 13.50 (lunch) and a la carte 24.00/
29.50 ℤ.
♦ Caters well for theatregoers: opens early, closes late. Buzzy eatery, quietly
decorated in white with subtle lighting. Varied International menu: Japanese
to Mediterranean.

X **Le Café du Jardin**   p. 37   EX   a
28 Wellington St, WC2E 7DD, ℰ (020) 7836 8769, *Fax (020) 7836 4123*
🖩. 🆖 AE ⓪ VISA
closed 24-25 December – **Meals** 13.50 (lunch) and a la carte 20.00/
29.50 ℤ.
♦ Divided into two floors with the downstairs slightly more comfortable.
Light and contemporary interior with European-influenced cooking. Ideally
placed for the Opera House.

X **Livebait**   p. 37   EX   u
21 Wellington St, WC2E 7DN, ℰ (020) 7836 7161, *Fax (020) 7836 7141*
🆖 AE ⓪ VISA JCB
closed 25-26 December, 1 January and Sunday – **Meals** - Seafood - 15.50
(lunch) and a la carte approx. 23.45 ℤ.
♦ Busy front bar and back restaurant both decorated with black and white
tiles. Energetic service and a menu offering fresh seafood in relaxed surroundings.

Victoria *Gtr London* – ✉ *SW1.*

🚹 *Victoria Station Forecourt.*

Royal Horseguards
p. 30   **LX**   a

2 Whitehall Court, SW1A 2EJ, ☎ (020) 7839 3400, *royalhorseguards@thistle.co.uk, Fax (020) 7925 2263*

�, *Ⅰ∱* – 📶, ⥤ rm, 🖥 📺 📞 – 🏛 200. 🅾 🆀 ⑩ 𝘝𝘐𝘚𝘈. ⌘

One Twenty One : Meals *(closed Saturday and Sunday lunch)* 20.50/27.50 and dinner a la carte 34.85/48.95 – ⌸ 18.50 – **276 rm** 369.60/399.50, 4 suites.

♦ Imposing Grade I listed property in Whitehall overlooking the Thames and close to London Eye. Impressive meeting rooms. Some of the well-appointed bedrooms have river views. Stylish restaurant, sub-divided into intimate rooms.

Crowne Plaza London St James
p. 36   **CX**   i

45 Buckingham Gate, SW1E 6AF, ☎ (020) 7834 6655, *sales@cplonsj.co.uk, Fax (020) 7630 7587*

Ⅰ∱, ⥉ – 📶 ⥤ rm, 🖥 📺 📞 �&. – 🏛 180. 🅾 🆀 ⑩ 𝘝𝘐𝘚𝘈 𝗝𝗖𝗕. ⌘

Café Méditerranée : Meals 15.00 (lunch) and a la carte 20.00/30.00 ⛾ – (see also ***Quilon*** and ***Bank*** below) – ⌸ 12.95 – **323 rm** 293.70/346.60, 19 suites.

♦ Built in 1897 as serviced accommodation for visiting aristocrats. Behind the impressive Edwardian façade lies an equally elegant interior. Quietest rooms overlook courtyard. Bright and informal café style restaurant.

51 Buckingham Gate
p. 36   **CX**   i

51 Buckingham Gate, SW1E 6AF, ☎ (020) 7769 7766, *reservations@51-buckinghamgate.co.uk, Fax (020) 7233 5014*

Ⅰ∱, ⥉ – 📶 🖥 📺 📞 🅾 🆀 ⑩ 𝘝𝘐𝘚𝘈 𝗝𝗖𝗕

Meals - (see ***Quilon*** and ***Bank*** below) – ⌸ 16.50 – **82 suites** 370.00/528.70.

♦ Canopied entrance leads to luxurious suites: every detail considered, every mod con provided. Colour schemes echoed in plants and paintings. Butler and nanny service.

The Goring
 p. 36   **BX**   a

15 Beeston Pl, Grosvenor Gdns, SW1W 0JW, ☎ (020) 7396 9000, *reception@goringhotel.co.uk, Fax (020) 7834 4393*

🚗 – 📶 🖥 📺 📞 – 🏛 50. 🅾 🆀 ⑩ 𝘝𝘐𝘚𝘈. ⌘

Meals 26.50/40.00 s. ⛾ – ⌸ 17.00 – **68 rm** 235.00/287.80, 6 suites.

♦ Opened in 1910 as a quintessentially English hotel. The fourth generation of Goring is now at the helm. Many of the attractive rooms overlook a peaceful garden. Elegantly appointed restaurant provides memorable dining experience.

41
 p. 36   **BX**   n

41 Buckingham Palace Rd, SW1W 0PS, ☎ (020) 7300 0041, *book41@rchmail.com, Fax (020) 7300 0141*

📶 🖥 📺 📞 🅾 🆀 ⑩ 𝘝𝘐𝘚𝘈. ⌘

Meals (residents only) a la carte 15.00/20.00 s. ⛾ – ⌸ 15.00 – **14 rm** 258.50, 4 suites.

♦ Take the lift to the 5th floor- London's first all-inclusive hotel. Relaxed and exclusive club-like lounge where meals and most drinks complimentary. State-of-the-art rooms.

The Rubens at The Palace
p. 36   **BX**   **n**

39 Buckingham Palace Rd, SW1W 0PS,   (020) 7834 6600, *bookrb@rchmail. com, Fax (020) 7828 5401*

🛗 ✻ ▦ TV ☎ – 🏛 90. ⓶ AE ⓿ VISA ✻

Meals *(closed lunch Saturday and Sunday)* (carvery) 16.95 ⓨ :
The Library : **Meals** (dinner only) a la carte 22.95/32.50 ⓨ – ⛱ 15.00 – **170 rm** 199.70/246.75, 2 suites.

♦ Traditional hotel with an air of understated elegance. Tastefully furnished rooms: the Royal Wing, themed after British Kings and Queens, features TVs in the bathrooms. Intimate, richly decorated Library restaurant has sumptuous armchairs.

Dolphin Square
p. 30   **KZ**   **a**

Dolphin Sq, Chichester St, SW1V 3LX,   (020) 7834 3800, *reservations@ dolphinsquarehotel.co.uk, Fax (020) 7798 8735*

🛗, ⓔ§, 🔲, 🚗, ✻, squash – 🛗 ✻, ▦ rest, TV ☎ 🚙 – 🏛 85. ⓶ AE ⓿ VISA JCB ✻

The Brasserie : **Meals** 14.50 and a la carte 19.90/29.45 **s.** ⓨ – (see also ***Rhodes in the Square*** below) – ⛱ 12.95 – **30 rm** 193.80/217.30, **118 suites** 229.10/528.75.

♦ Built in 1935 and shared with residential apartments. Art Deco influence remains in the Clipper bar overlooking the leisure club. Spacious suites with contemporary styling. Brasserie overlooks the swimming pool.

Jolly St Ermin's
p. 36   **CX**   **a**

Caxton St, SW1H 0QW,   (020) 7222 7888, *reservations@jollyhotels.co.uk, Fax (020) 7222 6914*

🛗, ✻ rm, TV ☎ – 🏛 150. ⓶ AE ⓿ VISA JCB ✻

Cloisters Brasserie : **Meals** *(closed lunch Saturday and Sunday)* (carvery lunch)/dinner 21.95 and a la carte 25.50/31.50 ⓨ – ⛱ 15.95 – **282 rm** 205.00/229.00, 8 suites.

♦ Ornate plasterwork to both the lobby and the balconied former ballroom are particularly striking features. Club rooms have both air conditioning and a private lounge. Grand brasserie with ornate ceiling.

Thistle Victoria
p. 36   **BX**   **c**

101 Buckingham Palace Rd, SW1W 0SJ,   (020) 7834 9494, *victoria@thistle.co. uk, Fax (020) 7630 1978*

🛗, ✻ rm, TV ☎ – 🏛 200. ⓶ AE ⓿ VISA ✻

Meals – (see ***Christopher's*** below) – ⛱ 13.95 – **361 rm** 245.00/262.00, 3 suites.

♦ Former Victorian railway hotel with ornate front entrance and grand reception. Harvard bar particularly noteworthy. Well-appointed rooms are generally spacious.

Thistle Westminster
p. 36   **BX**   **z**

49 Buckingham Palace Rd, SW1W 0QT,   (0207) 834 1821, *westminster@ thistle.co.uk, Fax (0207) 931 7542*

🛗, ✻ rm, ▦ TV ☎ – 🏛 150. ⓶ AE ⓿ VISA ✻

Meals 18.00/35.00 and a la carte 18.00/32.00 – ⛱ 13.50 – **134 rm** 197.00/261.00.

♦ Proximity to station and Palaces make this a popular destination for corporate and leisure guests. Comfortable and well-equipped bedrooms benefit from mini-bars and safes. Shelves with cook books for sale in restaurant.

🏛 Tophams Belgravia
p. 36   **AX**   e

28 Ebury St, SW1W 0LU, ℰ (020) 7730 8147, *tophams_belgravia@compuserve. com, Fax (020) 7823 5966*

|⑂| 📺 – ⚒ 30. ⓞ AE ⓞ VISA JCB. ℀

closed 24 December-2 January – **Meals** (dinner only) a la carte 17.00/22.50 **s.** – **38 rm** ⊑ 115.00/170.00.

♦ Family owned and run since 1937, this hotel has a certain traditional charm. Cosy lounges, roaring fires and antique furniture aplenty. Individually decorated bedrooms. Homely basement dining room.

🏛 Winchester
p. 36   **BY**   s

17 Belgrave Rd, SW1V 1RB, ℰ (020) 7828 2972, *winchesterhotel17@hotmail. com, Fax (020) 7828 5191*

without rest. – 📺. ℀

18 rm ⊑ 85.00/120.00.

♦ Behind the portico entrance one finds a friendly, well-kept private hotel. The generally spacious rooms are pleasantly appointed. Comprehensive English breakfast offered.

🏛 Express by Holiday Inn
p. 30   **KZ**   c

106-110 Belgrave Rd, SW1V 2BS, ℰ (020) 7630 8888, *info@hiexpressvictoria. co.uk, Fax (020) 7828 0441*

without rest. – |⑂| ⇥ 📺 ✆ ৬. ⓞ AE ⓞ VISA JCB. ℀

52 rm 105.00.

♦ Converted Georgian terraced houses a short walk from station. Despite property's age, all rooms are stylish and modern with good range of facilities including TV movies.

XXX Rhodes in the Square *(at Dolphin Square H.)*
p. 30   **KZ**   a

❀ Dolphin Sq, Chichester St, SW1V 3LX, ℰ (020) 7798 6767, *rhodesinthesquare@ sodexho.co.uk, Fax (020) 7798 5685*

▤. ⓞ AE ⓞ VISA JCB

closed Saturday lunch, Sunday and Monday – **Meals** 19.80/36.50 ♈.

♦ A calm atmosphere prevails in this richly decorated room. Raised tables to rear with sumptuous banquettes for more privacy. Interesting and assured modern British cooking.

Spec. Lobster omelette thermidor. Roast loin of lamb on creamed greens, reform sauce. Cherry and chocolate clafoutis, cherry ice cream.

XXX The Cinnamon Club
p. 30   **LY**   c

Great Smith St, SW1P 3BU, ℰ (020) 7222 2555, *info@cinnamonclub.com, Fax (020) 7222 1333*

▤, P. ⓞ AE ⓞ VISA

closed Christmas, Saturday lunch, Sunday dinner and Bank Holidays – **Meals** - Indian - 19.00/22.00 (lunch) and a la carte 29.00/41.50 ♈.

♦ Housed in former Westminster Library: exterior has ornate detail, interior is stylish and modern. Walls are lined with books. New Wave Indian cooking with plenty of choice.

XXX Quilon *(at Crowne Plaza London St James H.)*
p. 36   **CX**   i

45 Buckingham Gate, SW1 6AF, ℰ (020) 7821 1899, *Fax (020) 7828 5802*

▤. ⓞ AE ⓞ VISA

closed 1 week Christmas, Sunday, Saturday lunch and Bank Holidays – **Meals** - Indian - 12.95/15.95 (lunch) and dinner a la carte 25.95/30.95 ♈.

♦ A selection of Eastern pictures adorn the walls in this smart, modern and busy restaurant. Specialising in progressive south coastal Indian cooking.

XXX **L'Incontro** p. 35 **FT** u
87 Pimlico Rd, SW1W 8PH, ☏ (020) 7730 6327, *Fax (020) 7730 5062*
📖, **MO** **AE** **①** **VISA** **JCB**
closed Easter, 25-26 December and lunch Saturday and Sunday – **Meals** -
Italian - 19.50 (lunch) and a la carte 29.50/49.00.
◆ Cool, understated and comfortable with attentive service. Simple, unfussy,
traditional Italian cooking; set lunch good value. Private dining downstairs for
30 people.

XXX **Santini** p. 36 **ABX** v
29 Ebury St, SW1W 0NZ, ☏ (020) 7730 4094, *Fax (020) 7730 0544*
📖, **MO** **AE** **①** **VISA** **JCB**
closed Easter Sunday, 25-26 December, lunch Saturday and Sunday – **Meals** -
Italian - 26.00 (lunch) and a la carte 28.50/47.00 ⚑.
◆ Discreet, refined and elegant modern Italian restaurant. Assured and professional service. Extensive selection of modern dishes and a more affordable
set lunch menu.

XXX **Shepherd's** p. 30 **LZ** z
Marsham Court, Marsham St, SW1P 4LA, ☏ (020) 7834 9552, *admin@langans
restaurants.co.uk, Fax (020) 7233 6047*
📖, **MO** **AE** **①** **VISA** **JCB**
closed Saturday, Sunday and Bank Holidays – **Meals** - English - (booking
essential) 28.00.
◆ A truly English restaurant where game and traditional puddings are a
highlight. Popular with those from Westminster - the booths offer a degree
of privacy.

XX **Roussillon** p. 29 **IZ** c
❀ 16 St Barnabas St, SW1W 8PE, ☏ (020) 7730 5550, *alexis@roussillon.co.uk,
Fax (020) 7824 8617*
📖, **MO** **AE** **VISA** **JCB**
*closed last week August, first week September, 1 week Christmas, Sunday,
Saturday lunch and Bank holidays* – **Meals** 21.00/35.00 ⚑.
◆ Tucked away in a smart residential area. Cooking clearly focuses on the
quality of the ingredients. Seasonal menu with inventive elements and a
French base.
Spec. Mrs Beeton's Prince of Wales soup. Honey-roasted Yorkshire duck with
light spices. Spicy soufflé, gingerbread "soldiers" and maple infusion.

XX **Il Convivio** p. 36 **AY** a
143 Ebury St, SW1W 9QN, ☏ (020) 7730 4099, *comments@etruscagroup.
co.uk, Fax (020) 7730 4103*
🌳 – 📖, **MO** **AE** **①** **VISA**
closed 25-26 December, 1 January, Sunday and Bank holidays – **Meals** - Italian
- 19.50/31.50 and lunch a la carte 18.00/29.50 ⚑.
◆ A retractable roof provides alfresco dining to part of this comfortable and
modern restaurant. Contemporary and traditional Italian menu, with home-
made pasta specialities.

XX **Simply Nico** p. 36 **CY** a
48a Rochester Row, SW1P 1JU, ☏ (020) 7630 8061, *westminster@simplynico.
co.uk, Fax (020) 7828 8541*
📖, **MO** **AE** **①** **VISA**
closed Easter, 24-26 December, Saturday lunch, Sunday and Bank Holidays –
Meals (booking essential) a la carte 23.50/31.40 ⚑.
◆ Relaxed and discreet restaurant with a certain bistro atmosphere. Lunch is
especially busy. Short, Anglo-French menu. One of a small chain.

XX **Bank** p. 36 CX i
45 Buckingham Gate, SW1E 6BS, ✆ (020) 7379 9797, *westres@bankrestaurants.com, Fax (020) 7379 5070*
– ▤. MC AE ⓓ VISA
closed 25 December, Saturday lunch, Sunday and Bank Holidays – **Meals** 15.00 (lunch) and a la carte 25.00/31.85 ♀.
◆ The understated entrance belies the vibrant contemporary interior. One of Europe's longest bars has a lively atmosphere. Conservatory restaurant, modern European cooking.

XX **Boisdale** p. 36 AY c
15 Eccleston St, SW1W 9LX, ✆ (020) 7730 6922, *katarina@boisdale.co.uk, Fax (020) 7730 0548*
– ▤. MC AE ⓓ VISA
closed Sunday and Saturday lunch – **Meals** - Scottish - (live jazz at dinner) 19.00/22.45 and a la carte 19.00/34.80 ♀.
◆ Popular haunt of politicians; dark green, lacquer red panelled interior. Run by a Scot of Clanranald, hence modern British dishes with Scottish flavour: Crofter's pie.

XX **Christopher's** (at Thistle Victoria H.) p. 36 BX e
101 Buckingham Palace Rd, SW1W 0SJ, ✆ (020) 7976 5522, *info@christophersgrill.com, Fax (020) 7976 5521*
▤. MC AE ⓓ VISA
Meals - American Grill - 17.75 (lunch) and a la carte 32.00/40.45 ♀.
◆ Upmarket American grill in grand hotel dining room: ornate high ceiling and some stylish modern touches. Varied regional menu includes chowder, steak and lobster or crab cake.

XX **Tate Britain** p. 30 LZ c
Tate Gallery, Millbank, SW1P 4RG, ✆ (020) 7887 8825, *tate.restaurant@tate.org.uk, Fax (020) 7887 8902*
▤. MC AE ⓓ VISA
Meals (booking essential) (lunch only) 19.50 and a la carte 21.00/31.00 ♀.
◆ Continue your appreciation of art when lunching in this basement room decorated with original Rex Whistler murals. Forever busy, it offers modern British fare.

XX **Ken Lo's Memories of China** p. 36 AY u
65-69 Ebury St, SW1W 0NZ, ✆ (020) 7730 7734, *Fax (020) 7730 2992*
▤. MC AE ⓓ VISA
closed Sunday lunch and Bank Holidays – **Meals** - Chinese - 19.50/30.00 and a la carte 35.50/50.20 ♀.
◆ An air of tranquillity pervades this traditionally furnished room. Lattice screens add extra privacy. Extensive Chinese menu: bold flavours with a clean, fresh style..

X **Olivo** p. 36 AY z
21 Eccleston St, SW1W 9LX, ✆ (020) 7730 2505, *Fax (020) 7824 8190*
▤. MC AE VISA
closed lunch Saturday, Sunday and Bank Holidays – **Meals** - Italian - 17.50 (lunch) and dinner a la carte 19.25/32.00.
◆ Rustic, informal Italian restaurant. Relaxed atmosphere provided by the friendly staff. Simple, non-fussy cuisine with emphasis on best available fresh produce.

X **La Poule au Pot** p. 29 IZ e
231 Ebury St, SW1W 8UT, ✆ (020) 7730 7763, *Fax (020) 7259 9651*
– ▤. MC AE ⓓ VISA JCB
Meals - French - 16.00 (lunch) and a la carte 24.75/36.75.
◆ The subdued lighting and friendly informality make this one of London's more romantic restaurants. Classic French menu with extensive plats du jour.

International Dialling Codes

Note: when making an international call, do not dial the first «0» of the city codes (except for calls to Italy).

Indicatifs Téléphoniques Internationaux

Important : pour les communications internationales, le zéro (0) initial de l'indicatif interurbain n'est pas à composer (excepté pour les appels vers l'Italie).

from \ to	Ⓐ	Ⓑ	ⒸⒽ	ⒸⓏ	Ⓓ	ⒹⓀ	Ⓔ	ⒻⒾⓃ	Ⓕ	ⒼⒷ	ⒼⓇ
A Austria		0032	0041	00420	0049	0045	0034	00358	0033	0044	0030
B Belgium	0043		0041	00420	0049	0045	0034	00358	0033	0044	0030
CH Switzerland	0043	0032		00420	0049	0045	0034	00358	0033	0044	0030
CZ Czech Republic	0043	0032	0041		0049	0045	0034	00358	0033	0044	0030
D Germany	0043	0032	0041	00420		0045	0034	00358	0033	0044	0030
DK Denmark	0043	0032	0041	00420	0049		0034	00358	0033	0044	0030
E Spain	0043	0032	0041	00420	0049	0045		00358	0033	0044	0030
FIN Finland	0043	0032	0041	00420	0049	0045	0034		0033	0044	0030
F France	0043	0032	0041	00420	0049	0045	0034	00358		0044	0030
GB United Kingdom	0043	0032	0041	00420	0049	0045	0034	00358	0033		0030
GR Greece	0043	0032	0041	00420	0049	0045	0034	00358	0033	0044	
H Hungary	0043	0032	0041	00420	0049	0045	0034	00358	0033	0044	0030
I Italy	0043	0032	0041	00420	0049	0045	0034	00358	0033	0044	0030
IRL Ireland	0043	0032	0041	00420	0049	0045	0034	00358	0033	0044	0030
J Japan	00143	00132	00141	001420	00149	00145	00134	001358	00133	00144	00130
L Luxembourg	0043	0032	0041	00420	0049	0045	0034	00358	0033	0044	0030
N Norway	0043	0032	0041	00420	0049	0045	0034	00358	0033	0044	0030
NL Netherlands	0043	0032	0041	00420	0049	0045	0034	00358	0033	0044	0030
PL Poland	0043	0032	0041	00420	0049	0045	0034	00358	0033	0044	0030
P Portugal	0043	0032	0041	00420	0049	0045	0034	00358	0033	0044	0030
RUS Russia	81043	81032	810420	6420	81049	81045	*	810358	81033	81044	*
S Sweden	0043	0032	0041	00420	0049	0045	0034	00358	0033	0044	0030
USA	01143	01132	01141	001420	01149	01145	01134	01358	01133	01144	01130

*Direct dialling not possible   *Pas de sélection automatique

Indicativi Telefonici Internationali

Importante: per le comunicazioni internazionali, non bisogna comporre lo zero (0) iniziale dell'indicativo interurbano (escluse le chiamate per l'Italia)

(H)	(I)	(IRL)	(J)	(L)	(N)	(NL)	(PL)	(P)	(RUS)	(S)	(USA)	
0036	0039	00353	0081	00352	0047	0031	0048	00351	007	0046	001	**A Austria**
0036	0039	00353	0081	00352	0047	0031	0048	00351	007	0046	001	**B Belgium**
0036	0039	00353	0081	00352	0047	0031	0048	00351	007	0046	001	**CH Switzerland**
0036	0039	00353	0081	00352	0047	0031	0048	00351	007	0046	001	**CZ Czech Republic**
0036	0039	00353	0081	00352	0047	0031	0048	00351	007	0046	001	**D Germany**
0036	0039	00353	0081	00352	0047	0031	0048	00351	007	0046	001	**DK Denmark**
0036	0039	00353	0081	00352	0047	0031	0048	00351	007	0046	001	**E Spain**
0036	0039	00353	0081	00352	0047	0031	0048	00351	007	0046	001	**FIN Finland**
0036	0039	00353	0081	00352	0047	0031	0048	00351	007	0046	001	**F France**
0036	0039	00353	0081	00352	0047	0031	0048	00351	007	0046	001	**GB United Kingdom**
0036	0039	00353	0081	00352	0047	0031	0048	00351	007	0046	001	**GR Greece**
	0039	00353	0081	00352	0047	0031	0048	00351	007	0046	001	**H Hungary**
0036		00353	0081	00352	0047	0031	0048	00351	*	0046	001	**I Italy**
0036	0039		0081	00352	0047	0031	0048	00351	007	0046	001	**IRL Ireland**
00136	00139	001353		001352	00147	00131	00140	001351	*	00146	0011	**J Japan**
0036	0039	00353	0081		0047	0031	0048	00351	007	0046	001	**L Luxembourg**
0036	0039	00353	0081	00352		0031	0048	00351	007	0046	001	**N Norway**
0036	0039	00353	0081	00352	0047		0048	00351	007	0046	001	**NL Netherlands**
0036	0039	00353	0081	00352	0047	0031		00351	007	0046	001	**PL Poland**
0036	0039	00353	0081	00352	0047	0031	0048		007	0046	001	**P Portugal**
81036	*	*	*	*	*	81031	81048	*		*	*	**RUS Russia**
0036	0039	00353	0081	00352	0047	0031	0048	00351	007		001	**S Sweden**
01136	01139	011353	01181	011352	01147	01131	01148	011351	*	011146		**USA**

*Selezione automatica impossibile   * Automatische Vorwahl nicht möglich

*GREAT BRITAIN : Based on Ordnance Survey of Great Britain with the permission
of the Controller of Her Majesty's Stationery Office,* © *Crown Copyright 39923X.*

Manufacture française des pneumatiques Michelin
Société en commandite par actions au capital de 304 000 000 EUR
Place des Carmes-Déchaux – 63 *Clermont-Ferrand (France)*
R.C.S. Clermont-Fd B 855 200 507

Michelin et Cie, Propriétaires-Éditeurs 2003
Dépôt légal Janvier 2003 – ISBN 2-06-100703-1

**No part of this publication may be reproduced in any form
without the prior permission of the publisher.**

Printed in France 12-02

Photocompositeur : A.P.S. - Tours.
Imprimeur, brocheur : Imprimerie CLERC, St-Amand-Montrond

Illustrations Cécile Imbert/MICHELIN : pages 4, 6 à 10, 18 à 22, 28, 30 à 36, 40
Narratif Systèmes/Geneclo : pages 5, 17, 29
Rodolphe Corbel pages 14, 26, 38, 201.

In the same series ●

Dans la même collection ●

Altri titoli della collezione ●